I0820832

Never Mind the Happy

Never Mind the Happy

Showbiz Stories from a Sore Winner

MARC SHAIMAN

A REGALO PRESS BOOK
ISBN: 979-8-89565-224-4
ISBN (eBook): 979-8-89565-225-1

Never Mind the Happy:
Showbiz Stories from a Sore Winner

Cover Design by Jim Villaflores
Cover Photo by Robert Trachtenberg

Publishing Team:
Founder and Publisher – Gretchen Young
Managing Editor – Caitlin Burdette
Production Manager – Kate Harris
Production Editor – Rachel Paul

As part of the mission of Regalo Press, a donation is being made to Broadway Cares/Equity Fights AIDS, as chosen by the author. Find out more about this organization at *https://broadwaycares.org* .

This book, as well as any other Regalo Press publications, may be purchased in bulk quantities at a special discounted rate. Contact orders@regalopress.com for more information.

This is a work of nonfiction. All people, locations, events, and situations are portrayed to the best of the author's memory.

Regalo Press
New York • Nashville
regalopress.com

Published in the United States of America
3 4 5 6 7 8 9 10

I dedicate this book, no big surprise, to Bette Midler. Not just for all the shared escapades that make up so much of my story, but also for her connection to the two greatest gifts I ever received, those being two perfect Golden Retrievers, first Walli Woo and then Chops.

Scott Wittman and I found ourselves suddenly bringing home Walli after I purchased her right out of The Divine Miss M's arms during the auction at Hulaween, Bette's charity event to raise money for her New York Restoration Project. I found myself bidding against Estée Lauder (not someone from the company...the actual Estée Lauder!) Walli Woo was one of the world's most loved—and expensive—dogs, who lived a *very* glamourous fifteen years with Scott and me, and spreading her ashes in her beloved Atlantic Ocean was easily one of the saddest days of our lives.

And I am writing this dedication while sitting in Bette's kitchen in LA. I am here because, devastatingly, my husband Lou's and my cherished dog Chops passed away quite suddenly a few days ago at only eight years old, and Bette offered us the emotional rescue of leaving New York and staying at her beautiful home in California (where many of the stories that lay ahead take place). Blessed sanctuary.

(Two beloved dog deaths on just the first page! Well, the book *is* titled *Never Mind the Happy*.)

So, besides all the music and thrills that my work and friendship with Bette has afforded me for almost fifty years, she has also brought me great joy and comfort. Even just this week.

With love, I dedicate this book to her.

TABLE OF CONTENTS

PROLOGUE

It's February 24, 2019, and I am on stage with Bette Midler at the Dolby Theatre in Los Angeles, moments away from performing at the 91st Annual Academy Awards. On the other side of the closed curtain are 3,400 of the most powerful and successful players in Hollywood—plus another thirty million people tuning into the television coverage worldwide. One such player in the auditorium is Scott Wittman, my lyrical collaborator of almost fifty years, with whom I co-wrote the Oscar-nominated song "The Place Where Lost Things Go"—the very song Bette and I are about to perform. It has only been two months since Disney released *Mary Poppins Returns*—which has garnered my sixth and seventh Oscar nominations—and even though I am calm as I sit at the keyboard of the polished black grand piano, I am also conscious of what a fight it has been to get here.

A few weeks earlier, on the morning the Oscar nominations were announced, my husband, Lou Mirabal, and I sat on the couch in our Manhattan loft, our golden retriever, Chops, no doubt wondering why we were glued to the television at 8:30 a.m. instead of making her breakfast. A similar scene was playing out with Scott and his partner, Brian, at their apartment just six blocks to the south. *Mary Poppins Returns* had been a hit film, if not the billion-dollar blowout the studio had hoped it would be. Scott and I were very proud of the songs we wrote for the sequel to Disney's classic about a magical British nanny, but they had inevitably been compared to the unforgettable music from the original—so we didn't know if we should get our hopes up on the morning of the nominations.

Luckily, Oscar smiled and we were nominated for our song "The Place Where Lost Things Go," and I was also nominated for Best Score. We were all excited and relieved, perhaps nobody more than Lou, because he was the one who would have had to mop me off the floor if things had turned out differently.

I always say, though, that if showbiz puts you on a pedestal on Tuesday, it's only to have a better shot at your balls on Thursday. And right on schedule, after two days of elation, the producers of that year's Oscars telecast announced that of the five nominated songs, only two—one a duet by Lady Gaga and Bradley Cooper from *A Star Is Born*, the other by Kendrick Lamar and SZA from *Black Panther*—would be performed. Clearly, they wanted star power to boost the broadcast's ratings and, by cutting three songs, perhaps also trim a few minutes from its running time. But to say the remaining songs were not worthy of inclusion sent a message both to the public—and worse, to the Oscar voters, who had yet to cast their ballots—that they were not considered equal. It really was a low blow.

What those Oscars producers didn't anticipate, however, was just how much a dog with a bone I can be. First, I put together an appeal from the writers of the three orphaned songs (including my dear and foul-mouthed friend Diane Warren)—but that led to a dead end. Then, I went to Alan Horn, who was chairman of Walt Disney Studios at the time and who I knew from his years as Rob Reiner's producing partner. Since Disney owns ABC, the television network that broadcasts the Oscars, I thought he would be able to pull some strings—but he gruffly said, "The ship has sailed, there's nothing I can do." Well, maybe there was nothing *he* could do, but I was not going to give up.

I had met Bradley Cooper a few times due to our shared friendship with the great actor Victor Garber. Bradley had been to the home I then shared with Scott, my romantic partner for nearly thirty years, when he and Victor were filming the TV show *Alias*, and he had always been very friendly whenever I ran into him at other showbiz functions. I had also just recently become pals with Kevin Feige, Supreme Intelligence of the Marvel Cinematic

Universe. In fact, it was at an Academy event just a few weeks earlier (where we had all been schmoozing for nominations) when someone tapped me on my shoulder and said, "Kevin Feige would like to meet you."

"Kevin Feige would like to meet *me*?" I queried. I was in shock and couldn't believe, of all nights, that my Marvel-nerd husband wasn't with me. It turned out Kevin, who you would think is busy enough, also has time to be a serious film-score fanatic. And after enjoying a few minutes of him praising my work, I asked if we could take a selfie together so I could send it to Lou.

Not only are Bradley and Kevin two of the nicest guys in Hollywood, at that moment, being friendly with them was uniquely useful. After all, Bradley produced *A Star Is Born* and Kevin produced *Black Panther*—the two films whose Oscar-nominated songs had been anointed by the Academy to be performed. So, I reached out to them both to explain the situation, which they agreed was unfair, and each offered to do what they could to help.

I'm not privy to what happened next, but those two gentlemen clearly have their own superpowers, because only a day or so later, it was announced that all five songs would be performed. Thank you, Bradley, and thank you, Kevin—if you ever need a favor from someone *less* powerful, let me know.

And so, I made it onto the Oscars stage that year after all. Moments before our performance, through the curtain, I could hear the orchestra play a snatch of our movie theme, and then the crowd respond as Keegan-Michael Key was lowered from the ceiling of the Dolby Theatre clutching a Mary Poppins–style black umbrella.

"This evening's next nominee for best original song was written by Marc Shaiman and Scott Wittman for the film *Mary Poppins Returns*," he said. "In addition to lifting the Banks children's spirits through a series of magical adventures, Mary Poppins offers comfort and compassion with this tender lullaby, underscoring the notion that a loved one who is lost can still be very much present.

Performing 'The Place Where Lost Things Go' with Marc Shaiman on piano, please welcome the Divine Miss M."

(Both Bette and I thought—but of course did not have time to discuss in the moment—*What, he couldn't say her name?*)

Then the curtain lifted, Bette stepped into the spotlight as twenty-eight red umbrella lanterns descended against a stage backdrop of London's foggy skyline, and I started accompanying my favorite performer in the world—on a song I had co-written with my cherished collaborator—from a musical about my most beloved literary character—at the Academy Awards.

How did I get there? Well, as an old-school piano player might say, it went a little something like this...

1

WINDING BROOK WAY

One New Year's Day, my sister Joyce called my mother, Claire, and said, "Ma, I wanna be the first to wish you a happy and healthy New Year."

To which my mother retorted, "*Never mind the happy*!"

I tell this story to everyone who says to me, "Marc, you have had so many wonderful things happen in your life. Why do you always focus on the gloomy side? Why are you such an Eeyore?"

What can I say? It's in my blood.

Like my father before me, I was born in Newark, New Jersey. In fact, all four Shaiman children were born in Newark. And, bringing new meaning to the musical concept of "variations on a theme," three of us were born on the same day—October 22—but in different years.

I once did the math and realized we three were all conceived on either Valentine's Day or Washington's Birthday. My parents were either die-hard romantics, or American history was their kink. But my eldest sister, Karen, was born in April, so even Mom and Dad got off the rhythm method at least once.

My other sister, Joyce, and I are very alike. We are boisterous hams who love performing, and both sang solos in the talent shows at Terrill Junior High School. When our parents took us to the Garden State Arts Center for a 5th Dimension concert and they brought folks to dance on stage during their huge hit "Let the Sunshine In," Joyce didn't let the fact we were seated far from the stage stop her. She got up, ran down the aisle, jumped on stage, and boogalooed like she was about to enter a *sixth* dimension.

My brother, Ronnie, on the other hand, was more of an introvert. After college, he went searching for himself in Europe and Africa. He came home with a motorcycle and took me for a spin around the block, and on the turns, as my ankles seemed to skim the road, it cured me from ever needing to ride on a motorcycle for the rest of my life. Ronnie also came home with a shoebox full of beautiful beads from somewhere in Morocco. Always an enterprising young fellow, who clearly had not yet discovered my moral center, I stole a bunch of the beads and sold them to kids at school. One day I came home to find Ronnie waiting for me in the driveway. He hit me, which I totally deserved. And amazingly, from what I read about most brothers, that was our only physical dustup. And it was the last time I trafficked in stolen goods.

Karen was neither as quiet as Ronnie nor as loud as Joyce and me; she was the calm at the center of the storm. I remember lying in her bed for hours listening to The Beatles' *White Album*.

We all loved them, poring over the *Meet the Beatles!* album cover. One morning, while Joyce and I were walking to the school bus stop with another girl from the block, I desperately wanted to jump into their conversation to agree that Paul was "the cute one." But even at that young age, something told me I shouldn't express that opinion out loud. I somehow knew I wasn't supposed to have those feelings, or the ones I would get watching chiseled-jawed actor Dick Gautier when he played the well-built Hymie the Robot on TV's *Get Smart*.

But besides my siblings playing Beatles records, there was virtually no music ever in our house. My parents owned about three records, which they never brought out of their sleeves. One was some sort of cha-cha album, and the other two were by The Barry Sisters, two saucy siblings who performed popular Yiddish songs. At some point, a Herb Alpert & the Tijuana Brass album also appeared. Its cover photo was of a young woman wearing nothing but whipped cream, holding a single long-stemmed red rose, and licking her index finger suggestively. I stared at that image endlessly, wondering what it all could mean, completely unaware that my attractions to such an image would forever be directed exclusively toward the whipped cream.

My first inkling there might be something interesting about music was when, after seeing the movie, my parents bought me the soundtrack album of *Mary Poppins*. I listened to that cherished vinyl over and over again for years. My elementary school had virtually no music curriculum, but who needed a music appreciation class when you had the brilliant songwriting team of the Sherman Brothers as your teachers? And just as brilliant, I would later come to appreciate, were the perfect orchestrations of Irwin Kostal. When the first song started, I wondered why I got shivers up and down my spine. Spoiler alert: it's because the string section is playing a tremolo chord in the perfect register to give you goosebumps.

But lying on the floor of our house on Winding Brook Way in Scotch Plains, all these discoveries were still many years in the future. What set me on the path to find out was that one day I heard a magical sound coming out of a strange, boxy piece of furniture downstairs, and my life changed forever.

When I was around six or seven years old, Joyce began taking piano lessons. Once, after she had finished, my mother invited the teacher, Miss Andrews, to come upstairs for a cup of coffee. The family story goes that as they sat down, they heard the lesson being repeated even though they knew my sister had already gone outside.

So, they ran downstairs and saw little me sitting on the stool, reaching up to the keys, and playing Joyce's lesson by ear.[1]

Shortly afterward, I started taking piano lessons myself, and, augmented by marathons of practice and other training aids—including a then-ubiquitous book, *Teaching Little Fingers to Play*, with its battered red cover—my ability and confidence quickly grew. I was able to play as if the showbiz gods themselves were standing over me, egging me on. Even so, for a long time, the only ones who could appreciate that the Shaimans had birthed this tiny savant were the aunts, uncles, and cousins who would come by our house a few times a year.

When I wasn't practicing piano, I fine-tuned my persnickety palate at the cookouts our family held in the backyard. That is where I decided I hated the texture of barbecued foods, making my mother scrape off not only the crunchy grill lines from hamburgers, but also the crispy outer layer of hot dogs. To this day, my favorite

1. I learned this story from my mother and Miss Andrews almost fifty years later, when they told it to me the afternoon before The New York Pops honored Scott Wittman and me with a concert at Carnegie Hall in 2014.

two words in the English language are "children's menu" (with "comments disabled" running a close second).

That backyard lawn was also the stage for my first major production. One fall when I was very young, I threw a lit match into a pile of leaves my father had raked up and then ran away.

What happened next was that our neighbor, who lived just through the woods over the back fence, yelled, "Fire!" So, fire trucks descended on our little street and extinguished the blaze, which fortunately didn't do any more damage than leaving a burned patch on the grass. Apprehensive about the reviews for this particular show, I crawled into bed and pretended to be asleep, which was where my mother found me when she came home at four thirty in the afternoon.

"Oh, what happened?" I sleepily asked. "I don't know anything about what happened." And much to my surprise, she allowed this ridiculous denial to be the final word on the subject. Perhaps her ability to ignore the mess I made and the lies I told contributed in later years, like so many of her generation, to her willingness not to question Fox News.

My father made a good living with his business, Beverages Unlimited. It was a warehouse that customers could drive their car into to get their weekly supply of soft drinks, beers, or seltzer, along with pretzels, potato chips, and other salty snacks that encourage you to consume more of Dad's unlimited beverages. It offered the added convenience of someone loading the boxes into your trunk so you didn't have to lug them out to a parking lot yourself.

My parents only briefly tried to put me to work there when I was around eleven years old. My mother still brings up the story of when they tried to have me arrange cans in a certain order and I said, "Never bring me back here. I never want to do this ever again!" So I only lasted two days as an apprentice in the family business.

My father was an average suburban dad who, at least from his kids' perspective, mostly just went to work and came home again. Every so often he would demonstrate a hidden artistic flair that I'm not sure we appreciated at the time, like the pleasure he took from creating all the signage for the store himself, by hand.

But if at home he was a genial background presence who could be relied upon to tell corny dad jokes, my mother was his counterpoint. Of the two, she was definitely more of a stickler in her attitude toward raising the kids.

Something that irritated me for most of my childhood, for example, was that she would insist I "have a banana." Why this particular fruit met her daily nutritional requirement I don't know, but she would make me crazy by demanding it. The intensity of her insistence on me eating said banana before I could leave the table became a daily nightmare. The mantra "have a banana" was the "no wire hangers" of my home.[2]

Perhaps due to these Joan Crawford–esque aspects of life at home, I spent more time at the house of the Makowskis, our neighbors across the street. Of the three siblings, I befriended Matthew first. He and I shared a sense of humor but were also wildly different, in that he adored all sorts of sports and I did not. Next was his older sister, Noelle, whom I also befriended, perhaps to express my more feminine qualities. I clearly remember listening to Paul McCartney's first solo album with her in her room.

But the relationship that was deepest was with their middle brother, Mark, with whom I learned how to play every Beatles song on guitar.

Mark turned me on to all sorts of music, from David Bowie's *Ziggy Stardust* and Carly Simon's *No Secrets* to the Rolling Stones, Eric Clapton, and the mind-blowing *Jesus Christ Superstar*.

---

2 Years later, it was cathartic when I first played for Billy Crystal's stand-up act. At one point, he imitated his Jewish aunt, wailing, "I buy fruit, no one eats!" The audience dissolved into hysterics, applauding with recognition, and I thought, "You mean, it happened to everyone?" A weight was lifted. And I now "have a banana" every morning with my cereal!

The Makowskis didn't appear to mind me always being there, and even seemed to get a kick out of me. Except for their dad, that is, who would barely make eye contact with me when he came home from work before disappearing into his dark den. But my using their home as sanctuary from the plastic-covered couches in my mother's living room came to an end one fateful Christmas, when I had been in their house for many days without leaving. Mr. Makowski walked into Matthew's bedroom where I was doing something on my own—Matthew wasn't even there—and said, "Mr. Shaiman, I think it's time you pack up your marbles and go home." I can still see and hear it to this day. And I get it; I had truly overstayed my welcome!

But it was also Mrs. Makowski who rescued me one morning when she drove past the bus stop just as a bully punched me in the stomach. Luckily for a little gay boy, it was one of only two times I can remember being taunted due to clearly being "different."

The other time was when, unbeknownst to her, a jock friend of my sister Joyce wrote "FAG" on my piano sheet music, which my father tried to erase by gluing a piece of paper and painting over it. I remember feeling worse for my father than for myself; I personally was never bothered by not being "normal."

Along those lines, I think I suffer from the tiniest bit of undiagnosed OCD—just enough that I call it CDO so that it is in alphabetical order. As a kid, this manifested as mild trichotillomania, with me obsessively twisting and parting my hair. Sadly, I still do it, although it has become less pronounced as I age. (Less hair to work with!)

One Thanksgiving morning, I decided the small "widow's peak" I had at the top of my hairline (which I miss) had a little more hair on one side of it and I made it my goal to make it more even and started snipping away with my mom's manicuring scissors. I snipped, then had to snip some more to even it out, and on and on, snip after snip. I went into complete denial about how far I had gone until a few hours later, when Joyce and I went to the high school football game and a friend of hers sitting on a bleacher above me said, "Joyce, is your brother going bald?"

There is even proof of this unfortunate "hair don't." I played guitar for Mark Makowski at a junior high talent show a few days later, and there is a picture of me looking down at the guitar. You would think I was a balding Jewish businessman from the Garment District.

But also around the time of junior high, something else happened that truly changed everything.

2

THE SOUND OF MUSIC

'72–'75

In 1972, when my friend Cheryl Louden told me she was auditioning for *The Sound of Music* at the Scotch Plains-Fanwood Summer Theater Workshop, I decided to tag along. It was run by two local women with backgrounds in theater, Manya Ungar and Judy Cole. And it was Judy, the director, to whom I walked up and asked, "Can I audition to play piano?"

"Sure, kid," she barked. "There's the piano. Go play!"

So, I went over and played. I can't remember what piece, but I most definitely remember that when I finished and turned around, everyone in the auditorium was silent and staring at me. I can't blame them. I was only twelve years old, but I just might have summoned the ghosts of Al Jolson and Sophie Tucker with my little show-busy fingers. As Kiki Dee would have been singing around that time on my transistor radio, I had the music in me.

And from that moment at the Scotch Plains-Fanwood Summer Theater Workshop and beyond, musical theater took over my life. It was "So Long, Farewell" to my schoolwork, as I was never to return.

Judy started bringing me around to the community theaters where she directed shows, the first being *Funny Girl* for the Clark Players in Clark, New Jersey. "Everyone, here's our new musical director," she said, pointing at the pimple with two legs standing beside her. I was still just thirteen, and from the aghast looks on their faces, the cast was clearly certain Judy had lost her mind.

"This really has got to be a sick joke, that they brought in what looked like a nine-year-old," the lead, Vicki Tripodo, later recalled to a local newspaper.

But Judy was undeterred. "Marc," she commanded, "go to the piano and play." I followed her orders, scampered over to the piano like a trained monkey, and sight-read the score of *Funny Girl* on the spot. After that, no one questioned whether I had what was needed.

From there, it was one community theater production after another, which served as my equivalent of a college-level music education. It was thrilling learning to read and play from the piano/conductor scores, which were so much more intricate than the simple sheet music I had been buying up until that point from the Westfield Music Store. I could now put on the cast album for *Cabaret*, follow along with the piano/conductor score, and actually *see* the flute, trombone, and viola lines—all the different elements that made up the orchestration. This was how I began to understand the formal techniques behind the supercalifragilistically goose-bumpy music of *Mary Poppins* and other scores.

So, besides my piano teacher, Doris Andrews, my first mentors were Richard and Robert Sherman and Irwin Kostal. I'm happy that I had the good fortune, many years later, to be able to thank three of those people in person.

But community theater's gain was my junior high school's loss, because with music now coursing through my blood, I stopped studying and never handed in homework. I was barely passing my classes, being so deeply entrenched down in the auditorium at Terrill Junior High. Thankfully, *that* school had choruses and bands that I could sing in or play piano for. Eventually I started to create my own vocal arrangements, dragging girls down to the auditorium to try out some new three-part harmony I was imagining when I was supposed to be doing math—not to mention, some may have thought, the girls.

I was dreaming of three-part harmonies because to thank me for the work I had done on all the talent shows, my music teacher, Mr. Christensen, had given me Bette Midler's first two albums. He knew her 1972 cover of "Boogie Woogie Bugle Boy" had already set my head spinning. (That song had first been a hit for The Andrews Sisters, who also scored with "Bei Mir Bist Du Schön," which I would later record with Bette and whose original Yiddish version had likewise been a smash for—wait for it—The Barry Sisters.)

I have a distinct memory of being at a schoolmate's house as everyone else romped outside in the pool, while I sat in his living room next to the radio, just waiting for "Boogie Woogie Bugle Boy" to get played again by WABC. This Bette Midler, whoever she was, had a propulsive charm that leapt out of the radio and grabbed you by the lapels, almost dragging you to your feet to dance. I was absolutely in love.

Ironically, even though I didn't realize it at the time, I had already seen my new idol on Broadway. In 1968, when I was eight years old, my parents took me to see *Fiddler on the Roof* at the Majestic Theatre just off Times Square in Manhattan—because *it is the law* for suburban Jews to bring their children to see *Fiddler on the Roof*. I honestly don't remember seeing the show, but I do remember obsessing over the souvenir booklet that came home with us. Most of all, I was incredibly drawn to one certain actress in the pictures, the girl playing Tzeitel. Her face was so expressive, and the way that she smiled up at Motel the Tailor stole my heart. Reader, that actress was Bette Midler.

Unfortunately, one of the other laws of suburban Jews, and of show business in general, is that for every *plotz* there's a *zetz*. (For the gentiles in the audience, a *plotz* is a moment of excitement, while a *zetz* is a punch in the gut.)

You see, there was this kid named George in my junior high school who was the kind of nerd who carried a briefcase to every class. He found out The Carpenters—the Pepsodent-y brother/sister duo who were then topping the charts with their cheerful hit "Sing"—were coming to town and seeking local kids to join them on stage to perform the children's choir part on that song. And somehow, this kid got us the gig.

"Well, Mr. Christensen," I said to my music teacher, being the Boy Wonder to his Batman, "I will figure out all the harmony on that record. This is going to be great."

So I transcribed the harmonies—even the three-part harmonies at the end that were tucked down in the mix—wrote it all out, and taught it to the girls' choir. We rehearsed and rehearsed, me biting my fingernails until they were nothing but tender red crescents, until it was perfect. And when everything was finally just how I wanted it to be, I felt like a twelve-year-old Napoleon, all set to conquer the world.

But when it came time to go to the Garden State Arts Center for the concert, not only was I told there was no room for me on the bus, but also no money to buy me a ticket for the show. A friend's mom took pity on me and bought me a ticket. It was a clear July night with a breeze—a miraculous break from the rain and New Jersey's swampy humidity—and I sat in that enormous open-air amphitheater in Holmdel, watching Karen Carpenter do an actual double take when the kids sang those subtle three-part harmony chords. And then I watched as my music teacher was whisked backstage. I can still see it in my head, him rushing by our seats and being brought to the side door, while I just sat there, not at all part of the evening, nor of the celebration. I had never felt lonelier or more left out. Holmdel, it turned out, was my Waterloo.

"So, this is showbiz," I thought. It may have been my first big *zetz*, but hang on, little me, there would be many more to come.

Now, if I have one talent even greater than my aptitude for music and lyrics, it is my ability to sulk. I sulked for *months* after that Carpenters concert, refusing to play for the talent shows or anything down in the auditorium. And I ruthlessly froze out Mr. Christensen, any goodwill generated by his previous gifts of the Bette Midler albums long forgotten.

Eventually, gradually, I got over it. Or at least I got over it enough. I even made my peace with David Christensen, who for three years had certainly been a solid mentor to me. I suppose even mentors are only human, and Lord knows, if I have ever been one myself, I surely have not done it perfectly. (Unlike, say, the three-part harmonies I orchestrated for "Sing." *Which. Were. Perfect.*)

Over the next few years, I found myself under the tutelage of a renowned local talent named Norman Krisburg, who directed just about every other community theater production I was involved with (and christened me with the nickname "Knuckles"). If they had made a movie about Norm at the time, Kirk Douglas would have played him. I don't think I ever knew what he did for a day job, but he had served in the navy during World War II and when night came and rehearsals started, he was *the man* in charge. His vitality and concentration were remarkable. I did *Cabaret* with Norm, plus *Fiddler on the Roof, Godspell, Jesus Christ Superstar,* and *West Side Story*. Each of them was a learning experience as he guided different troupes through their paces, always putting on a show that left the audience enriched and the cast in love with the work and each other. So many of the great people I did those shows with are still in my life, and I in theirs.

By putting on regional productions of these classic shows, I was slowly learning all the important lessons of musical theater. They taught me about building storytelling structure, especially through song; about the importance of exquisite accompaniment and orchestrations; and also, the importance of casting.

By the time I turned fifteen, I had begun learning about other things as well. That was the age when I came to accept and enjoy that I was gay. I always say that as a teenage boy, there were four things I tried once and never went back for seconds: coffee, alcohol, cigarettes…and pussy. In fact, I had become quite the Pied Piper, drawing out all the possibly gay friends in school and community theater. Since I was not of age, I hope the statute of limitations will protect my various paramours, but I was probably more sexually active at fifteen than at any other time of my life. (File that under "good news/bad news.")

My first conquest was fellow Midler-fanatic Bruce Conroy, whom I met through community theater and quickly became obsessed with. He worked at a hair salon that had a little side room where I eventually seduced him...or he seduced me...or we seduced each other. But I was infuriated when, months later, he brought someone else to a rehearsal who I'd correctly guessed was a romantic rival. My friends and I were driving off afterward to swim in a lake, but along the way I stopped at a payphone and called the salon before getting back in the car, leaving the phone dangling off the hook so it would ring indefinitely. My diabolical plan was that the incessant ringing would ruin the mood in the side room, where they must have gone to be alone—but that Bruce would not be able to answer the phone because he wasn't supposed to be there after hours. Years later, he confirmed that my teenage, *Dynasty*-like scheme had worked.

Bruce was just one of many lifelong friends I made through community theater.

Although we were far from Broadway, I met wildly talented people like Vicki Tripodo, her mother, Harriet Saltzman, and my fellow harmony-lover, Jamie Rose. I had the blessing of visiting Jamie's house for the holidays—I call it a blessing because her mom and four aunts had been a renowned singing group, The DeMarco Sisters. They may never have had iconic hits like the Andrews, McGuire, or DeCastro Sisters, but they kept their heads above water in show business for many years. And these five sisters effortlessly sang the *tightest* five-part harmony you can imagine. At Christmas, if they could stop fighting about the seven fishes for a moment—this was a big, Italian, musical family, prone to great drama—they would sing through their repertoire around the couch, a cappella, and I had my first eargasms. If you want proof of God, whatever God is to you, sit in a living room and experience the level of natural talent bestowed on this family.

And, because she is never far from the story of my life, there is even a Bette Midler connection.

Like many people, I experience sense memories when I hear certain recordings, and when Bette's fantastic cover of Jackie Wilson's "Your Love Keeps Lifting Me (Higher and Higher)" comes on, I am immediately taken back to Norm's house one afternoon, prepping for our upcoming show. Like me, Norm had just gotten Bette's second album, and I have a distinct memory of sitting in his living room listening to "Higher and Higher." He went over to his record player and kept repeating the song, unable to stop raving about the magnetic energy emanating from this woman. (I must say, the energy is *also* coming from Barry Manilow's thrilling arrangement.) So just at that moment in that living room, I had three important mentors guiding me: Norm, Bette, and Barry.

Many years later, Norm came to see my musical, *Hairspray*, on Broadway after it had opened to ecstatic reviews. When I greeted him in the audience during the curtain call, being a director to his bones, he gave me notes. The next time I saw him was in the hospital when he was nearing the end of his life. He seemed uncomfortable during the visit, perhaps because he didn't like anyone to see him when he wasn't in control. I pray he knew—he must have—how much he meant to an entire musical tribe of suburbanites who loved theater. Both Norman Krisburg and Judy Cole gave that thrill to so many people.

Norm left us in 2007, and Judy Cole passed away only a few days short of her ninety-fifth birthday in 2023. The very last thing she left her apartment to do was be my guest at the invited dress rehearsal (a kind of friends-and-family preview) for my Broadway musical, *Some Like It Hot*. I wanted her there as a bookend to the invited dress rehearsal for *Hairspray* that she had attended in 2002. At that afternoon's performance of *Hairspray* twenty years earlier, in front of a theater packed with Broadway performers and creators, I introduced Judy to the crowd, explaining who she was and what she meant to me. I knew everyone there had benefited from having a Judy Cole in their life, someone who recognized their talent and encouraged them to pursue a career in the arts. You can only imagine the sustained, raucous standing ovation the crowd gave her. I was so blessed to have been able to give Judy that moment, and for her to finally receive an ovation in a packed Broadway theater.

I went to see Judy in her hospital room during the final weeks of her life. On my first visit, she was not awake. Her caretaker, Anna, told me she had not been "present" for a few days.

I gently whispered, "Judy, it's Marc." No reaction.

So, I whispered once more, even more softly, barely a murmur, "*...Marc Shaiman...*"

Then Anna fog-horned, "JUDY! IT'S MARC! MARC SHAIMAN!"

Judy wasn't dead yet, but even if she had been, Anna's voice would have woken her up. And to my delight, her eyes opened.

She couldn't speak but looked up at me, her eyes brimming with a lifetime of emotions. I looked right back, speaking without words, not only for myself, but also for every other kid from the Scotch Plains-Fanwood Summer Theater Workshop, saying *thank you*. And then her eyes closed again.

There's the piano, kid. Go play.

3

MANIFESTING MIDLER

'75–'77

From the moment I first heard "Boogie Woogie Bugle Boy" emanating from my radio in 1973, I became completely obsessed with Bette Midler. Outside of my junior high school dance band, I had never really been exposed to the big band sound, and now suddenly here it was, pouring out of my AM radio like sunshine. The music of the 1940s—perhaps to offer refuge from all the horrible things that were then happening in the world—just seemed to radiate pure joy. In the early '70s, amid the tie-dyed T-shirts, bell-bottom pants, and Volkswagen beetles, nostalgia was all the rage. And suddenly, there was Bette, singing three-part harmony with herself, with an infectious vitality that was unusual for pop radio then or even now.

Her records quickly replaced the *Mary Poppins* soundtrack on my little turntable and Bette's posters went up on the walls of my suburban bedroom. I devoured every song from her first three albums. I had never encountered a performer like her—one who could be hysterical, sensual, raucous, and bittersweet all on just the first side of an album. And then you would turn it over and she would do it all again on side B. The heartbreak in her voice on songwriter John Prine's exquisite "Hello in There" could move my little thirteen-year-old heart beyond measure, and then her ebullient theme song "Friends" would pick me right back up.

I was also musically proficient enough to recognize how the arrangements by her gifted musical director, Barry Manilow, were as responsible for my delirium as Bette's vocals. The pair were masters at taking songs you already knew and blowing them up to become showstoppers. Girl-group songs like "Chapel of Love" were amplified into joyous celebrations of themselves, while they remade a song like "Superstar"—whose soothing but white-bread version was made famous by The Carpenters—into a harrowing exploration of unrequited love.

I started following her career, and in 1975, when I was fifteen, I read in a school copy of the *New York Times* that she was coming back to Broadway with a new concert called *Clams on the Half Shell*. (And yes, I was the one kid reading the *New York Times* in my homeroom, even if I was maybe only looking at the Arts & Leisure section.) I knew I had to go see her in person, so I helped myself to some of the cash under the sink in my parents' bathroom, cut school for the millionth time, and boarded a bus to New York.

Scotch Plains was only fifty-five minutes from Manhattan, and there were buses leaving all day to get there. So, the journey wasn't as intimidating as it might have been for some naïf blowing in from the prairie, like Jon Voight in *Midnight Cowboy*. But still, the city was more dangerous then, so maybe I should have been cautious about going alone.

Nonetheless, my longing to see Bette Midler live in concert on Broadway was stronger than my survival instincts, so I snuck off to New York, arriving at Port Authority in the late morning. That notorious bus terminal on Eighth Avenue was right in the middle of the midtown badlands, one block west from Times Square. The city seemed grayer back then, as if everything was asphalt-colored with a layer of graffiti on top. So, I had to take a deep breath and gather all my courage before scurrying along 42nd Street past the hookers, drug dealers, and porno theaters, not stopping for an instant until I was safely on Broadway.

I went to the Minskoff Theatre and bought one ticket—leaving me with hours to kill. Fortunately, a nearby cinema was showing *Funny Lady,* Barbra Streisand's sequel to *Funny Girl,* and although I had already seen it twice, I went in and watched it two more times. During one of those screenings, however, a stranger sat next to me and placed his hand on my thigh. This freaked me out and I moved to the other side of the theater, but he followed me and once again put his hand on my leg. Now, I was no shrinking violet, so after a bit more of this, I finally just shrugged and thought, "I've seen enough of this movie." By the time I entered the lobby of the Minskoff that night, I was already enjoying the gayest day in my fifteen years on the planet: Barbra Streisand followed by Bette Midler, with an unexpected assignation in between.

Naturally, Bette was the highlight of the day. She had taken a few years off from live performing, so her return to Broadway was a big deal; the audience was primed and the theater was abuzz with excitement. The house lights dimmed, drumming began, and, even now, I can still picture Bette's backup girls, The Harlettes, with only their hands sticking out of the beaded curtain, pointing stage left as they sang a cover version of "The Bitch Is Back." And with that song as her entrance music, out came—oh my God, there she is, right in front of me—*Bette Midler*!

I was in absolute heaven, completely transfixed. Listening to Bette's records could hardly prepare me for the electricity of her live performance. She strutted back and forth across the stage and would keep the audience in hysterics until she smoothly switched gears and sang a ballad that brought us to tears. As she sang, I imagined myself running down to the stage, pleading, "Oh, Miss Midler, I know every note, of every arrangement, of every song, on every album of yours. Please let me play for you." In this daydream, I then sat down at the piano to play and was, of course, fantastic. And perched atop the piano, she'd cross her legs and look out to the audience with an expression that said, *Damn, he's good*! Nice dream.

A year or so later, I went into the city with Bruce Conroy to see an Off-Broadway musical called *Boy Meets Boy*—a title that ended up being prophetic. This time, I didn't have to skip school to go to Manhattan, because, by sixteen years old, certain that high school was a waste of time, I had already passed the exam and received my general equivalency diploma. After the show, we ran into some other friends, and the four of us stepped into a nearby bar on the corner of Seventh Avenue and Grove Street in the Village. It was a little basement piano bar called Marie's Crisis Cafe,[3] and what with it being 4:30 in the afternoon, we were the only four people there, so of course I went right to the piano and played.

The bartender stopped sweeping the floor, looked up, and like right out of an old-timey movie said, "Hey kid, you're good! Stay right there." He ran to The Duplex, a cabaret bar down the block, and came back a minute later with five people. They were rehearsing an act called "Cocktails for Five" and needed a funnier piano player. So, they asked if I knew "Together Wherever We Go" from the musical *Gypsy*, and I went right into it in the style it was written for the show. But one of them stopped me and asked if I could play it again but "cheesy." This was a few years before Bill Murray did his character Nick the Lounge Singer on *Saturday Night Live*, making "cheesy" show business a bit. And I had never really known anyone else who shared that sense of humor about how the old guard could take every song, no matter how un-show-bizzy it seemed, and make it sound like it was written for a Las Vegas lounge act. At community theater cast parties, I would sometimes say, "Okay, here is how

---

3 Although it may not be as famous as the Stonewall Inn, which is only 450 feet away on Sheridan Square, Marie's Crisis Cafe is one of the most culturally and historically important gay bars in New York City. The 1838 townhouse whose basement it occupies is on the site of the former home and death-place of Thomas Paine, a Founding Father famous for his revolutionary pamphlet series "The American Crisis." The current venue is thought to have been a gay bar since 1890; renamed Marie's in 1929, the "Crisis" part of its nickname was historically apt, camp, and just kind of stuck. As a meeting place for Broadway's LGBTQ+ creative community for more than a century, its significance cannot be overstated.

a song sounds on the radio—and now, here is how a Bar Mitzvah band would play it!" In the same way, I figured that was what these folks wanted to hear, and I played "Together Wherever We Go" like Steve Lawrence and Eydie Gormé would have bedazzled it on *The Merv Griffin Show*.

"That's it!" they all yelled, and I got the job.

The director of the act—the one who asked me to play it "cheesy"—was Scott Wittman. He was talented, tall, and good looking, with black curly hair and a moustache—just my type. It turned out that my seeing *Boy Meets Boy* earlier that day would be the prelude of a romantic hit that, when it got started a couple of years later, would run for almost three decades.

In the meantime, Scott and his friends, Billy Gallo and Tracey Berg, who were two of his collaborators in "Cocktails for Five," had an apartment up on West 79th Street between Columbus and Amsterdam Avenues. It was a two-bedroom in an elevator building, and I would stay with them on the weekends to play for their act. My parents clearly had a lot of faith in my street smarts, because I don't remember them fretting over my new life of playing for a nightclub act every weekend in the city. I felt I was exactly where I wanted to and should be, laughing with new friends whose sense of humor perfectly matched my own. And that Scott guy was awfully cute!

Another early job I got in the city came via one of the acting teachers from the summer theater course I took in Pittsburgh when I was fifteen. I guess at that point my dreams went beyond the piano and I thought I might also be fated to become a performer. I attended with my fellow *Sound of Music* auditionee, Cheryl Loudon, whose stage mother, Harriet, got us both into the program at Carnegie Mellon University.

There was a very intense Israeli teacher there named Rina Yerushalmi, who suffered no fools. Most of the students were intimidated by her, but I thought she was fantastic. She was like an Israeli

Maria Callas, who did not treat me or any of the other teenagers like a kid.

A few months after that summer course, right after I had left school on my sixteenth birthday, Rina called me at my family's house in New Jersey. In her fabulously thick accent (think Anna Magnani by way of Golda Meir) she said, "I'm doing an evening of Beckett, a combination of his stories at the La MaMa Annex. I want the sound effects to have musicality, and I thought you'd be perfect for the job."

So, I would take the bus from Scotch Plains, arrive at the Port Authority in Manhattan, and head down to East 4th Street, where this very, very experimental production was rehearsing. My only memory of the sound effects I did "with musicality" was the shoes and keys of a prison guard—a true precursor to the matron in *Hairspray*.

I think the production ended with a thud after one performance. But it rehearsed for a couple of weeks, and my parents saw me going into New York and getting paid for a job, even though it was probably only five dollars.

That job enabled me, at only sixteen years old, to tell my parents I wanted to move into Manhattan. "What am I, gonna chain him to the piano?" my mother exclaimed to anyone who questioned their choice to let me leave home so young. But they didn't fight me because I had already started coming into the city to work.

A few months later came that fateful summer day, seeing *Boy Meets Boy* and meeting Scott Wittman and his friends. Not only did I start playing for their act, "Cocktails for Five" at The Duplex, but John Michel, the bartender who ran Marie's Crisis, also offered me a job on the spot.

So, in 1976, my parents helped me move into a closet masquerading as a studio apartment on West 22nd Street. My father, God bless him, even helped the movers push my upright piano up the rickety, crooked stairs.

I worked at Marie's Crisis from approximately September of 1976 through January of 1977. I knew all the Broadway music of the time and before, as well as the Judy Garland and Barbra Streisand numbers that were constantly requested. And I was a wiz at transposing, so I could put the songs in men's keys, although most of the guys unfortunately insisted on singing them in Judy's and Barbra's keys.

I think this was the origin of my disdain for very drunk people. You haven't paid your dues until a queen with the breath of an alcoholic cougar chastises you for lowering the key of "Come Rain or Come Shine."

But I was going home with a big wad of cash at the end of every week. I told my parents I was playing piano for a nightclub act at a piano bar, but did not encourage them to come in. They seemed to intuit, "Let's not." Marie's Crisis was basically a gay bar, and at that point, I still was not out to them. (Although, to be fair, the Bette Midler posters on my bedroom wall offered a clue.)

In 1976, sixteen-year-olds weren't coming out on TikTok. It was actually quite a few years later that I came out to my parents, and to her credit, it was my mother who dragged it out of me—no pun intended.

I had lied to John Michel about my age to get the job. Actually, I lied twice. As my October birthday approached, I "confessed" to him I was seventeen going on eighteen, when in fact I was sixteen going on seventeen. Although I looked my age, my piano-playing ability and bizarrely expansive music knowledge meant nobody ever questioned me.

However, when they lowered me from the balcony above the piano in a diaper on New Year's Eve, I knew it was time to go. I turned my back on the weekly wad of cash and took a chance that other opportunities would come my way.

One unexpected opportunity for creativity presented itself alongside Sal Piro, a friend from New Jersey community theater who would often come into the city to stay with me at the time. One night in 1977, while walking though the West Village, we passed the Waverly Theater, which had just started midnight showings of *The Rocky Horror Picture Show*.

"I've heard this is great," Sal said. So we lined up.

We immediately hit it off with a few other folks on line, including Louis Farese, a kindergarten teacher from Staten Island who is credited with being the first person to talk back to the movie. As Susan Sarandon, portraying Janet, walked through the rain, Louis yelled, "Buy an umbrella, ya cheap bitch!"

The ad-lib went over so well with the audience that we started writing other lines to go between the film's dialogue, then creating props, and eventually performing the songs before and during the movie.

And that is how, quite innocently, we gave birth to a cultural phenomenon. Audience-participation screenings of *The Rocky Horror Picture Show* cropped up all over the world, and although I finished my run after some eighty evenings, it turned into Sal's life's work and passion. He became president of the *Rocky Horror* fan club and spent the next forty years being a guru to millions of fans. Time Warp to 2023, when he passed away—his outré life achievement earned him an obit in the *New York Times*.[4]

Playing for Scott's comic revue, starring his friends Billy Gallo, Tracey Berg, Lisa Passero, and Mary Fulham, also introduced me to the rest of their tribe. As fate would have it, Ula Hedwig, one of Bette Midler's back-up girls, lived across the hall from Scott's apartment. They had just finished a tour with Bette where she had let them open the second act with their own song, and they were now looking to do an independent act. And because I (a) knew all about the harmonies they'd want from my fervent study of Bette's

4 In 1978, I worked with *Rocky Horror*'s Dr. Frank-N-Furter himself, Tim Curry, as he prepped his first solo album. As we rehearsed around my piano on 79th Street, I surreptitiously called Sal on my bedroom phone so he could hear I was truly "not dreaming it, but being it!"

records and the other albums those led me to; (b) sorta lived across the hall, but mostly (c) would work for next to nothing, I got the gig to become their musical director. This meant I helped choose the songs for their act and worked out the harmonies and band arrangements, which was truly a dream assignment.

The act was a huge hit at New York's premier cabaret at the time, Reno Sweeney on West 13th Street. It was a cramped, smoky room with a stage at the back laid in checkerboard black-and-white linoleum tiles, and the Harlettes packed it every night. Then Bette said that if the girls would go back on the road with her for her forthcoming Copa Tour, she would let them open her show with a half-hour version of their new act. And so, I was flown to Los Angeles to teach Bette's band the Harlettes' act at a well-known rehearsal hall called SIR (a.k.a. Studio Instrument Rentals), where the band sits up on a stage—a small but important detail of my fantasy.

After finishing the Harlettes rehearsal, I sat on the couch in the back of the room and, lo and behold, Bette Midler herself came in to start her own rehearsal. Her explosive performance persona, "the Divine Miss M," may be known to fans worldwide, but offstage she is more focused—if you came across her in a restaurant reading a book, you might even think she was a librarian. Onstage she is a lightning bolt, but in rehearsal she is more like a light bulb: always looking for a way to make the performance better. Watching her cross the room, my head and heart were exploding. Could I have ever imagined being this close to someone whose posters had plastered my bedroom wall just two years ago?

At some point, she asked her newly hired band, who were all strangers to her repertoire, to play "No Jestering," a reggae number from her third album, *Songs for the New Depression*. There was no music for it in their folders and they were stymied. One of the Harlettes, Charlo Crossley, walked over to Bette and whispered in her ear while pointing to me. Then Bette yelled out, "Hey! Can you play 'No Jestering'?"

And I actually got to walk up to a stage, exactly like in my daydream back at the Minskoff Theatre, and say, "Oh, Miss Midler, I know every note of every arrangement of every song of every album of yours. Please let me play for you!"

I am not a very courageous person; I hate roller coasters and heights and would never enter a place where there was a chance of trouble. But my self-confidence when it came to Bette Midler, her material, and my ability to play it well was sky high. After all, I had spent the last four years playing along to all her records and I knew, as I told her, every note. So, I sat at the piano and played "No Jestering"—if I may say so—*flawlessly*.

Bette must have agreed, because she said, "Stick around, I could use you."

My return flight home was quickly postponed. And if all this wasn't enough to blow my mind, Bette decided, either due to frugalness or because she liked having a piano player close at hand night and day, that instead of putting me up in a hotel, she would move me into the guest room at her small house in Beverly Hills which she was renting from the actor Richard Chamberlain. And I'm not talking about staying in a guest house out back, I am talking about the guest room down the hall.

Suddenly I was living with and having breakfast at the kitchen table every morning with my idol, working on her Copa Tour. The big sister/little brother relationship that still exists today was born in that house. Just one memory from that time is the night Tom Waits came over and taught us his new song "Rainbow Sleeve," the three of us sitting on a piano bench, with me to his left and Bette to his right.

When people talk about manifesting something for themselves, I always tell this story, because somehow I managed to make my ultimate dream come true when I was still only seventeen years old.

I believe it was my destiny or, as the Jews call it, *bashert*. When I returned to New York, my friend, Zora Rasmussen, a wonderful singer and comedian, took me to a place she had discovered called the Gypsy Tearoom. It was across the street from Madison Square Garden and had a bunch of psychics who would read your cards. Slightly skeptical, I went along with Zora, and when my turn came, I was seated with a fellow who looked like he still lived in his parents' basement. Neither Zora nor I said a word to him about anything, and when he read my cards, I was unimpressed, since everything he said sounded vague and generic. Then he said, "Drink up your tea so I can read the tea leaves." Inside, I rolled my eyes, but I swallowed the tea and passed him the cup. He looked into it, and this guy who resembled a shut-in who wouldn't know pop culture from popcorn said, "I see the smiling face of Bette Midler."

Like I said…*bashert*.

4

GOD SAVE THE CITY

'76–'82

My work on the New York cabaret circuit in the mid-1970s included playing for the multi-talented Zora Rasmussen and her ex-husband, Robert I. Rubinsky. Robert I., as he was always known, was in the original cast of *Hair* and had a kinetic performing style all his own. He had started writing lyrics in that same style and asked if I'd set some of them to music.

His idea was for a musical about the inhabitants of a welfare hotel in Midtown: hustlers, hookers, drag queens, bag ladies, and Bowery bums, plus the Rich Lady who would comment on them all. He wanted to humanize these characters in a show called *Dementos*. Thus began a years-long loop of one step forward, two steps back.

After writing enough songs to try out in front of friends and business associates, we gathered a cast and started holding "*Dementos* presentations" in rented rehearsal studios. They were always well received; the cast and material meshed, and the down-at-heel characters blended humor and emotion nicely. As Robert I. wrote in one of his lyrics:

THE PEOPLE YOU THREW AWAY
YOU HURRY BY EACH DAY
THE PEOPLE YOU HURRY BY
BUT DON'T WANNA SEE

I MAY BE LIVING APART
BUT I FEEL IN MY HEART

AND I KNOW IN MY HEAD TOO...
I'M JUST LIKE YOU

Various folks would come and go on *Dementos*: producers who wanted to help but didn't have the means; directors who liked but couldn't figure out how to present our songs. Finally, a man named Rick Grimaldi appeared. He worked at a management company headed by Bill Aucoin, who made his fortune managing the rock group Kiss. Rick eventually left Aucoin to focus on our show.

He hooked us up with director Ron Link (known for directing Tom Eyen's outrageous plays Off-Broadway) and in 1980, an actual Broadway production was being put together. We were slated to open a new theater space underneath City Center!

We rehearsed with a cast including Loretta Devine and Cleavant Derricks, who would go on to be original cast members of *Dreamgirls*. But we found that although the songs Robert I. and I wrote had emotional punch, the show lacked a clear storyline. This was probably why it never gelled. It would have been better if we had followed Robert I.'s original concept of a concert-style presentation, but everyone kept trying to shoehorn the songs into a plot.

Finally, an ad for *Dementos* appeared in the *New York Times*' Arts & Leisure section, making the whole thing seem real. But a few days later, we got a phone call from Rick saying not to come to rehearsal that day. He said he "hit a small snag" and we should "give him a beat." We got the same call the next day, and the next. Eventually, he admitted he lost his investors and we were up the proverbial creek.

Devastating.

Our only hope of keeping the production alive was a Hail Mary backers' audition that would have to happen right away. So, I did something many others had done but I'd never wanted to do: I called Bette Midler to ask if she could front me the money.

I had a tax rebate coming and promised I could pay her back promptly. But I knew by asking for money, I had joined a long list of folks who hit her up and that it would tarnish our relationship. Which it did. Because we did the backers' audition (at Studio 54!)

with hardly any rehearsal or a proper sound check, and nothing came of it. So, the tax rebate was suddenly all the money I had to live on, and I couldn't immediately repay Bette as promised.

Doubly devastating.[5]

Dementos would have two more resurrections before it finally died. New producers came aboard, Gerald Duval and Candy Leigh, who had a relationship with the original manager of the Rolling Stones, Andrew Loog Oldham. His idea was to record a live cast album, but again, when the day came, we were not prepared. The band was under-rehearsed, and the performers' vocals and harmonies were less than perfect, as was the entire recording setup. Then, the musicians had to bring Oldham up on charges with their union in order to get paid. Have I mentioned the word *devastating*?

You would think by then we'd have given up. But in 1983, Robert I. met Norman René, who ran an Off-Broadway theater on West 28th Street called The Production Company. Norman decided to take a chance on our poor misbegotten show.

When it premiered, we got an "okay" review in the *New York Times* that was lukewarm on the musical, but raved about our amazing cast, which included Charlayne Woodard and my eternal friend, Annie Golden.[6]

After the Production Company production, it was finally time to close the book on *Dementos*. I did continue to perform some of

---

5 A few years later, my Harlette friend Ula Hedwig, hoping to end the years of awkwardness between Bette and me due to my inability to pay her back when promised, brought her to a revue of my songs at The Westside Arts Center. At the end of the show, I tearily spoke of Bette and how I had broken a promise to her and she stood up and just as tearily wailed, "You don't owe me the money anymore!" And as fate would have it, from having just started working at SNL, I was finally able to pay her back the following week.

6 A few years earlier, when I was King of the Broadway Audition Pianists, I had played for Annie when she auditioned both for *Hair*'s first Broadway revival (which was not a success), and Miloš Forman's film version (in which her solo ended up on the editing room floor). Since Annie had first been noticed at legendary punk club CBGB as the lead singer of the band The Shirts, I knew she was perfect for the role of *Dementos*' punk-poetess, Spike Heel. So, I called Barneys department store, where I discovered she was working, and asked if she would be in our show. I can't take credit for her resurgence in theater, but I am very happy to have been the guy who diverted her from selling men's socks.

its best songs in my revues, culminating in the shows at The Bottom Line that later got me noticed by the *New York Times*. But their '70s style became dated, and the way we presented the characters might get us cancelled today, even with the dignity we tried to bestow upon them.

Years later, when *Rent* and *The Life* were both playing to acclaim on Broadway, I had to look away from the marquees and even their ads in the papers. It was just too painful to see those shows had pulled off what we had tried to do with *Dementos*. I guess we were simply too early.

A few years ago, when Covid turned Manhattan into a ghost town, I went into the vaults and found a live recording of my friend Jenifer Lewis singing the show's finale, an anthem to New York called "God Save the City." An editor friend of Robert I.'s, Eric Marciano, cut it into a beautifully poignant video set to visuals of what was going on in New York and cities all around the world. It took a global, hundred-years pandemic to make it happen, but for a moment, *Dementos* lived once more.

5

IT TAKES AN EAST VILLAGE

'80–'84

Artistic expression of all kinds, however low-budget or short-lived, flourished in New York even as Ronald Reagan's presidential election victory ushered in a national wave of conservatism. In 1980, our friend, writer Marge Gross, told Scott and me she had discovered a wonderland of weirdness in the basement of 57 St. Mark's Place in the East Village.

Underneath a Polish church was a unique space called Club 57. A group of irony-obsessed creatives at the forefront of the '80s art wave had taken over the basement and were curating events that skewered pop culture.

Habitués included soon-to-be-celebrated artists like Jean-Michel Basquiat, Keith Haring, and Kenny Scharf; visionary performer Klaus Nomi; and theatrical punks with names like Wendy Wild and John Sex. Ann Magnuson, the performance artist who helped start the club, said it was filled with "pointy-toed hipsters, girls in rockabilly petticoats, spandex pants, and thrift-store stiletto heels [and] suburban refugees who had run away from home to find a new family. [They] liked the things we liked—Devo, Duchamp, and William S. Burroughs—and (more important) hated the things we hated: disco, Diane von Fürstenberg, and *The Waltons*."

At that moment, Scott and I, and many of our performer friends, felt like we had no place to belong. We were too quirky for Broadway, especially the huge English musicals then taking over, but too theatrical for mainstream music. We weren't getting shows produced or record deals. But at Club 57, we could exercise our imaginations, no matter how ridiculous those ideas might seem to anyone outside our little troupe. It was like coming home—if your home was an otherworldly, pansexual, nonconformist fever dream of creativity and expression.

Scott's first idea was to bring dinner theater to Manhattan. He unearthed a trifle of a play called *Boeing-Boeing*, a 1960s farce about a wannabe Don Juan who juggles dating three stewardesses based on their flight schedules. The extremely cheesy show was perfect for the tone of Club 57. (Decades later, it was revived on Broadway to great success; it's a pain in the ass to be ahead of your time.)

We served macaroni and cheese to the gays and stoned fashionistas who stumbled in—and if Scott thought the pacing was too slow, he would throw ice cubes at the actors from the DJ booth.

Scott insists that while cleaning up the basement dressing area, he once yelled, "Someone tell that Keith Haring to move all these drawings!" If only we had kept a few, I would own the company publishing this book.

Next up was Scott's inspired production of Euripides' *The Trojan Women*, transplanted to the fiery ruins of the MGM Grand Hotel in Las Vegas.

All of our friends brought out their best (or worst) impressions: Tracey Berg as Joan Rivers playing Hecuba; J.P. Dougherty as a bloated ghost of Elvis playing the messenger Talthybius; Laura Kenyon as Lainie Kazan as Andromache, and me as her infant son, Astyanax. Laura and I made our entrance with me playing "Don't Cry Out Loud" on a Casio keyboard hanging from my neck as I suckled on her breast. It was an instant hit, drawing limos containing agents and trendsetters. Even Hollywood producer Allan Carr came down and tried to buy the show (and Scott). But Club 57 was there for fun, and no matter how popular one show would become, we would just think of something else to do.

One of my favorite shows was our bootleg production of *The Sound of Music,* which starred Andy Warhol superstar Holly Woodlawn (a trans pioneer who was the subject of the first verse of Lou Reed's "Walk on the Wild Side") as Maria. J.P. Dougherty portrayed both the Mother Abbess and Captain von Trapp, showing how quickly a habit can be thrown over a naval captain's uniform. John Sex and Wendy Wild turned young lovers Rolf and Liesel into Aryan punk rockers. And we had sets on every wall of the clubhouse, so Scott invented "Rotation Theater." He would yell, "Rotate!" after each scene and the audience would boisterously turn their folding chairs to watch the next scene. If there had been an Obie for Audience Choreography, we would've been a shoo-in.

Our highly edited and highly illegal version of the script had Maria singing:

COCAINE THAT STAYS ON MY NOSE AND FALSE LASHES

and

WHEN THE DOG BITES, WHEN MY PEE STINGS

Besides being the musical director and playing the piano, I sold tickets at the door each night with an old black T-shirt and white paper towel on my head, converted into a nun's wimple. I was constantly surprised at how agents would huff and puff, expecting to be comped to a show put on by starving artists that only cost a few dollars. How happily I refused to admit them until they coughed up the five bucks!

Scott was a voracious reader. One day, he came home from the bookstore with a huge coffee-table volume on the history of Barbie's fashions and proclaimed, "This is a musical!" So, we sat down and quickly wrote an original musical called *Livin' Dolls*, a beach-party romp about how Barbie met Ken. We had collaborated on a one-off sketch song before, for the comedy group The High-Heeled Women, but this was the first musical Scott and I wrote together.

Our show was not trying to be about "the patriarchy" or other themes running through the outrageously successful *Barbie* movie that came out in 2023. It was just a simple tale of how all them dolls first got together during a vacation in Waikiki. Barbie meets Ken, Midge meets G.I. Joe (yes, we cross-bred from Mattel to Hasbro), and Chatty Cathy meets Poindexter (who was a precursor to Ken's "friend" Allan). Even Barbie's pet poodle, Fifi, met the Creature from the Black Lagoon, who just happened to play a mean sax.

With our friends playing all the parts, singing to the musical accompaniment I created with Man Parrish (the first guy I knew to be making music with synthesizers), the show was another huge hit—if you are grading on the curve of what kind of hit you can have in the basement of a Polish church in the East Village.

At that time, I was also working as a pianist at the Public Theater on *Gallery*, a theatrical revue of the songs *A Chorus Line* lyricist Ed Kleban had written over the years. Fellow Broadway lyricist Richard Maltby Jr. was directing it after just having had enormous Broadway success with *Ain't Misbehavin'*. One night I got Richard and legendary Public Theater impresario Joe Papp to come over to St. Mark's Place to see our show. Much to our shock, they loved it. Within days, Richard beat Joe to the punch and convinced Lynne Meadow and Barry Grove, who ran the Manhattan Theatre Club, to put it up as the final show of their season.

At that time, their theater was located on the Upper East Side, and, well, their elderly audience didn't quite know what to make of our East Village musical. The old joke is that "the Manhattan Theatre Club sleeps two hundred." One night, when our friend J.P. Dougherty was ebulliently enjoying the show, an ancient subscriber left a note on his seat at intermission saying, "Shut up or go home!"

These people liked to enjoy their comedy *in peace*.

More problematic than the geriatric audience was that Mattel refused to grant us the rights to Barbie and Ken. "Barbie doesn't speak; she never will," they told us—although apparently they changed their minds for Margot Robbie. The show simply lost its appeal when it became about "Candy and Paul" instead. So, although it got okay reviews (the notoriously acerbic critic, John Simon, of all people, loved it), *Livin' Dolls* did not become our ticket to Broadway.[7]

After the sad chapter at the Manhattan Theatre Club, Scott and I headed back to Club 57.

We had another hit with *Trilogy of Terror*, co-written with and starring our friend Laura Kenyon, who at the time was on Broadway

---

7 Fast forward to sometime after *Hairspray* opened, Scott and I got a letter from Mattel, asking if we were still interested in doing that musical about "Barbie and Ken" we had once inquired about. I was in LA and set up a meeting. Could this finally be the big break for our Barbie musical? Well, the guy never showed. I learned later he had been stuck on the 405 Freeway. Nothing came of it after that, despite getting the letter we had been waiting twenty years for.

in the musical *Nine*. (We "borrowed" the title from that Karen Black TV movie, the one with the crazed, spear-stabbing voodoo doll.) Laura played all the lead parts, with Vicki Schrott as "the assistant" and nine-year-old Cameron Johann, who was also in the cast of *Nine*, playing all of Laura's love interests.

Eventually, the Polish church closed Club 57 and we scattered. Scott and I kept busy creating cabaret acts around town for talented friends like Christine Ebersole, Lonette McKee, Debbie Shapiro Gravitte, Ellen Foley, and the great Ann Reinking.

I also found myself involved with two theatrical projects that were wild successes downtown, the first being *Leader of the Pack*, a revue of classic Ellie Greenwich songs from the '60s that featured the comeback of Darlene Love. The other was another revue called *Haarlem Nocturne*, created by and starring the indomitable André De Shields.

Sadly, both shows suffered the same fate as *Livin' Dolls* in that they were brought "uptown" by eager producers who managed to strip them of the downtown energy that made them hits in the first place. You can take the show out of the East Village...and as it turns out, you can also take the East Village out of the show.

Concurrently, Scott also started doing larger, one-night extravaganzas at all the major dance clubs in the city which I would sometimes musical direct. We did insanely fun shows at the Palladium, Limelight, and especially Danceteria. John Sex starred in Scott's bootleg production of *Peter Pan* and many spectacular revues, like *Nude Faces of '85*. Scott's burlesque revue, *Les Girls*, starred our trans friends as the burlesque queens, and our lady pals cross-dressing to become the male top bananas.

Despite a conservative national mood, the East Village in the early '80s provided a haven for those defying gender taboos. Holly Woodlawn and Alexis Del Lago were embraced without question as women, decades before trans acceptance spread beyond the LGBT community. Other friends like Lady Bunny and Lypsinka were taking drag to a new level. And then there were friends like Joey Arias, who appeared in Scott's one-night blowout at the Palladium called *Pagan Place*, which also featured the exuberant young Jerry Mitchell (our future *Hairspray* choreographer) leading the chorus.

Many years later, Scott and I would be blessed to collaborate with creators like Bridget Everett, Cole Escola, and Murray Hill, whose bold sexuality and gender fluidity—always mixed with tremendous humor—would echo our fearless days in the East Village.

"Rotate!"

6

A FUR CHUBBY AND A MINISKIRT

'82

In 1982, Scott and I were licking our wounds from the disappointment of our Barbie and Ken musical, *Livin' Dolls*. And we were flat broke. But we were always working (usually pro bono) on someone's cabaret act, and somehow a B-movie and theater actress who shall remain nameless—let's call her "Briana Moonglow"—got our number and asked if she could hire us to put together her nightclub act.

We knew it was going to be a cheesy affair, but Miss Moonglow was not untalented, and we needed the gig. So, we said yes.

For weeks and *weeks*, Miss Moonglow would come over to work at our loft with her scary, mobster-y boyfriend, Tommy. We not only had to please Miss Moonglow, but also Tommy, whose talents clearly lay in literally breaking legs.

One weekend, when it was time for Scott and me to deliver a "Born in a Trunk"-style number to describe her career, we actually dropped acid to get through writing it. Don't judge, it was the '80s! We were young, and Tommy was looming! How else could we come up with lyrics like…

SIX YEARS OLD AND EVERYTHING'S TERRIFIC
SIX YEARS OLD AND I'M IN SOUTH PACIFIC!

Not to mention this classic quatrain:

I PLAYED ANITA ONCE (*musical bump*)
CREATED BY CHITA ONCE (*musical bump*)
RECREATED BY RITA ONCE (*musical bump*)
I GOT SO TIRED OF ALL THOSE BUMPS!

And yes, we knew that "bumps" did not rhyme with "once," but tell that to the acid. And our employers loved it.

They also kept talking about getting this big agent from William Morris—I can't recall his name, so let's call him "Sol Schmegeggy"—to book the act. Somehow, they got him to come down to our Dickensian loft in deserted (at that time) SoHo. After buzzing "Sol" in, he somehow didn't understand we would come get him in the hand-driven elevator, and this tiny, *ancient* man walked up three flights of stairs. Once he got to our door, he collapsed—very much like Mildred Natwick in *Barefoot in the Park*.

Luckily, he collapsed into the first chair he spied, which was this strange little wicker chair next to our front door that was only big enough for a doll. (Don't ask me why we owned such a thing—money we did not have, but kitsch comes cheap.)

Once "Mr. Schmegeggy" caught his breath, we extracted him from that miniature chair and sat him down in the middle of the loft in a canvas butterfly chair into which he practically disappeared.

Miss Moonglow then climbed up on the wooden coffee table and, grabbing a little Venus de Milo statue to hold like a mic (I'm not making *any* of this up), proceeded to do the entire act for this somnambulant relic of showbiz past. Forty minutes later, as she hit the final note, he woke with a start and proclaimed, "She's a fireball!"

So, with "Sol Schmegeggy" of William Morris allegedly now on board, the next step was to hire an arranger to create band charts better than I could at that time. We booked musicians for a read-down of the charts, which went as well as we could have hoped. Then it was time for everyone to get paid: Scott and me, the arranger, and the musicians.

You guessed it. Our calls stopped being returned.

Then one day, as Scott and I were painting the loft, they showed up, demanding the band charts.

"Not until you pay us or, at the very least, the arranger and the musicians!"

A physical struggle ensued amidst the paint tray and brushes, between two broken-down gay writers, Miss Moonglow (who was wearing—I kid you not—a fur chubby and a miniskirt) and Tommy, who was scary on a good day, so you can imagine how terrifying he was then.

But Scott and I were so demoralized, we clutched that box of music charts as long as we could, until finally Tommy had them in hand. Down three flights of stairs they ran, with us in hot pursuit!

The bar across the street was patronized by off-duty garbagemen, who must have been a little shocked when these two gaylings ran in (me in tears, of course) yelling, "Help, we're being robbed!"

God bless those garbagemen; they ran back into the street with us, brandishing pool cues, and I got my hand on Tommy's car door. But I couldn't hold on, and Tommy and Miss Moonglow sped off. I was left crying in the street, very much like Sophia Loren in *Two Women*.

I brought them up on charges at the Musician's Union, but since we had not been doing any of this with a signed contract, we were outta luck. At this point, I flew to my parents' home in Florida and had a mini nervous breakdown.

Then, half a year later, Miss Moonglow had the *chutzpah* to do this act in New York, at Freddy's Supper Club. Scott and I solicited all our wonderful friends to call in bookings for opening night (just like Lucy, Fred, and Ethel did when Ricky got fired from the Tropicana). We sold out the joint! One friend even said, "Bob Fosse is coming with a table for twelve. We might be a little late, please hold the curtain for him."

Success! No one showed! The *New York Post* even wrote an article about it, saying "some cranks" spoiled Miss Moonglow's opening.

Let me be clear that I am ashamed we acted so childishly. But we had really been laid low by the entire experience, and...well, karma's a bitch.

Cut to: More than a decade later, Scott and I were living the good life in LA. One night, driving past a cabaret on Santa Monica called The Gardenia, we saw a familiar name on the marquee: "Wednesday—Miss Moonglow"!

Is it possible, we wondered, *she is still doing that act?* We snuck into a darkened corner the night of the show, and sure enough, she did the entire act. Right down to, "Six years old and everything's terrific/Six years old and I'm in *South Pacific*!"

For a minute, I thought we were on acid again. We tried to slip out unnoticed afterward, but she spied us and ran out to greet us, as if none of the above had ever happened.

God bless Miss Moonglow, and all those like her. Showbiz is cruel, and we all do what we must to hang on.

Some of us just do it in a fur chubby and a miniskirt.

7

SATURDAY NIGHT LIVE '81–'15

I'm going to be a complete cliché and start this chapter by saying, "The first time I tried cocaine was up at *Saturday Night Live*."

But at first, my various stints at *SNL* only involved pot. A whole lotta pot.

After the show's first five groundbreaking years, the original cast, writers, and many senior staff left. But in 1981, a fantastic musician named Tom Malone, who played trombone in the original band, was promoted to musical director. Tom is one of those geniuses who can play practically every instrument on Earth.

Luckily for me, though, he wasn't the thing that all comedy shows need: a funny Jewish guy at the piano. It's a law!

So, with no one at the piano—Jewish or otherwise—whenever a musical idea would come up, a freelance piano player/arranger was called in. The first year I went up to the *SNL* studios on the seventeenth floor of 30 Rockefeller Center, a landmark Art Deco skyscraper in Midtown Manhattan, was 1984. Tom was an avid marijuana enthusiast, and no one at that time ever needed to twist my arm to get high, so he and I would sit in the music office and smoke. And smoke. And smoke.

The only sketch I remember working on (who could remember anything after ingesting that much marijuana?) was setting out the arrangement for Julia Louis-Dreyfus singing in a spoof of Linda Ronstadt's new album of standards with the famed arranger/

orchestrator Nelson Riddle. That was probably the first time I sat down and analyzed a Nelson Riddle orchestration, but it certainly wouldn't be the last.

The following year, producer Dick Ebersol (who is barely mentioned now but produced the show for five years, including the Eddie Murphy years) pretty much cleared the decks and brought in a bunch of comedy all-stars including Billy Crystal, Martin Short, and Christopher Guest.

My sense of humor completely meshed with those three guys. I've remained friendly with Christopher, who went on to create brilliant mockumentaries like *Waiting for Guffman* and *Best in Show*. But my close relationships with Billy and Marty have continued far past their one year on *Saturday Night Live*.

My most vivid memory from that year is when Ringo Starr hosted. I remember being at the table read on Wednesday thinking, "Sure, a Beatle is sitting right over there, but if only it was Paul or George or the late John Lennon."

After the read-through, someone suggested Billy do his phenomenal Sammy Davis Jr. impression (which is now outlawed) in the opening monologue. Ringo and "Sammy," in Rat Pack fashion, could sing each other's hits. So we all piled into the music room, and from the piano I said to Billy and Ringo, "You know what would be helpful? If we start with you guys first singing your actual songs, not each other's, just for us all to remember what they are before we trade off."

Billy sang a few measures of a bunch of Sammy Davis Jr. hits, and then it was Ringo's turn. This was before he started touring with his All-Starr Band, which reintroduced audiences to him performing his solo and Beatles hits. But at the time, no one had seen or heard Ringo sing any of those songs in the flesh for almost two decades.

So, I began playing "With a Little Help from My Friends" and then *Ringo fucking Starr* started singing and my blasé attitude was quickly obliterated by a bolt of electricity that went from the base of my spine, straight up my back, around my head, back down through my arms and legs, and repeated over and over again.

SNL creator Lorne Michaels returned to the show in 1985. His first year back was a bit of a disaster, but the second year, he hired a brilliant cast including Phil Hartman, Jon Lovitz, Dana Carvey, Dennis Miller, Nora Dunn, and Jan Hooks.

Luckily for me, the new musical director was G.E. Smith, a rock 'n' roll guitar virtuoso, but—once again—not a funny Jew at the piano. So, not only was I back, but also they hired me full time as a writer on the show. Full time as in Writers Guild membership and going down to the lady behind the window every Friday to get a paycheck. It was my first steady job. Associate producer Dinah Minot hired me and told the other writers, "You guys should put your heads together with Marc for anything having to do with music."

But this is the Marc Shaiman story, so every stroke of luck is counterbalanced with its opposite. Which was the case here.

Today, practically every *SNL* host partakes in a huge musical number. But at that time, music in sketches was poo-pooed by the writers. In fact, I will say it is the only gig I've ever had where I felt treated like "the fag at the end of the hall."

None of those tall, WASP-y Harvard/Yale types wanted anything to do with me, and I was too intimidated to pitch them any ideas of my own. They were just too unapproachable. It was depressing as I just sat in my small office making a lot of long-distance phone calls on NBC's dime, which, before cell phones, was an exotic perk.

Finally, one day Jan Hooks, Nora Dunn, and the married writing team of Bonnie and Terry Turner knocked on my door. The Turners were Southern and much friendlier than most of the frosty Ivy Leaguers on the other side of the seventeenth floor. The four of them presented an idea based on an act Jan and Bonnie had developed in Atlanta, involving two lounge-singer sisters who put together nonsensical, and endless, medleys.

"Would you like to create a medley with us?" they asked.

I would say I ran to the piano, except my office was so small I was already seated at the piano. But I was finally excited. So, with Nora taking over Bonnie's role in the duo, the girls were named "Liz and Candy Sweeney" and we set to writing. Our first medley consisted of themeless, musical non sequiturs that we imagined being performed on the black stage of a made-up cable TV show. Something about it clicked, and as the weeks went by, we wrote more sketches with specific themes relating to where the sisters were performing.

At the read-throughs, the tall white guys would roll their eyes: "Oh God, not another Sweeney Sisters sketch!"

And I'm the first to admit what Paul Shaffer said to us the week he hosted, and the Sweeneys did a sketch, is true: "Oh right, you girls like to work long."

But despite the mixed messages backstage, the Sweeney Sisters had become what everyone on *Saturday Night Live* aspires to create: recurring characters. Not only was I doing something completely in my wheelhouse, but I also appeared on-screen with the girls as their accompanist, "Skip St. Thomas."

Unfortunately, *SNL* musical sketches and performances are rarely shown as repeats or posted online, due to the structure of who owns the rights to the music. So, the Sweeney Sisters are only cherished by a certain generation (dare I say mostly of gay men and the women who love them), while remaining unknown to those who came after.

Fortunately, however, the only sketch you can find online is also the best. "The Christmas Bell Medley" is where we hit our peak. I post the one grainy YouTube version every Christmas, as do an awful lot of other people. Someday, I'm going to get a pristine copy from NBC and insist on permission to post that.

The Christmas episode that included the bell medley, hosted by William Shatner, is actually pretty iconic for, among other things, the *Star Trek* sketch. Shatner also appeared as Oliver North, then in the news for the Iran-Contra scandal, in the show's "cold opening," which had the male cast members singing new lyrics to the '60s hit "The Ballad of the Green Beret," which I co-wrote with future senator Al Franken. It was a big hit at the top of the show, and then the Sweeney Sisters' medley was also a hit midway through. I left 30 Rock that night probably the proudest I'd ever felt in all my time there.

That same year, Bill Murray came back to host and resurrected his lounge lizard character "Nick." I was thrilled to become his accompanist. Unfortunately, Bill didn't want to rehearse very much, and although I'm happy to be free and loose, when it comes to live television, it's preferable to have a solid idea of what the hell you'll be doing.

He was also in another sketch playing an out-of-shape Hercules with drooping "man boobs." So, one of the strangest memories from my time at *SNL* is chasing Bill Murray under the bleachers during dress rehearsal as he ran from one sketch to another wearing prosthetic man boobs, trying desperately to get him to answer a few questions about what we were about to do on live television. If you find the "Nick the Lounge Singer in Prison" sketch online, you can tell I'm glowering at him a bit!

In the break after my first full-time season, Lorne Michaels produced the Emmy Awards and asked Nora, Jan, and me to create a Sweeney Sisters medley to open the show. It included a rendition of the *Mary Tyler Moore Show* theme, which the girls bellowed right into Mary's face—as she beamed right back at them.

And when Mary Tyler Moore hosted *SNL* the next year, the first thing she said at the Monday night meeting was: "The only thing I insist on is being in a Sweeney Sisters sketch!" So, we wrote her in as the prodigal third sister, returning to the fold. She even pulled a mic out of her purse and joined in with, "Clang, clang, clang went the trolley," the Sweeneys' theme song.

Growing up in the '70s, I *loved The Mary Tyler Moore Show*. Later, in the '80s, NBC re-ran them in the middle of the night, two or three episodes at a time. Just when you thought, *I* have *to go to sleep,* the intro started again and you simply had to watch one more. I believe I rewatched all seven seasons of the show in those crazy middle-of-the-night reruns, so the Sweeney Sisters leading me to working with her felt like a fantasy.

"Clang, clang, clang!"

8

SUDDENLY, NOTHING IS THE SAME

The AIDS Epidemic

'81-

I am not a person who easily remembers dates, but one that is firmly implanted in my mind and heart is December 8, 1980: the night John Lennon was murdered.

We first heard he had been shot when someone called our East Village performance space, Club 57. I rushed home to our television set, unable to believe the news. Not that it would have been any less shocking at another time, but Lennon's latest record had just been released and he appeared to have finally made peace with himself and the world. How could this happen?

But as Scott was still not home, sitting alone in our SoHo loft watching the news was far too solitary a way to take in what was happening. So, I called my Harlettes compatriot and fellow Beatles fanatic, Ula Hedwig, and she invited me to join a growing group of friends who were gathering at her apartment on the Upper West Side. It was there we took in the unfathomable news that John Lennon had been pronounced dead at Roosevelt Hospital, not too many blocks from where we were sitting. We remained at Ula's the rest of the night, consoling each other, speechless, crying; all of us feeling the profound loss not just of this musical hero, but also of our own childhoods. The Beatles' music had coursed through our youth and sparked so many of our own creative aspirations. Too young to have been truly affected by the political assassinations of the '60s, Lennon's murder was the darkest event of our lives.

Little did we know what the following fifteen years would bring.

In the days following Lennon's death, like every other songwriter across the universe, I wrote a song about how I felt.

"SUDDENLY"

SUDDENLY, YOU SAY GOODBYE
NO EXCUSE, NO REASON WHY
SEEMS TO ME
THAT NOTHING'S EVER HAPPENED JUST LIKE THIS BEFORE
AND I DON'T FEEL YOUNG ANYMORE

SUDDENLY, YOUR SMILE IS GONE
MEMORIES WILL HAVE TO CARRY ON
SEEMS TO ME
A LITTLE PIECE OF EVERYONE HAS DIED
A PART INSIDE

SUDDENLY, YOUR SONGS ARE EVERYWHERE
I CAN FEEL SUCH SADNESS IN THE AIR
BUT I WILL TRY
TO LIVE UP TO ALL YOU THOUGHT WE COULD BE
JUST A PART OF HUMANITY

BUT WHEN I THINK OF HOW YOU TRIED
HOW YOU LIVED, AND HOW YOU DIED
SEEMS TO ME
HUMANITY SHOULD HIDE ITS FACE IN SHAME
CAUSE SUDDENLY, NOTHING IS THE SAME

I sang the song to my friend Orrin Reiley, a Broadway actor and singer, who encouraged me to include it in the revue of my songs I was performing on Sunday nights at the West Side Arts Center.

Orrin was our friend Laura Kenyon's first husband, and he was a gorgeous man—strikingly tall and full of humor. Laura and Orrin had long since divorced by the time he came out as gay, but they were still as tight as could be, soulmates till the end. And unexpectedly, the end came heartbreakingly soon, because Orrin was one of the first of our friends to contract AIDS. We watched him go from having movie-star good looks, with mischief always dancing in his eyes and on his tongue, to a weakened shell of himself.

What is this disease that is suddenly attacking our community? we all wondered. Along with: *Am I next?*

Orrin's beautiful eyes grew vacant over the following months, and we witnessed his suffering until the horrible day Scott and I got the news that he had passed at home. We went to his apartment to sit with Laura and Orrin's roommate, our friend Victor Garber, all of us shell-shocked. Entering his room and seeing that once-vital body empty of his spirit shook us like a nightmare from which we couldn't awaken. Before long, the men from the coroner's office appeared, and I know Orrin would have laughed when they had no option but to balance him upright in his body bag in the tiny elevator to take him away. I don't know if any other unsuspecting tenant of the building had called for the elevator as Orrin made his way down to the lobby, but showman to the end, he would have relished seeing their reaction to his final exit.

Suddenly, one person I knew after another was being diagnosed, falling ill, and dying. At revues of my music, I continued singing my John Lennon song, but now also in tribute to Orrin and all the other friends disappearing from our lives.

For the next fifteen plus years, my community was bombarded by a constant cycle of fear, death, and crushing grief. Later generations, fortunately, don't know what it's like to turn to the obituaries first thing every morning when you're not yet thirty years old, learning to decipher the codes that let you know the twenty-eight-year-old who died so suddenly of cancer, pneumonia, or some other nonspecific disease had most likely been claimed by AIDS. Lifelong partners were often ignored completely in the mainstream tributes and notices or, at best, acknowledged by the limp euphemism "longtime companion." This was a time when no family wanted the word *AIDS* in their child's obituary, while others disowned them and wouldn't even come to their funerals.

On the wall of my music studio, I started keeping a list of those I had lost, from casual acquaintances to great friends with whom I shared years of laughter and collaboration. Over the years, that list swelled to one hundred and thirty-four names of friends, colleagues, and first loves. It wrecks me that I can no longer put faces to some of the names on this list, whose memories I have tried so hard to hold onto. Most names, however, still summon not just faces, but also recollections of their spirit, humor, talent, life. Their losses deprived us of untold art and design, music and dance; plays that will never be produced and books that will never be written. How wondrously crowded my life would be today if they were all still here, where they belong.

Like many who made it through, I carry survivor's guilt. Why was I inexplicably allowed to live and continue to use my talents when so many like me were cut down? When I moved to LA in the late '80s, I met so many new friends, but soon almost all of them were getting sick. Early on, I spent almost every waking moment at the home of my new friends George Guim and Michael Crane, laughing hysterically while dissecting pop culture and the performers we loved. Then George was diagnosed and started that hideous decline. I remember going to visit him at the hospital only to find him wandering the halls in his flimsy paper gown, unaware of where he was. And then there was the terrible morning Michael called me and told me through sobs that George had just passed. I raced over to their house in the Valley where George lay in the hospital bed that had been brought into their living room. Michael, who would himself die of AIDS a few years later, was in and out of the room, inconsolable. Then came the knock on the door, and I watched again as the men from a funeral home came to collect another friend. I stayed by George's side as they wrapped him in his shroud before placing him inside the body bag, zipping it up, and putting him on the gurney to roll away. These are images that stay burned into your soul.

I'm sorry to have mentioned friends in body bags twice already, but that was what life was like at the time. I lost about every one of the friends I met when I first moved to Los Angeles, and almost all our collaborators from the East Village. And not just the friends and chosen family we found upon moving to New York, but dear friends from my New Jersey community theater days, including my best Parish Players of Plainfield pal, David Pasacrita, with whom I discovered at fifteen, well, a lot of things, but especially the full scope of Judy Garland's career and repertoire. We spent countless hours together in his bedroom listening to his record collection, and around a piano after *Godspell* rehearsals, David singing Garland's "Judy at the Palace Medley" at the top of his lungs and vocal range.

There was also Bruce Conroy, my first passion, who wouldn't let me come to him in his final days; he did not want me to see him like that. I told his lover, Frank, that Bruce shouldn't be concerned with how he looked, but Frank said Bruce refused to let me come to say goodbye, which was his choice. Some people prefer to stay away, but I was never one to say, "Oh, I don't do hospitals," and I won't judge those who do say that. Well, who am I kidding? I judge, I judge. I remember going to St. Vincent's Hospital—whose location in Greenwich Village made it perhaps the global epicenter of the AIDS crisis—to visit the beautiful, and I mean truly beautiful actor Christopher Stryker. But lying in that hospital bed, with his face ravaged and swollen, he looked like an unrecognizable species. Assuming his mind had gone the way of his body, I whispered, "Chris, it's Marc Shaiman," and he barked, "I know! Whaddya think I am, blind?"

Memorials (a.k.a. Celebrations) became a new form of creative expression, and there was a certain gallows humor among the survivors. So, you might be appalled to hear yourself saying, "So-and-so's memorial was so much better," or, "Oh dear, she really shouldn't have sung that in that key." Or the most horrible thing we often found ourselves noticing: "Where is his family? Why is no one here from his family?"

I often thought I should have written a country-western song with the title "If Only Tears Were Calories, Just Think How Thin I'd Be." But nowadays, when I hear about friends or relatives dying, I am horrified to sometimes not have the tears flow, at least not the way they used to. I think—no, I know—that AIDS hardened me. I will still cry at a movie (just ask my husband, Lou) or when hearing a certain piece of music ("Sunday" from *Sunday in the Park with George* is a certain trigger for the tear ducts), but something in me died with every death, and I would never, ever be the same.

In 1994, Scott and I were honored when AIDS Project Los Angeles asked us to direct and music direct that year's Commitment to Life concert. APLA was a foundation created when Hollywood, after the death of Rock Hudson, finally "acted up" in their own way and did an awful lot to raise money for research, housing, and education.[8] The year Scott and I did the concert was a most star-studded affair, with Tom Cruise, Tom Hanks, Whitney Houston, Bruce Springsteen, Barbra Streisand, Hillary Clinton, Lauren Bacall, Liza Minnelli, Debbie Reynolds, our friend Jenifer Lewis, and even the Rockettes.

Even though the concert was a stupendous success, I'm still reminded of a telling moment that happened behind the scenes. It has long been understood in show business that no matter who else shows up for free at a benefit, the musicians always get paid. For this concert, we had gotten APLA to agree to a full orchestra, which

8 The AIDS Coalition To Unleash Power, known by its acronym ACT UP, was a direct-action AIDS pressure group founded in New York City in 1987 that spread to several cities across North America, including Los Angeles. It focused on street protests and civil disobedience and preferred to work outside establishment channels.

was going to be expensive. But because of how personally meaningful the cause was to me, I stood up during a recording session for the film I was doing at the time and asked the orchestra if they would talk amongst themselves and possibly, hopefully, agree to do this concert pro bono. Their de facto leader, a virtuosic musician with whom I had a wonderful relationship at all our sessions—but here shall remain nameless—contacted me later and said, "Sorry Marc, we just can't set that precedent, the musicians are going to have to be paid union rates."

Now, I am also a musician, and admittedly I make a nice salary, so perhaps I'm privileged, *but come on*! What is with this "the musicians always get paid" mantra, especially extremely well-paid musicians like those who populated the Hollywood movie music scene? But I had to accept his objection and move on.

Which is why one particular moment the night of the concert pierced my heart. It was when Tom Cruise came on stage and asked everyone in the Universal Amphitheatre to call out the names of people they had lost. It was an incredibly poignant moment; at first only a few people started, but others quickly joined, and it soon became an emotional cacophony of names. It was as cathartic a group moment as I have ever had, and as I choked out my own list of names, I noticed the musician who denied us a break whispering the name of his brother.

I'll forever wonder how his own brother's death didn't lead this man to try and make an exception to an inflexible rule. But that was one of the sad and strange things about AIDS, how its stigma allowed shame to enter the grieving process. And, along with my inappropriate judging, my heart went out to him.

At a previous APLA benefit concert in 1991, Bette had been given their Commitment to Life award for her fundraising. Her theme song "Friends" had always been performed at an upbeat, feel-good tempo, but that night, we slowed it down to emphasize the eerily prophetic lyrics written twenty years earlier about some mysterious fate robbing you of your friends.

I don't really believe in an afterlife—I suspect the idea came about because humanity just has too much of an ego to believe we could possibly cease to exist—but if there *is* an afterlife, I cannot wait to once more see these friends:

DANNY FORTUS
ORRIN REILLY
JOHN SIMINETTI
JAMES SEGALL
DON YOWELL
KEITH AVEDON
WAYNE MATSON
CHRIS ADLER
GREGORY CONNEL
BOB DE ANGELES
RICHARD AMSEL
BILL ELLIOT
JOE MASIEL
JERRY MOORE
STEVE ROTH
JAY GROSSMAN
ROBERT WARNERS
MAX DREW
WAYLAND FLOWERS
HOWARD JEFFRIES
SETH ALLEN
RON FIELD
SHOOTER
KIM MILFORD
RICHARD HOWE
PATRICK GOLDEN
DR. BRUCE
CHARLES HUNT
BRUCE SAVAN
ANDY KATZ

BILL HENNESSY
FRITZ HOLT
ALAN BUCKSBAUM
KENN DUNCAN
MIKI ZONE
CHRIS STRYKER
WILFORD LEACH
BILLY ORIGO
MICHAEL RHONE
RICK RICHARDSON
LARRY GALLAGHER
RONN FORRELA
GILBY LA CHAPPELE
BILLY PORTER
PATRICK REAGAN
EDDIE STONE
JERRY BLATT
ANDY REES
W.C. CONWAY
JAMES KIRKWOOD
MARK OATES
GREG MULLINS
MARK HENRI
KEITH HARING
BRUCE CONROY
BRUCE CLIBORN
CHARLIE WHITESIDE
MARTY TURK
ED MILLUS
ROB PLATZ

PETER DALLAS
GARY KEEPER
ETHYL EICHENBERGER
JOHN SEX
TIM BUTLER
WILLIAM FLEET LIVELY
TOM HAWK
TOM EYEN
HOWARD ASHMAN
LARRY KERT
HOUIE MONTAUG
GERRI RAGNI
BRUCE HUBBARD
GEORGE GUIM
AVERY AUSTIN
CURT DAVIS
ED LOVE
LEWIS FREIDMAN
A.J. ANTOON
VINCENT MICRO
CLOVIS RUFFIN
SHARON REDD
RICK GRIMALDI
CHRIS HUGHES
DANNY DRAGON
LENNY DEANS
CHICO KASINIOR
PETER ALLEN
TOM RUBNITZ
KENNY SACHA

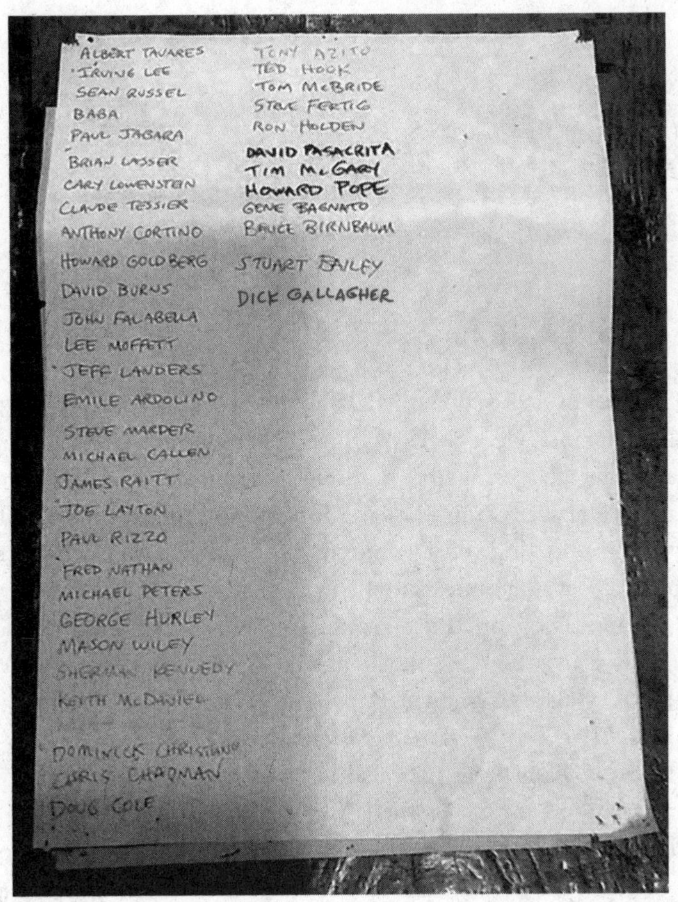
ALBERT TAVARES
IRVING LEE
SEAN RUSSEL
BABA
PAUL JABARA
BRIAN LASSER
CARY LOWENSTEIN
CLAUDE TESSIER
ANTHONY CORTINO
HOWARD GOLDBERG
DAVID BURNS
JOHN FALABELLA
LEE MOFFETT
JEFF LANDERS
EMILE ARDOLINO
STEVE MARDER
MICHAEL CALLEN
JAMES RAITT
JOE LAYTON
PAUL RIZZO
FRED NATHAN
MICHAEL PETERS
GEORGE HURLEY
MASON WILEY
SHERMAN KENNEDY
KEITH McDANIEL
DOMINICK CHRISTIAN
CHRIS CHAPMAN
DOUG COLE
TONY AZITO
TED HOOK
TOM McBRIDE
STEVE FERTIG
RON HOLDEN
DAVID PASACRITA
TIM McGARY
HOWARD POPE
GENE BAGNATO
BRUCE BIRNBAUM
STUART BAILEY
DICK GALLAGHER

9

BARBRA IS UPSET

'88

In the fall of 1988, when Michael Dukakis was running for president against George H.W. Bush, I was booked to accompany Bette Midler at a campaign fundraiser organized by the Hollywood Women's Political Committee. (You may not be astounded to learn we were supporting the Democrat.) A couple of weeks before the October 16 event, Bette called to say that Barbra Streisand would also be appearing on the bill, and the committee wanted to save money by using the same musicians to support both artists. "Would you be okay also playing for Barbra Streisand?" Bette asked.

Would I be okay playing for Barbra Streisand? I mean, if only Liza Minnelli or Diana Ross had also been on the bill, they would have given me my own float in the LA Pride Parade.

I knew her name as a kid, but it wasn't until I was a teenager that I was able to fully appreciate the phenomenon that is Barbra Streisand. It's not just that her voice is a natural wonder of tone and range—although it is—but also the drama and humor she brings to her performance are capable of connecting with the audience's own deepest emotions. This interpretative gift is what separates superstars from the merely stupendously talented. When I first listened to *A Christmas Album* and she sang the high note in "Ave Maria," I didn't just cry, I ejaculated tears, which shot straight out of my eyes too forcefully to even touch my cheeks. And then she did the same thing three tracks later in "The Lord's Prayer," and it happened again. Truly, this was the greatest Jewish Christmas miracle since Irving Berlin wrote "White Christmas."

What Barbra and Bette have in common is that they started as outsiders—looking and acting differently from the people they grew up with. But rather than conform, they celebrated their differences and became stars because of it; they made themselves beautiful. I think this is a quality that gay men and other outsiders recognize in themselves—and are drawn to when it's interpreted on stage. Both artists also worked with music that evoked nostalgia, drawing inspiration from the fascinating women of Hollywood's golden age, from Mae West and Rosalind Russell to Carmen Miranda and Judy Garland. Yet they always found ways to elevate and update the material as Bette did so flawlessly with "Boogie Woogie Bugle Boy." At the height of Beatlemania, Barbra was singing "Bewitched, Bothered and Bewildered" live at the Bon Soir nightclub in Greenwich Village, as if to say, *Let's not forget about the Great American Songbook.*

So, all you can do when Bette Midler asks if you'd "be okay also playing for Barbra Streisand" is try not to squeal the answer.

The next day, Barbra's sheet music (her "charts," as we call them in the trade) was sent over to me. This was not long after she had done the *One Voice* concert in the backyard of her Malibu ranch in front of a star-studded live audience, and later, millions of television viewers both on HBO and globally. That had been the first moment in a very long time she had sung in public—if appearing in your own backyard can be considered public—and it was these *One Voice* charts that I received. At band rehearsal, after completing Bette's material, I put the Streisand music in front of the musicians and started to record. My plan was to out-Streisand Streisand and critique the recording of the rehearsal with the same degree of perfectionism for which she was famous.

Later that night, I listened to the rehearsal tape and notated *everything*. "Oh, the keyboard came in a little loud at the top of that verse," and, "That transition into the modulation could be a little smoother." The next morning, I sent the tape and my cover letter off to her manager, Marty Erlichman, who had discovered Barbra singing at that Greenwich Village nightclub when she was only nineteen years old, and who had been her fierce protector ever since. I was told he would pass the tape and letter on to her.

The charts for the event had come from Marty's office, along with the request that I get the music written out a half step lower, so that Barbra would have a choice of key in which to sing. Setting the key for a singer in this way is like the final fitting for a tailored dress—it makes sure the material is perfectly aligned with where the artist's voice is at that moment. The songs were "America the Beautiful" and one of her signatures, "Happy Days Are Here Again." The chance to play the latter for Barbra Streisand—can you believe it?—made me truly Hollywood's happiest homosexual.

A few days later, as I was lying in bed, the phone rang. But I was still half asleep, so I let the answering machine in the next room pick up and couldn't quite tell who was leaving a message. But when I played it back a short while later, there was *her* voice, unspooling from the tape like a velvet ribbon. "Hello, Marc? Hi, it's Barbra Streisand. You did good! Give me a call to discuss, my number is ________ well, actually, call me at ________. No, call me at ________ instead."

You've got to love a superstar who has so many phone numbers she can't decide which one to have you call her on. So, I took a deep breath and called one of those numbers. *She answered.*

"Hello, Barbra? It's Marc Shaiman, Bette Midler's musical director."

"Oh yeah, hi, the tape sounded good." She was very friendly, we made small talk, and she made me feel comfortable enough to tell her I had enjoyed her recent duet "Till I Loved You." She had just released the single with her then-beau, Don Johnson, who at the time was very hot as the star of *Miami Vice*.

"I think you did a great job of matching your voices so that yours didn't overpower him," I said.

"Oh good, thanks," she replied. I then inquired if they planned to make a video to go with the single. And with her answer, I felt the showbiz earth shift under my feet, because she said, "Oh no, that would be giving them too much."

If *them* meant the general public—"civilians" as Hollywood types call them—that must mean that *I* was an *us*. I was in!

Plans were set up for rehearsal, all seemed to be going well, and the next day, I got a call from the music copyists. These are the folks who actually write out the music by hand—or these days by computer—which is a very intense and complicated craft, and they truly are the unsung heroes of the music business.

"Hey, Marc," they asked, "where should we send the bill for transposing and printing out Barbra Streisand's charts for this event?"

"Gee, I don't know whether it should be the Hollywood Women's Political Committee or Barbra herself, since the transposed charts will go back to her," I said. "Let me ask."

I hung up with the copyists and called Marty Erlichman's office. When he picked up, I simply repeated their question, asking, "Where should the copyists' bill for the transposed charts go, to the Committee or to Barbra?"

I swear on a stack of Barbra Streisand albums that was it, that's all I said. He said he'd get back to me.

Later that morning, my phone rang. I picked up and it was the late, great Marilyn Bergman—*whom I worshiped*. Marilyn was a revered lyricist who, with her husband, Alan, wrote some of the most gorgeous and intricate lyrics of all time (like their first Oscar winner, "The Windmills of Your Mind"), many of them for Barbra Streisand (like their second Oscar winner, "The Way We Were"). Not only were the two women very close, but Marilyn was also the queen of the Hollywood Women's Political Committee, for which the *One Voice* concert had also been a fundraiser.

Her voice was a deep, throaty baritone—sultry and authoritative. Think of honey mixed with sand, then dipped in molasses. "*Maaarc,* it's Marilyn Bergman." She paused. And then very slowly, "Marc. What did you say to Marty Ehrlichman about the bill for the charts?"

I began to get an awful feeling like some kind of serpent was waking up and turning over in my stomach. "Um, I just asked him where the bill should go, to the Committee or to Barbra?"

"Well," she said, "Marty told Barbra the Committee refused to pay the bill, and she's very upset. It looks like she's gonna cancel."

"Oh my God," I answered, trembling. "I never for a moment said anything like that, never insinuated anything like that. It was a simple question of where to send the bill!"

We hung up, and I was devastated. I will gladly beat myself up over all the mistakes I make in any given day, but I was certain I had done nothing wrong here. Nothing I said had been inaccurate; I couldn't have been clearer, but now it looked like my one simple phone call to Marty Erlichman had ended my gay dream of playing for Bette Midler *and* Barbra Streisand on the same night. I spent the rest of the morning in despair.

Luckily, I got word later that day it was all a simple misunderstanding that had been resolved. Whew!

However, a day or two later, my phone rang and again, it was that sonorous, canorous, imperious voice. "*Maaarc,*" she rumbled, "Marilyn Bergman." The serpent napping in my stomach lifted its head to see what was up. "Tell me again *exactly* what you said to Marty Ehrlichman about the bill for the charts."

"Marilyn, there's nothing different I could say to you now than what I told you on our first phone call. I simply asked, on behalf of the copyists, where they should send the bill."

"Well," she said, "Barbra is still upset, and she may only sing one song instead of two."

Luckily, the next call was equally as commanding but much less dramatic. "*Maaarc*...Marilyn Bergman. Barbra is going to sing both songs, and is curious if the rehearsal studio could house her trailer."

"Well, that's a question I've never been asked," I replied. "Let me find out." I called the studio and was told that they could indeed open the garage doors wide enough for her (well, her driver) to bring her trailer right inside the rehearsal hall.

Cut to the big day: I am on gay cloud nine, driving—nay, floating—down Sunset Boulevard in a convertible, headed to the rehearsal studio *where I am going to play for Barbra Streisand*. To get further into the mood, I put on one of my favorite Streisand records, the *People* album, which opens with "Absent-Minded Me," featuring some of the most glorious vocals and orchestrations ever set to vinyl.

So, I am merrily singing along—yes, in a convertible with the top down, screw the haters—when the phone rings. Car phones had just started trending, and I had one of those huge monstrosities to my right. I answer. From some subaqueous, primordial place, so low only the snake in my belly could hear it, comes: "*Maaarc*. Marilyn Bergman."

My heart stopped.

"Tell me again, *word for word*, what you said to Marty Erlichman about the bill for the charts."

"Oh my God, Marilyn, what else is there for me to say? I've told you over and over again!"

"Well," she said, "I hope it doesn't come up today. Barbra is on her way to the studio right now."

So I pulled into the parking lot fearful that our famously exacting star would arrive already in a bad mood. It was a large rehearsal complex in Hollywood, a neighborhood which in real life is a shopworn, low-rent part of central Los Angeles where a lot of this kind of behind-the-scenes work gets done, and far from the glimmering "Hollywood!" of public imagination. Despite the fact we were only eight musicians, they had given us a huge room, with loading doors that opened onto the street, big enough to accommodate Barbra's trailer. You have to admire a movie star who doesn't work anywhere their trailer doesn't fit. But she's Barbra fucking Streisand, what's she supposed to do, get in a Honda and drive herself?

The band was scruffy but professional. (In their line of work, scruffy *is* professional.) We ran through all the material, both Bette's and Barbra's charts, and then the garage doors opened, in came the trailer, and from it, she emerged. Seeing her in person for the first time, I had a sensation not unlike the first time I had been in Bette Midler's divine presence: On one level, she's another person coming to work in street clothes, but she looks just like Barbra Streisand; *oh my God it* is *Barbra Streisand*!

Despite the imbalance of star power in the room, we greeted each other and got right to work, running through both songs twice. I have never had a problem finding the confidence to quickly settle into a working rhythm with even the biggest stars. In fact, over the years I have found that even huge talents can also be a little nervous at rehearsal, singing in front of a room full of strangers, and wanting to do their best. Everybody can get butterflies, I guess—the only difference is that Barbra Streisand's butterflies fly private.

Underneath the professionalism, however, accompanying Streisand was still an almost out-of-body experience for me. I played the iconic piano intro to "Happy Days Are Here Again" and when she started singing, I did my best to control my emotions. But it was difficult because, at that moment, I was elated in a way I would only experience a few other times in my life—hearing Scott's and my names announced at the Tony Awards, for example, or on my wedding day to Lou. Accompanying Barbra Streisand, my soul swelled like a balloon and then zipped joyfully around the ceiling as if propelled by escaping air—trailing a string with a little paper bow tie in its tail: this one a folded bill from the copyists.

The day of the gig—loftily titled "Voices for Change '88: A Celebration of America"—was a week before my twenty-ninth birthday. We arrived early at a Beverly Hills estate known as Greenacres, a classic Italianate 1920s mansion built by the silent film star Harold Lloyd but then owned by *Revenge of the Nerds* movie producer and Interscope Records founder Ted Field. A mix of Hollywood and Washington swells gathered on the lawn, including Chevy Chase, John Kerry, Reverend Jesse Jackson, Ann Richards, and the candidate's wife, Kitty Dukakis.

The event, kicked off by Ashford & Simpson singing "Solid (As a Rock)," went well—certainly better than Dukakis did on election night three weeks later. Bette, as always, was a smash. And Barbra was...Barbra. Her voice was like a cashmere blanket making everyone feel warm in the crisp fall air, and, at least that night, all our liberal political fantasies seemed possible.

The morning after, I sent her a note saying, "It was good for me, how was it for you?"

She wrote a lovely reply, saying, "It was good for me too. If I ever decide to work again, I'll look for you."

Well, she did decide to start concertizing again around the world pretty soon after that, but she never came looking for me. That's fine, I was kind of busy myself, and my one encounter with Barbra Streisand and pals was all I needed. I was perfectly satiated and had learned an important lesson about avoiding land mines when working with great talent and the people who surround them. Everyone is so protective of both the star and their own place in their orbit that it's like playing chess: You have to develop the skills to anticipate every possible move that might affect your own ability to get your job done.

Actually, I did have one other encounter with Barbra Streisand about ten years later. The renowned record producer Arif Mardin (with whom I had collaborated on many of Bette's records) called to ask if I could suggest a piano player to go with him to Barbra's house to set keys for an album he was about to produce. Did I manage not to squeal when I volunteered myself? I don't recall.

"Marc," he said, "you are a big Hollywood composer. I really just need a piano player."

"Arif, pick me up at my house. I'm already outside on the street waiting for you."

So, off we drove to Malibu. I did not sense she either remembered or recognized me from the Dukakis gig, nor would I have expected her to. I can't tell you how many times someone is insulted that I don't remember them from the one day I met them on a project years ago, which is just unfair. If you're lucky, show business has you going from project to project, meeting and working with at least fifty new people every three months, and it all becomes a blur. I was not offended that she didn't remember me.

But I will tell you that when she sang through "The Star-Spangled Banner" with my friend Mervyn Warren at the piano (who was also there to set a key for the cut he was arranging and producing), she got a word wrong. *In the national anthem.* I can't remember which one, but Merv had the balls to say, "Um, Barbra, I think you mixed up some words there."

The room fell silent—I think even a squirrel outside the window gasped.

Finally, Barbra, after a long pause, unwilling to take Merv's word for it, called out to her longtime assistant: "Renata! Call Washington, have them fax me the lyrics!"

I don't know who she expected Renata to call in Washington—maybe the Library of Congress, or the president himself—but I just sat there like the Cheshire Cat and smiled. You gotta love her, and I do.

10

SKYLARK

Continuing Adventures with Bette

'85-

Besides arranging, producing, and writing lyrics for Bette on films like *Beaches, For the Boys, Hocus Pocus,* and *The First Wives Club,* I worked with her on many electric live performances. One of the perks of doing that is the unique view from the piano of the beaming faces of the audience.

After living at her house in preparation for the Copa Tour, when I heard Bette was putting together a world tour in 1978 I called her from my apartment in New York to offer my services. But she said she was only hiring local people from LA.

I bemoaned this fact for exactly five minutes before I ran to the bank, emptied out my meager account, got in a cab to JFK Airport, bought a ticket with the cash I had just withdrawn, and moments after landing, called Bette from a phone booth at LAX to say, "Okay, I'm in LA. When and where do rehearsals start?"

The lesson I learned from the experience is that in Hollywood, *chutzpah* pays off!

In December 1985, Bette called to say she booked *The Tonight Show* to publicize a comedy record we had just recorded live at The Improv called *Mud* Will *Be Flung Tonight*! In the first half of this appearance with Johnny Carson, Bette would perform "Fat As I Am," the original song she and I had written with our frequent collaborator, Jerry Blatt.

It goes a little something like this:

FAT AS I AM
THAT CAMERA'S GONNA ADD A TON TO MY CAN
THIS IS THE WAY THEY SAY GODZILLA BEGAN
HOW DID I GET AS FAT AS I AM?

ALL OF MY SINS
ARE NOT AS NUMEROUS AS ALL OF MY CHINS!
I COULD AUDITION FOR THE DOUBLEMINT TWINS
NO ONE IN THE BIZ IS AS FAT AS I IS

AAH, BUT WHAT'S A CAREER
WHEN YOU PUT IT NEXT TO KNOCKWURST AND BEER
THEY COULD PARK A DC-10 ON MY REAR
GOD KNOWS I'VE GOT THE GAS

THERE GOES THE CHAIR
BUT TO TELL THE TRUTH, I'M TOO FAT TO CARE!
I ATE A MEATBALL OFF THE FLOOR RIGHT OVER THERE
AH, YOU DON'T GIVE A DAMN
WHEN YOU'RE FAT AS I AM!

For her second number, Bette chose to sing "Skylark," a song that starts her second album. As a teenage fanatic with a piano in my bedroom, I had played along to it many, many times—right down to the very '70s-style fade-out at the end where I would play the chords quieter and quieter and quieter until I was barely pressing the keys.

We rehearsed for this appearance at her house. Bette said, "I don't remember how I sing 'Skylark,'" walked over to her vinyl collection, put on her second album, and we rehearsed *along with* the record. And the fifteen-year-old still living in me has an aneurism, because it's just like it was back in my little room at home, playing along with the record, but now the actual Bette Midler has joined in.

In 1985, we created a short film for a David Letterman Christmas special adapting a song from the *Mud* album called "Why Bother?" The record version was dirtier, but the sanitized TV adaption was fun to film, and I was certainly the thinnest I've ever been, judging by this picture.

Bette played a beat-down nihilist, bemoaning the fate of the world and always coming to the conclusion: "Why bother?" I was her beatnik piano player, improvising atonally (and obnoxiously) to underscore her malaise. On this cut, Bette looks at me and says, "There are millions of piano players in the world. Listen to the chump *I* got…*why bother*?" And then a little later, "There are eighty-eight keys on that piano. This motherfucker knows five of 'em…*why bother*?" Given that Bette's nickname for me was "the little worm"—earned since I "wormed" my way into her world tour back in 1979—I assume she rather enjoyed saying those lines!

In March 1995, I even traveled with Bette to the White House. We were thrilled to be part of a live NPR radio show for the Clintons, broadcast directly from the East Room. After the concert, we all mingled, you know, just *schmoozing* with the president of the United States. Bill Clinton was so charming, so charismatic and magnetic, that you were drawn right to him. At one point, I couldn't believe I had found myself in a group of about six people, listening to him talk.

And talk.

And talk.

It started to remind me of the high school classes I barely attended. And so, ten long minutes later, I could not believe I found myself slowly creeping away from the group to find a more superficial conversation.

Later, in 2005, I got to play a classic song at her annual party, Hulaween—whose name winks at Halloween by way of Bette's native Hawaii. The celebrity-studded charity costume bash raises funds for the New York Restoration Project, an organization she started to clean up streets and parks.

I had musical directed a few of those evenings, but that night I was attending as a civilian. I went backstage to say hi, and Bette told me she was singing a duet with the night's featured performer, Elton John. I happened to be sitting there when Elton walked in (dressed as the Devil) and Bette said to him, "Okay Elton, we're singing 'Your Song' in my key, right?"

Elton calmly replied, "I don't know how to play in any other key except mine." And off he went to get ready.

Panic ensued, so I said to Bette, "I can play 'Your Song' in any key."

After a messenger was sent to Elton's corner, he came over and said, "I understand your man can play it in your key, that's fine.

It'll be more fun for me to sing it in a different key and harmonize with you."

So that night, the boy who came of age in the '70s listening to Bette Midler and Elton John albums got to play for both of these icons at the same time. In this picture taken afterward, I look sorta happy, doncha think? Actually, we *all* do!

There were endless other benefits, of course. And unfortunately, also endless memorials—so many nights singing for the friends we lost to AIDS. Like the tribute in 1989 for dear Jerry Blatt, the eccentric genius who worked alongside Bette for so many years; the evening in '95 for Joe Layton, the brilliant director who guided her *Clams on the Half-Shell Revue* on Broadway, and the memorial in '93 for Peter Allen, when Bette so exquisitely sang his "I Could Marry the Rain" and "Tenterfield Saddler."

It was my honor to collaborate with Bette on these nights, as her artistry provided catharsis to so many people. But what we mostly do together is laugh.

After paying my dues as music supervisor on "Wind Beneath My Wings" and associate producer on "From a Distance" (another

Grammy-winning Song of the Year I found for her), I worked my way up to finally co-producing her entire album, *It's the Girls*!

But in between, one of the cuts I was most happy to have produced and arranged for her was on her *Bathhouse Betty* album. It's a song with music by my late, great friend Dick Gallagher, who also passed away from AIDS, called "Laughing Matters." And I can't think of a better song to describe my relationship with Bette.

11

LEGENDS! In the Depths with Mary Martin and Carol Channing '85–

One day, while gathering material with Bette at her home in Los Angeles, the phone rang. It was Ahmet Ertegun, the pioneering producer and president of Atlantic Records.

I only heard Bette's side of the conversation, but she suddenly said, "I've got just the guy for you. He's sitting right here."

After hanging up, she explained, "Ahmet is co-producing a play called *Legends*! that is in previews downtown at the Ahmanson. It stars Carol Channing and Mary Martin. The play's not going very well, and they want to add a song at the end of the show. They need an arranger. They're gonna call you. Now—let's get back to work!"

Call me they did, and I went to meet Mary Martin at the place where she was staying in West Hollywood. I couldn't believe I was sitting, talking, and playing piano for this legend of Broadway musical theater. I must have passed the audition, because the next day I was driving to the Ahmanson Theatre to teach Mary and Carol Channing my arrangement of the standard, "Ac-Cent-Tchu-Ate the Positive."

That was a *long* drive that I would have to get used to because both ladies had reached an age when learning new material didn't happen as fast as it once did. Not to mention they were rehearsing and performing in a play that had changes coming in every day. The playwright James Kirkwood (who, in his book about this debacle, *Diary of a Mad Playwright,* called me "the world's most expensive piano player") was still feverishly trying to fix the play. New lines were coming in daily, and Mary finally had to get an earpiece into which an assistant stage manager could whisper prompts.

(It was rumored that she started getting police dispatches in her ear and reciting them back in the middle of scenes. Given the state of the script, this might have been an improvement.)

So, I sat for hours at the piano in a rehearsal room down in the depths of the Ahmanson, Mary to my left, Carol on my right. Carol had a quirk of drawing a black dot on the tip of her nose, which I guess someone once taught her brought attention to the center of her face. And she was growing frustrated at how long it was taking sweet Mary Martin to learn this arrangement. My favorite memory is when I was pounding out the last verse of the song and Mary turned to Carol and said, "Oh Carol, doesn't he play that 'Mississippi Mud' rhythm *wonderfully*!"

The director, an English gentleman named Vivian Matalon, had gone away for a while—although *escaped* might be a better word. The day he returned, he attempted to stage the number on the set, and it became a free-for-all, with everyone chiming in about how to do it. Now that the train was entirely off the rails, everyone wanted to be the engineer.

By this point, I had become frustrated with the entire enterprise, and when Mary's personal assistant piped up to say something to me about the arrangement, I snapped, "I don't even know who you *are*!" And although it was *her* assistant, I caught Mary smiling at me, with a look that seemed to say, "Ooh-wee, I love a good dust-up at rehearsals. Stick to your guns, honey!"

The show got legendarily bad reviews wherever it toured for the following year. The most accurate one may have come from my friend, performer Peter Allen, who, on opening night in LA, turned to me afterward and said, "Darling, it was positively science fiction!"

But I got to work with those *actual* legends, and I wouldn't trade the experience for anything. I must admit, however, almost forty years later, I'm still haunted by the black dot in the center of Carol Channing's nose.

12

PEOPLE COME AND GO SO QUICKLY HERE! '87–'88

Whenever I'm asked to name the first piece of music that affected me emotionally, my answer is, "The theme to *Million Dollar Movie*."

Growing up, every night, WOR-TV Channel 9—which served New York City and its suburbs—showed a film. It was introduced by a moody black-and-white montage of late-night Manhattan, with a lonely Edward Hopper vibe, set to "Tara's Theme" from *Gone with the Wind*. I couldn't identify the piece as a young boy; I just knew it was spectacular music.

One shot in particular always moved me: a pay phone with the handset hanging off the hook, slowly swinging from side to side. Its poignancy was my first lesson in how music and image can combine to create emotion. Couple this seminal childhood experience with Bette Midler's movie career now taking off, and perhaps it's not surprising that I ended up writing film scores.

Down and Out in Beverly Hills and *Ruthless People* had been huge smashes for Bette and Disney's Touchstone Pictures. In 1987, she was back in New York filming *Big Business*, a mistaken-identity comedy with Lily Tomlin, each of them playing twins.

She called me out of the blue one Friday and asked, "Can you help me come up with a yodel that fits over music a steel band is going to be playing in the scene I'm shooting on Monday?"

"Sure," I said, "come on over." Phone calls out of the blue with requests like 'Can you help me with a yodel?' are what really put a life in show business over the top.

So, I did a crash course in yodeling, Bette came over with the cassette of the steel band, and we worked it out. I didn't yet know anything about matching music to movies. But when I accompanied Bette to the set that Monday, I was surprised to find out both she and the band would be recorded live on the street. Nothing was pre-taped, and there was nothing to keep the tempo the same in different takes, which would have helped with the editing.

Luckily, it went well. The producer of the film, Michael Peyser, and director Jim Abrahams (fresh from *Airplane*!) thanked me for, as they said, "saving the day." They were so friendly that I blurted out, "How does a person get into scoring movies? Can I audition?"

They laughed at my naivete and said, "It's not really a thing you audition for, but thanks again for getting us through today."

But they did fly me to LA to co-write, arrange, and record the song Bette sang in the movie while…milking a cow. Oh, the glamour!

As I was doing this work on *Big Business*, the film *Broadcast News* came out, in which I had a small role. A year earlier, a fellow musical director named Glen Roven called to say that his casting director friend, Paula Harold, was looking for two piano players for a new movie that was being directed by James L. Brooks (who had just had a monster hit with *Terms of Endearment*). The characters were two overzealous jingle writers who appear in the middle of the movie for one bizarre minute of screen time. Paula put us on video and much to our amazement, we got the gig. And even more amazing is that we made the final edit of the movie!

Glen and I worked out how to play, physicalize and vocalize the news theme written for the film, including our exclamation at the end, "BIG FINISH!" The scene was a standout and *Broadcast News* was an immediate icebreaker for every conversation I had while working on Bette's songs for *Big Business*. I was suddenly a part of a hit Oscar-nominated movie and who knows, maybe that was part of the equation that led to, a few months later, Michael and Jim calling to say they had never forgotten my question. They were going to send me a few scenes that, if I wanted, I could write music for as an audition.

I plopped my TV set onto the piano, a VHS player underneath, without any knowledge of click tracks or how to record music that lines up to film. I just did what I had always done since first attending cast parties: play appropriate (or inappropriate) music whenever a person entered the room.

I started keeping track of signposts, such as when Lily placed her hand on the doorknob. I knew I needed to be on the downbeat of a certain measure for the next few seconds of music to lay in perfectly with the scene. In this way, I found subtle visual cues to know where I had to be as I played. If this sounds like a task requiring a certain degree of "CDO," then I'm explaining it perfectly.

The music I wrote was in the mode of Alfred Newman's classic score to *How to Marry a Millionaire*, a 1950s-Hollywood-style for movies set in New York, a style itself inspired by Gershwin's "Rhapsody in Blue."

I wrote out the music and went into a studio with a bass player and a drummer, and God bless them for being able to follow me as I chased Lily Tomlin's hand and Bette Midler's feet. Then, I sent the recording to Jim and Michael.

Imagine my shock when they called and said, "We love what you sent. We want you to do the movie! Here's the plan that we have devised with Chris Montan, the head of music at Disney. We are hiring both you and Ralph Burns to score the movie together."

Ralph Burns was a legendary arranger, Bob Fosse's go-to music man, who'd won Oscars for his score adaptations for *Cabaret* and *All That Jazz*.[9] Their plan was to have young meet old; I'd offer a new

9 "Score Adaptation", the category for adapting existing music that Ralph won those Oscars for, the same category Marvin Hamlisch won for *The Sting*, was eliminated the year before I got to Hollywood and scored *When Harry Met Sally, Sister Act* and *Sleepless In Seattle*. Arrghh!

perspective while he would be the seasoned expert, and somehow together, we'd create a cohesive score. I was thrilled to work with Ralph—not only a musical genius, but also a social pioneer as an openly gay man who came up in the jazz world of the '40s and '50s and nonetheless managed to be accepted and cherished.

Around the time I got the call from Jim and Michael, I was doing a concert at the Bottom Line in New York of the best songs from the five musicals I had written up until then. It was ironically named "Marc Shaiman: The First Fifty Years," winking at the fact I had already done so much in my twenties. The night before I was to fly to LA was the last of my run, and I stood up on the piano to tell everyone I was flying to Hollywood tomorrow. Celebration all around!

Stephen Holden in the *New York Times* even wrote up the show, including the line, "Broadway's loss is Hollywood's gain, as Marc Shaiman heads west."

I flew to LA and immediately rented a car, a piano, and a house on my own, since Scott was in Germany working with the singer/actress Ute Lemper. I also went to the Guitar Center on Sunset Boulevard where a patient fellow took me through the new equipment that was hitting the scene: the synthesizers, the sequencers; all of it connected by a mystifying computer language called MIDI. It was a lot to absorb, but I was ready for the challenge.

The much bigger challenge turned out to be when they sent me the movie with the "temp track."

The temp track is pre-existing music a director and his editor will place into a movie as they are editing and previewing it. A movie without music is like a dead fish: you simply can*not* show it without proper music underneath. So, over the years, music editors have kept libraries of every single note ever recorded for film and, rather brilliantly, cut together a *temporary* score for previews.

These temp scores, I soon learned, are the bane of the film composer's existence. After living with it for months, everyone involved falls in love with the temp, and composers are too often nudged (or forced) to simply copy it. Often, I can figure out what a new movie was temped with—and then go and watch *that* movie and figure out what *it* was temped with. It's a vicious cycle.

Nonetheless, it helps a director express to the composer what he's thinking—and if you're lucky, your director will be open to something more than just a recreation of the temp.

So I was shocked when I listened to the temp score for *Big Business* and heard music from *Beverly Hills Cop* and *Fletch*. Composer Harold Faltermeyer was all the rage at that moment, and they wanted his style, even though it was absolutely nothing like the music I had written that made them hire me in the first place. "Oh, no, Marc," they explained, "the music you sent showed us how talented you are, but the movie has to sound contemporary, and this is the style we want you to work in."

It was a bit like saying, "We love what you did. Do something else."

If you thought I was perplexed by all this, imagine how Ralph Burns felt. He, who was probably around seventy, had been working at the highest levels for decades, and was not used to being told to emulate the flavor of the month.

Ralph had been very sweet to me, explaining technicalities like "click tracks" (which is figuring out a tempo for the music you're gonna write for a scene, so you know where important pieces of action will fall). We split up the "cues" (each separate piece of music written for a movie) and went to work in our own homes.

Trying to follow the guidelines for something contemporary, I wrote a long cue for a New York shopping montage in the style of *Saturday Night Live*—which might not have been Harold Faltermeyer, but was at least a sound that wasn't '50s Hollywood. Ralph was writing in *his* own style, as was his prerogative. One of Ralph's cues and one of my cues were going to be placed into the temp score for the first test screening. Every movie previews in front of a guinea-pig audience to see if the laughs are landing, if certain scenes or lines need to be recut, and to basically find out if it works.

But Ralph had become frustrated at being told to copy the temp score, not to mention having to record music on synthesizers and supply it to the editing room. He was used to going in with an orchestra once the film was completed, not having to deal with creating temp "mockups." So, one day at the sound mix for the first test screening, Michael and Jim came over and told me Ralph had decided to leave the project. It was all now in my hands! They were optimistic, even celebratory about my prospects, but I do remember my inner Dorothy thinking, "My, people come and go so quickly here."

At the first test screening the following night, I sat right behind Chris Montan, the head of music who'd hired me and had continued to be incredibly supportive. The movie played well, although I still felt its music was uninspired. After the film ended, Chris was talking animatedly with someone beside him and then turned around and, I swear, was as pale as a ghost.

He said, "Go home, I'm going to call you in the morning."

Gulp.

The next morning, Chris told me someone from the studio at the test screening did not like the style of music in the temp. "Oh my God," I said, "you know I agree with them a hundred percent. Who was it?"

Long pause. Then, "It was Jeffrey Katzenberg."

He was the head of Disney and Touchstone at that time, so it was about as bad a piece of news as you could get. Chris went on to say that when Katzenberg asked, "Who is going to be scoring this movie?" and heard it was a novice who had never even scored a student film, he said, "No way, you're gonna have to fire him."

I pleaded with Chris to convince Katzenberg to let me show him I could write music that was not in the Faltermeyer style. (I should say here that I *love* Harold Faltermeyer and his music, it's just that I didn't want to copy him.) Katzenberg agreed, but the only time he could give me later that week was a 6:30 a.m. appointment.

Okay!

So I picked three scenes from the movie and figured out three different styles to score them with, writing and "synthesizer orchestrating" nine separate cues.

I also begged them to let me be at this 6:30 a.m. showing of my cues, because I knew film music had to be mixed—brought up and down under dialogue to work properly. Katzenberg agreed: I could come in and run the fader, but then had to leave the projection room so they could speak freely.

A sound man came over to my house to record my cues. He brought a Nagra machine, which, up until the computer age, was equipment that used timecode to correctly align music with movies. Except the Nagra broke two-thirds of the way through and only six cues got recorded, meaning only two of the three style choices I had prepared would make it to my big 6:30 a.m. meeting. Good Lord, why me?

I got to Disney Studios at dawn, I was brought into Katzenberg's screening room to meet him (he was very cordial), and with Michael and Jim also there, they rolled the scenes as I mixed the music from a sound deck in the back. I then left and sat alone in the waiting room.

It didn't take them long to emerge, looking like three surgeons coming out of an OR to give the family the bad news. Katzenberg said he was very impressed with my music and understood why they had wanted to hire me. But at this moment, he felt these guys needed an old hand who would tell them the best way to score the movie and not say, "I could try it this way or this way or that way." It turned out that by preparing different ideas, I had inadvertently shown Katzenberg I would not be the strong arm he wanted. And so…I was off the picture.

I feel terrible for whoever was behind me on the 101 Freeway that morning as I drove back home to Laurel Canyon in my rented convertible. I was weeping so copiously they must have thought, "Why is it only raining on *my* car?"

Jim and Michael called me later to say, "Don't give up. You're so talented, something good is going to happen for you soon." I had been hearing that about my theater stuff for so long that I was not in the mood to hear it again about another avenue of show business. But they did say they were going to keep my shopping-montage cue in the movie. Luckily, by this time I had already been hired to help choose songs for Bette's next movie, *Beaches,* and also had *When Harry Met Sally* lined up.

Not too long after that tearful day, and the great success of those two films and their respective soundtracks, I was called into another meeting with the very same Jeffrey Katzenberg—at a more reasonable time of day. He and his team pleaded with me to use my relationship with Bette to get her to agree to taking over the role that had been written for her in *Sister Act,* because Whoopi Goldberg was giving them such trouble with her demands.

As I sat in that meeting I thought, "Gee, what a difference a year makes."

13

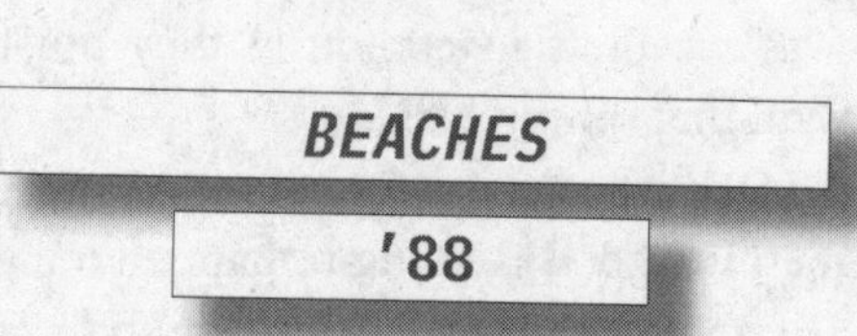

In 1988, I was hired as the music supervisor for *Beaches*, a Bette Midler film and soundtrack that would become extremely meaningful to us both, as well as to millions of others.

Beaches celebrated the decades-long friendship between Cecilia Carol "C.C." Bloom, an aspiring Broadway actress, and Hillary Whitney, an ACLU lawyer—played in adulthood by Bette and Barbara Hershey, and as children by Mayim Bialik and Marcie Leeds. It portrayed the ups and downs of female friendship, which was an unusual subject for a big studio film at the time, and came with an emotional wallop of an ending that has kept it a favorite with fans for almost forty years.

My job as music supervisor was to go through the script with Bette and help choose songs she felt passionate about and that helped to tell the story. These songs would then be produced and recorded by Arif Mardin.

Considering the two young characters meet under the Atlantic City boardwalk, it didn't take an Einstein to realize the song "Under the Boardwalk" would be a candidate for inclusion. No one balked when I suggested it—and in my showbiz experience, no one balking is sometimes the biggest thumbs-up you're going to get. (Career tip: If you require lots of day-to-day positive feedback, look to other industries.)

Bette then played me a recording of old-time movie star Ann Sothern singing a Cole Porter song (which Ethel Merman premiered on Broadway in *Panama Hattie*) called "I've Still Got My Health." It was self-deprecating but upbeat, and perfect for the witty, brassy C.C. to perform as part of her nightclub act during a low point in her career: "My best ring, alas, is a glass solitaire / But I still got my health, so what do I care?" One by one, we continued choosing the other songs, and it was producer Teri Schwartz who brought in Alberta Hunter's recording of "The Glory of Love," thinking the song could work as emotional bookends to the film.

Under Arif's guidance, Bette and I would lay down piano/vocal demos of the songs. If chosen, they would then get further arranged and orchestrated by him, me, and other musicians. But the very first piano/vocal recording Bette and I made of "The Glory of Love" was considered a keeper, and I was tasked with writing an orchestration that would work with my piano part.

This was the first orchestration I had ever written, and I was very nervous. But I was even more nervous about conducting it in front of an orchestra, because I had also never done that. If the song had been performed to a steady beat it would have been easy to conduct, but our version was rubato—meaning out of tempo—and it's only because I played the piano on the original track that I felt I could follow myself well enough to keep the orchestra in sync.

At the top of the session, I said to the musicians, "I have never done this before, and I have no ego about it, so please tell me anything I'm doing wrong or anything I can do to help you."

After we finished the first take, one of the cellists pulled me aside and said, "Marc, it's called a *down*beat for a reason." It turns out I had been raising my hand upward for the first beat of the measure—completely ignoring the term "downbeat." Who knew it was a literal thing! Luckily, the rest of the recording went well, and that afternoon's work is what you hear on the album. If the music sounds different when you watch it on screen, it's because we re-recorded my orchestration with an even larger orchestra for the movie. At *that* session, I finally knew my up from my down.

On *Beaches,* I discovered I could suffer from "red-light fever," which is when a normally capable musician tightens up when the red recording light goes on. I am extremely confident as an accompanist; put me on stage with a great performer and I am at my best, more at home than at home. But with little experience in the recording studio, on *Beaches* I could get close to perfect, but seemingly, no cigar. I found this out when Arif and Bette told me that my piano track on "Baby Mine" (a tender lullaby adapted from 1941's *Dumbo*) would be replaced on the second pressing of the album with the exquisite session virtuoso, Randy Kerber.

This disheartening news came after the album—a hit—was out. But it followed an even bigger disappointment while I was working on the film. When I arrived at the studio prepared to record the piano part for "I Think It's Going to Rain Today" that I had meticulously arranged, I discovered Randy sitting at the piano. He was playing what I had written out and listening to a tape of me rehearsing with Bette. Obviously, Randy had been chosen to play on the recording, but no one had been thoughtful enough to tell me. Then, someone from the music department, tone-deaf to the awkward situation, said: "Marc, Bette is running late and you know her phrasing so well. Would you please sing so that Randy can rehearse?"

Ouch. Oof. Oy.

I was embarrassed and humiliated. But always the good soldier—especially if it grants me license to sulk about it in print forty years later—I went into the vocal booth and sang Randy Newman's powerful song about feeling like the world is a dark and disloyal place. And I did not have to reach deep for those feelings, because they were all right there on the surface. I sang it through twice, and if it had been a movie, the camera would have started outside the scratched glass recording booth and slowly circled as I emoted an Academy Award-worthy performance. You should've heard my reading of these lines:

TIN CAN AT MY FEET
THINK I'LL KICK IT DOWN THE STREET
THAT'S THE WAY TO TREAT A FRIEND...

And right after that moment, as I was silently walking back into the control room with my head hung low, one of the big kahunas of the film arrived.

She saw me and said, "What are *you* doing here?"

"*What am I...?*"

Big *zetz*. Double-*zetz*. Game, *zetz*, match.

And then I had to get outta there. Off I fled in my convertible, tears streaming all the way home. In the movie adaptation of my life, the same guy from when Jeffrey Katzenberg fired me will again be stuck behind me on the freeway, still wondering why he's the only one with rain on his windshield on an otherwise sunny day.

Can a moment like that make you want to quit the business? Yes! Do you quit? No! Do you grow cranky and bitter, filling your memoir with unforgotten slights? I plead the Fifth!

But there was no time for me to pout since we had more spots to fill and more songs to place into the movie. (In scheduling future gigs, I allotted adequate time to pout.) Our song, "Otto Titsling," got the spot for the bawdy Broadway musical which makes C.C. a star.

The name of Bette's character will always remind me of the line I had for my cameo in the opening minutes of the movie. The first scene was going to be filmed at the Hollywood Bowl, with Bette as C.C. singing "Under the Boardwalk," and our director, Garry Marshall, asked if I would like to play piano onscreen. My mind immediately went to what my mother would say whenever she called me after I was on the Regis Philbin *Morning Show,* which was, "Marc! Stop biting your nails!"

You see, almost every time someone sings on a TV show, the director will invariably start with a shot of the piano player's fingers on the keyboard during the intro, and then dissolve to the singer's face when she is about to sing. I suddenly thought, *What if this scene in* Beaches *starts that way, with a big-screen close-up of my fingers? Oh my God, I'm gonna actually have to listen to my mother.*

I used to bite my nails so terribly that I had never even known there was supposed to be a little white rim at the end of them. *Eewww*. So, a few days before filming, I went to a salon in the Valley and asked for the manicurist to apply some fake nails. At first the woman thought I was a drag queen and started putting on long nails and I said, "No, no, I want man nails, I'm just trying to cover up my own."

The manicurist rolled her eyes, probably thinking I was too embarrassed to admit I had a drag act, but gave me what I wanted. And after showing off my new nails on the set the day of filming, Bette's producing partner, Bonnie Bruckheimer, kept teasing me, telling me I should throw both my hands up around my face to show off my nails as I said my one big line, imploring the star to come back to the stage: "C.C.! C.C.!"

Ironically, there was no big close-up of my fingers, but there is a happy ending to this mini saga: I couldn't bite the fake nails, and once they fell off some weeks later, I had been cured. It never occurred to me to bite my nails again.

As pre-production work progressed, there was still one slot open for what everyone hoped would be an original song, because only an original song can be nominated for an Oscar. Lord knows, I and every other songwriter in town wanted a chance to write a song for this spot.

One day, Bette came over to my house in Laurel Canyon with co-producers Bonnie and Teri as well as director Garry Marshall, to go over our song choices. When the slot for the original song came up, I suddenly remembered one I had learned a few years earlier.

Sometime in the mid-'80s, my friend Jackie Judd, a manager and producer who was always on the lookout for talent, brought Scott and me to hear a singer from down south named Jerome Olds. He was doing a gig at a club in the Village and sang the most glorious song by Jeff Silbar and Larry Henley, on a subject that no other song had ever really addressed, called "Wind Beneath My Wings."

At the time, I didn't know it had already been a country hit for Gary Morris, or that it had even won Song of the Year at the Country Music Awards. This certainly underscores how country music and pop radio lived in different worlds at the time, since this gorgeous song was completely new to me. And it was magnificent. Jackie brought Jerome over to our SoHo loft one day and he sang it again, and I memorized the whole song from just hearing it twice.

Fast forward a few years to the *Beaches* music meeting in my house. I said to everyone, "I just thought of a song that will serve as a perfect template for what we need in this spot. Let me sing it for you, I think it really points the way to what we're looking for in an original song."

My rented upright piano was against the opposite wall, so my back was to the team when I sang "Wind Beneath My Wings" as expressively as I could. Although my singing voice has often been called a Jewish cry for help, my years of being a Bette Midler disciple have taught me to sing with emotion, and I gave it my all. And the part of me who wanted a chance to write an original song for this spot probably wished I had *not* given my all, because when I finished and turned around, all four of them were in tears. From that moment, "Wind Beneath My Wings" held claim to the spot.

Well, that's not completely true, because *also* from that moment, as she has often recounted in interviews, Bette questioned the song. Bette questions all things, always wondering, "What else ya got?" I remember she once stopped in the middle of recording the vocal for "Wind" and said, "Marc Shaiman, you are leading me down the garden path with this song, and I will never let you forget it!"

But luckily, she sang on and the rest, as they say, is her story. And although I did not have any financial stake in the album or the single, and my credit was only as music supervisor, not as co-producer, Bette recognized that I had sat shoulder-to-shoulder with Arif for the entire process. When the song hit number one (her first!), she wrote me a lovely check and also sent Scott and me on an all-expenses-paid trip to her home state of Hawaii.

That extremely generous gesture took *some* of the sting away from not receiving royalties from this mega hit for the rest of my life. Aloha *oy*!

I also had the *chutzpah* to rewrite some lyrics in *Beaches* to better fit Bette's character. I changed a line with an outdated reference in Cole Porter's "I've Still Got My Health," switching "I ain't quite as sleek as the chic Norma Shearer," to "My ship ain't come in, but I grin while I bear." And then, thinking about the illness of Barbara Hershey's character, I changed a lyric in "Wind" from "I never once heard you complain," to "A beautiful smile to hide the pain." In the studio, Arif and I egged on Bette from the control booth as she created the soaring, majestic ending—"Fly, fly, fly high against the sky"—which instantly became iconic. And it was she who created all the wonderful asides, adding "That's your way," "For so long," and "Of course I know" into the song. And now that's the way everyone sings it. I used to wonder if the songwriters were upset that we made these minor adjustments—but since "Wind Beneath My Wings" ended up being named both Record and Song of the Year at that year's Grammys, I had to imagine they were okay with it.

Many times, when listening to the radio in the car, I will shout to Lou, "Sense memory!" So often a song first heard in youth sticks in your brain, inextricably linking it with memories of a specific time and place. Whenever I hear Seals and Croft's "Summer Breeze" I am suddenly in a car parked in front of my childhood neighbors, the Makowskis. If I hear "Turn Around, Look at Me" by The Lettermen, I am at a snack bar on the boardwalk at the Jersey Shore, and when I hear "I Need You" by the group, America, I am at the Blue Star Shopping Center in my hometown. But more than just being connected with a location, "Wind Beneath My Wings," played at countless graduations, birthdays, and funerals, has surely given millions upon millions of listeners their own warm sense memories. I know that "Wind" has a place in millions of hearts, and I take great pride in having been part of Bette's perfect recording of it. It is a profoundly loving song, and when Jeff Silbar and Larry Henley created their masterpiece, they gave people a way to express an emotion that had never before been put to music and lyrics.

What a legacy.

14

WHEN BILLY MET MARC

One of the relationships formed at *SNL* that changed my life was my friendship with Billy Crystal.

I have a lot to thank him for, like introducing me to Robin Williams. In 1986, Billy brought me in for the first HBO telethon Comic Relief to arrange a number for a sketch called "Betty's Boys" in which they played two "flamboyant" backup dancers practicing a Vegas routine. We would all be thrown into a cancellation dungeon if it aired today.

Billy also introduced me to Oscar. Not the Grouch, but the statue—or at least the ceremony where they give them out (to everyone but me).

I was delighted when Billy invited me to join the team that wrote the humorous medleys that always opened his Oscar hosting duties. As a kid inspired by everything from Allan Sherman ("Hello Muddah, Hello Fadduh") to *Mad* magazine's hilarious song parodies ("Sung to the tune of..."), I had been writing funny lyrics to existing songs since I first sat down at a piano. So, I was all set for this gig of gigs.

It is rather daunting to write for the Academy Awards, knowing it is being seen—they always claim—by a billion people around the world. One might imagine that kind of pressure could dampen the fun of the process. Not with this bunch—Good Lord did we howl when writing with Billy.

The writers (including the ubiquitous Bruce Vilanch), Billy, and I would laugh ourselves sick by suggesting incredibly inappropriate lyrics—before eventually getting realistic about what the censors would allow. Those medleys also allowed me to arrange and orchestrate alongside a great team of co-orchestrators and then have that phenomenal Oscars band play their asses off no matter what we put in front of them. Another thrill I would have every year was singing Billy's part during the orchestra's first read-through.

The first year Billy hosted, I was not billed as a writer but rather under "Special Musical Material." So, I was not included when the writing team was nominated and—surprise!—won an Emmy.

That might have been the first time people working on one awards show won an award for it on another awards show. My billing got fixed the second year, but Scott had been frustrated with my not being present at our rental house in Laguna, and I was so sure that lightning wouldn't strike twice—and to keep the peace at home—I did not attend the next Emmys.

Lo and behold, Billy and his writing team won again, this time with me included. But I was not there to get up on stage. My friend Toni Basil called the next day to say, "I've been working my whole life in this fucking business, and you win an Emmy and don't even show up?!"

For a decade, those Oscar medleys were a chance for me to exercise my more theatrical side. After all, the Broadway songwriter in me was not being called upon in my other film work. But when I first met Lin-Manuel Miranda, while working on *Mary Poppins Returns* years later, he started the conversation by singing:

> IT'S A WONDERFUL NIGHT FOR OSCAR
> OSCAR, OSCAR
> WHO WILL WIN!?

So, I was inspired by *Mad* magazine's song parodies, and Lin-Manuel was inspired by ours. (I like to think of "It's a Wonderful Night for Oscar" as being my *Hamilton*.)

When Billy began filming *When Harry Met Sally*, directed by his best friend Rob Reiner, he asked what Rob was planning for the music. Rob replied that he wanted to use standards from the Great American Songbook. Billy, mensch that he is, told him, "Have I got the guy for you!"

Billy likes to call me "Rain Jew," comparing me to Dustin Hoffman's character in *Rain Man* for my ability to somehow remember and play just about every song that has ever been written. Some people have a photographic memory, but I guess mine is phonographic. I'm not even sure how I do it; I just somehow retain every song I hear. What can I say? I am a human Spotify.

So, Billy set me up for a meeting with Rob. I brought with me a Rodgers and Hart songbook I have had since I was a teenager (which, I'm afraid to say, I think I borrowed from a friend's piano in New Jersey and never returned) because I knew the final lyrics to "I Could Write a Book" perfectly fit the movie:

THEN THE WORLD DISCOVERS AS MY BOOK ENDS
HOW TO MAKE TWO LOVERS OF FRIENDS

Rob hired me, and while the job didn't utilize my composing skills, working on *When Harry Met Sally* taught me how music is timed, recorded, and placed into a movie. I worked alongside a great music editor named Scott Stambler, and he, Rob, and I chose the songs and/or the recordings that were used in the film.

At the same time, Rob's friend Bobby Colomby—former drummer for the classic band Blood, Sweat & Tears turned Columbia Records executive—told us about a new, very young jazz artist the label had recently signed. Maybe this Harry Connick Jr. would be perfect to perform some part of the soundtrack.

I'm sure I was thinking, "Wait a second, I thought *I* was the piano-playing prodigy hired for this movie!" But when Rob and I heard Harry's first record, *20*, we realized he'd be a welcome addition to our team. So I was sent up to Seattle, where Harry was performing with his trio, for a meet and greet.

In truth, I bet Harry's first thought about me was the same thought I had about him: *Who needs this guy*? But I told him what Rob and I were up to, and we made plans for Harry to come down to LA and be part of the recording.

But when Harry and his trio came in for that first day at the recording studio, which was a Friday, exactly what I feared might happen did.

To smoothly segue into the other recordings we were using in the film, we needed the songs we were laying down that day to be played in certain keys so as to end on specific chords and to be played at precise tempos. This ensured we got to the end of the song at the exact millisecond necessary.

Creating music for film is as much about mathematics as it is notes, chords, and emotions. In addition to putting in a lot of time figuring all this out, I had also recorded a temporary version with my own fingers and style.

Well, things got very egg-shelly in the studio, as Harry did not like some guy laying out strict guidelines for him simply to color in. But somehow, with everyone biting their tongue before saying something that could cause a real blowup, we got through the day. Harry's creativity flourished and I still got the ins and outs we needed.

What is going to happen on Monday? I wondered as I drove home. We would then be recording cues with a full orchestra and have no time for "friendly" arguments about what we were doing. The clock is ticking at a film scoring date, and the budget would explode if every measure of music was up for debate.

Monday came around, and I took to the podium to conduct the first cue of the day. It was music under the first New Year's Eve scene in the movie, when Harry and Sally are dancing with each other and begin to realize that their friendship could become more than platonic. (Ironically, Scott and I had the exact same experience at a previous New Year's party, which led us to become more than roommates.)

The scene had been filmed to a Sinatra recording, and I knew I had to cop that vibe for Billy and Meg's movements and emotions to match. It was also the spot we had decided to use "I Could Write a Book," and my tempo ensured that those lyrics about "how to make two lovers of friends" would fall at just the right moment as Harry and Sally recognize a change in their relationship.

I had sweated over the musical arrangement, trying desperately to follow in the footsteps of the legendary arranger/orchestrator Nelson Riddle. Would Harry like what I had prepared, or would this session become reminiscent of a scene out of *Who's Afraid of Virginia Woolf?*

To have complete separation of his vocals, Harry was in the vocal booth, which at this studio was located behind me. So, I couldn't see him but could only hear his voice. As I watched the footage of the scene, I counted in the orchestra and prayed.

God heard my prayer. Just moments into Harry's vocal, the friction of that Friday session vanished. And as the orchestra perfectly nailed the style, Harry and I firmly and fully fell in love with each other. I had found my Frank and he his Nelson (if you'll forgive my hubris). The rest of the day went smoothly, and we all heaved a sigh of relief.

Beside Harry and me on the soundtrack—it's me playing "It Had to Be You" the first time we hear it in the movie, as Harry and Sally reconnect in New York—the film was chock-full of legendary recordings of illustrious stars singing those classic songs.

Now, there are certain deals a record company makes to license music for use in a movie, but completely different terms for the use of those same recordings on a movie's soundtrack album. Luckily for Harry and me, most of the recordings, especially the ones with Ella Fitzgerald, were deemed too expensive to license for the album. So, Bobby Colomby said to us, "If you guys want to throw together an album *inspired* by the music in the movie, go ahead. Here's a few dollars."

We were *inspired* to say yes.

Harry and I met at a recording studio in New York City a few weeks later. For the movie, we had contributed usually about thirty-two measures of this or that, but for this album, we got to do our own full versions of the songs.

I did three big orchestral charts: for the great Duke Ellington song "Don't Get Around Much Anymore," the classic Gershwin tune "But Not for Me," and the old chestnut that became Harry and Sally's theme in the movie, "It Had to Be You." The New York musicians were phenomenal (including the noted Count Basie saxophonist Frank Wess), and it all felt great—especially "It Had to Be You." There was just a sense of magic in the air.

And let me tell you one final thing about that recording, something I've pointed out to musician friends over the years: The engineer had the first and the second trumpet players sharing the same mic, but I was too inexperienced to notice that, let alone worry about it. I only discovered when we went to mix the recording that, when the orchestra takes over the melody in the instrumental midway through the song, the second trumpet player is louder than the first trumpet part. And it *drives me crazy*!

I chose to go with an angular chord for that moment, and the second trumpet harmony note only works if the melody in the first trumpet above it is good and strong. Luckily, I think because listeners know the tune so well, everyone's brain does the work and hears the melody stronger than it actually is on the recording. But if you are with me when that record comes on, you'll know why I leap out the door right before that measure—which is a real problem when I'm driving.

Despite that off-balance trumpet moment, the soundtrack was a huge success. It was quite the launching pad for both Harry and me, and I am forever grateful to whoever negotiated Ella Fitzgerald's licensing deal back in the day, because the inability to use her recordings created an open door that Harry and I walked through into platinum record heaven and our first Grammy nominations.

I spent the next few years working with Harry. We collaborated on another album, *We Are in Love*, toured all over, and even played a stint at the Lunt-Fontanne Theatre on Broadway. On the *We Are in Love* album, there ended up being another moment that called for a "fix it in the mix" moment, and on this occasion, I acted in time.

Well, almost in time.

Harry was a purist and would not cut between takes; it had to go on the record exactly as recorded live. Which sometimes resulted in a lot of takes.

Well, as we were preparing for the sessions, Harry said he was bringing up a drummer from New Orleans named Shannon Powell, whom I would love (and did end up loving). But what Harry did *not* tell me was that Shannon did not read music. Now, it's one thing to do a jazz gig and have musicians play instinctively, but when you are recording a full orchestra and have written an arrangement that calls for the drummer to know exactly what's going on in all departments of that arrangement, the drummer not being able to read music is...problematic.

So here I was with a full orchestra in front of me, including brass players who have to blow their brains out on every take. They are not used to having to start all over again, endlessly, as a drummer learns the arrangement on the spot, by ear. On a big band chart, the drummer will very often hit the snare in tandem with the major brass licks, which gives those licks greater impact. So with the brass players glaring at me, instead of being on the conductor's stand, I ended up standing in front of Shannon's drum set, trying to telegraph when the brass were going to play a lick that he should underline.

I was dancing and gesticulating like Ann-Margret hopped up on amphetamines. *Bip*! *Bop*! *Bap*! You shoulda seen me go!

Somehow we got the job done without a mutiny in the trumpet section. A few days later, Harry, our engineer, Joel Moss, and I went off to mix the record—and just getting Harry to mix the record and not leave all levels exactly as recorded was a big deal. We had booked a small mixing studio in the hills north of Los Angeles. It did have a small "live" room that musicians played in long ago, but that was in disarray because the studio now only booked the control booth for mixing.

As we listened to the recordings, I grew frustrated at the many spots where, despite my dancing prowess, Shannon had not been able to catch the brass licks. I wandered outside the mixing booth and suddenly saw a snare drum through the window of the "live" room, which was stacked with abandoned clutter.

I investigated but could not find a drumstick, so I tiptoed into the studio's kitchenette and retrieved a fork. I went back into the control room and said, "Joel, set up a mic to record in the studio. And Harry, you're just going to have to turn your back or walk away for a few minutes because I can't take it anymore and I'm going to use this snare and this fork to overdub drum hits to go with the horn licks."

Harry was so bemused he stayed in the control booth while I went out to the studio and started overdubbing. It only took about a minute for him to come into the studio and say, "Hey man, your time stinks, let me do that!"

I am happy to report that I can listen to that album now and not make out when it is Shannon at the live session, or me or Harry playing the snare drum with a fork. But all the horn hits are there in the drum part!

And none of my time and success with Harry could have happened without good ol' Billy Crystal.

Billy and I have worked together on so many other projects: just one of the many once-in-a-lifetime moments he has afforded me was, when filming a performance for the HBO special *Midnight Train to Moscow*, I got to play Tchaikovsky *in* Russia to underscore Billy's "Chaplin in Moscow" pantomime (my childhood piano teacher Miss Andrews would have been so proud!) And in 2012 all of my worlds converged when I scored *Parental Guidance*, starring both Billy and Bette. (On a call, my mother once asked what I was up to and I told her, perhaps with too much self-satisfaction, "Well, I rehearsed with Billy Crystal all day and recorded with Bette Midler all night," to which she responded as only a Jewish mother can: "So, maybe through *them* you'll meet someone im*port*ant?")

Most recently, *much* to Billy's surprise, my husband Lou indoctrinated me into becoming a New York Yankees fan. When I text Billy from Yankee Stadium, he can hardly believe the same Marc who would nod off whenever he went into one of his Yankees stories was now reciting stats for this year's roster. We even went to a game together and, since I know the organist at Yankee Stadium, I ran up to the organ and the crowd that day heard the *City Slickers* theme as they cut to Billy in the stands!

When people ask me for advice on how to have a career like mine, I tell them, "Meeting Billy Crystal when you're in your twenties is a must."

15

TALENT IS TALENT

(Says Rob Reiner)

'89-

In 1989, shortly after *When Harry Met Sally*, Billy Crystal made an HBO special called *Midnight Train to Moscow*. I enjoyed scoring its dramatic storyline in a cinematic fashion. Rob Reiner came to a screening and called me the next morning.

"Hey, buddy, you wanna score my next movie? It's a psychological thriller called *Misery*."

I didn't try to talk him out of this idea, but I was bewildered he would think I had the chops to do such a thing—a sentiment that happened to be echoed by my brand-new agent, Richard Kraft.

While I was working on *When Harry Met Sally* and *Beaches*, the music contractor (who hires the musicians and takes care of payroll) was Sandy DeCrescent, a powerful figure in the Hollywood orchestra scene. She recognized I was suddenly getting all this work and asked, "How come you don't have an agent? I'm gonna hook you up with Richard Kraft. He's perfect for you."

I even resemble Richard, who was expecting a child at the time. So, when I stepped into his office, he said it was like meeting his unborn embryo. Then he asked, "What do you want to do?"

I blurted out, "I wanna score movies. I wanna be famous like Paul Williams! I wanna be on talk shows and *Hollywood Squares. I wanna be the gay Marvin Hamlisch*!"

Based solely on the fact that I was getting work and sorta looked like him, Richard signed me, never having heard a note of my music. And then Richard had to negotiate with Rob Reiner for *Misery*.

Even though he was representing me, Richard said to Rob, "You've only heard his arrangements, what makes you think Marc can compose an original film score?"

And Rob replied, "Richard, talent is talent!" So that became Richard's mantra when negotiating on my behalf.

Billy Crystal had just finished *City Slickers*, which he starred in and co-wrote, and had suggested me to its director, Ron Underwood. All the top composers were up for the job, but Ron liked my spirit. Richard gave him the "talent is talent" spiel and he hired me.

In quick succession, I was hired to score the movies *Misery*, *The Addams Family*, and *City Slickers*, without having written a single note of original movie music except for about five minutes in Billy's HBO special. Where did I get the *chutzpah* to think I could do this?

But back to Rob's thriller, which always reminds me of the joke, "Why don't Jews drink? Because it interferes with their misery!"

Since *Big Business,* I had started purchasing all the equipment necessary at that time to score movies: synthesizers, computers, and wiring that allowed me to compose on a real piano. I can't work on an electronic or digital keyboard; I crave an actual piano under my fingers. So, with a TV set up on top of the piano and VHS tapes of the current edit of *Misery,* I started writing music.

I was once again confronted with a "temp score." But this time it was helpful, being made up mostly of soundtracks by the film-score giant, Jerry Goldsmith. Although Lord knows I wasn't capable of copying him, it was like having a brilliant teacher coaxing me along. I began to see how orchestral music could have many groupings, each doing their own thing at the same time. Cellos and basses may be rumbling along on a frighteningly low melody, as the woodwinds are pecking like a riot in a chicken coop, while the high strings are sustaining a cluster of odd, disconcerting notes. I was learning as I was listening.

Rob started coming over to hear what I was up to and, amazingly, liked what he heard.

Up to this point in my career, I was an inveterate pothead. I smoked all the time and for everything. I smoked before a meal, I smoked before a movie, I smoked before sex, I think I even smoked before I smoked. But most of all, I smoked before arranging or writing music and lyrics. I truly couldn't con*ceive* being creative without getting a little high first.

But suddenly I was scoring this movie, which involved getting to work right after breakfast and working throughout the day and into the night. Film scoring requires finding the right tone, rhythm, notes, and harmonies to play the emotions and plot of the movie, while figuring out the complex mathematics all of it involves. Not to mention it was the birth of using synthesizers and sequencers to write music directly into the computer, all of which I was learning at the same time.

By Wednesday of the first week, I realized there was no way I could score a movie after smoking a joint before ten in the morning, which would make me want to quit for the day by noon. So, I decided to try to write music, and do all that math and press all those buttons, without smoking first. And I got through the first day! Then I figured I'd try another day, which led to the next day, and then suddenly it was the weekend. And I thought, *Well, let me keep on this path.* Therefore, it's thanks to Rob Reiner that I quit pot cold turkey and freed myself from the misconception that I had to get high before creating.

Nail-biting, pot-smoking—all my bad habits were eradicated by America's leading comedy film directors.

At the time, I was living in a rental house at the end of a spooky dirt road in Laurel Canyon, and while watching the scenes of Kathy Bates freaking out on James Caan, screaming and shaking his bed—over and over at high volume—I often wondered whether people walking their dogs past my window were thinking, *What the fuck is going on in that house*?

Once I had this music written with the rudimentary orchestral sounds the synthesizers of that time could render, a skilled, patient conductor and orchestrator named Dennis Dreith entered the picture. He was able to take the music I was writing in very irregular time signatures and make it conductible and sight-readable by an orchestra.

It wasn't easy work. For example, during the final battle-to-the-death between Kathy and James, I followed the onscreen action and emotions by literally banging on my piano like a child having a tantrum. And then figured out, moment by moment, how that banging could be turned into notes. I wrote every note of music in the movie, but without Dennis' ability to transfer those notes from the computer and make them reality, my career might have self-destructed at the first recording session. Thank you, Dennis, for making *Misery* a delight!

My creative relationship with Rob would ultimately lead to scoring over twenty of his films, including the plum assignment *A Few Good Men*. What luck that my parents came to visit me in LA on the day Jack Nicholson shot the scene with the iconic line, "You can't handle the truth!" We watched as he gave a full performance on every take, even when the camera turned away to film reactions by Tom Cruise and others. Moments like that really show why certain people become—and remain—stars.

When Rob made *The Story of Us* with Bruce Willis and Michelle Pfeiffer, he told me that Eric Clapton had agreed to write some songs for the movie that would serve as the underscore. "Buddy," Rob asked, "would you be willing to help him form what he is writing into underscore?"

"Work with Eric Clapton? Uh, *yes*."

(What was I gonna say, "No, I'm holding out for Dylan"?)

Two moments with Clapton stand out in my mind. One was the day he and Rob came over to my home studio to talk through the music. When we finished, I really had to get back to the other job I was on, the *South Park* movie. But Eric wanted to keep playing his guitar, looking to jam. I was *really* under the gun to deliver a cue to an orchestrator, and am not a good jammer, so, believe it or not, I politely told them to get lost!

The other Clapton moment occurred during the recording sessions for the film when I was rehearsing a string chart for Eric's end title song. In one spot, I had the high strings forming a C-minor major seventh chord, which is very film-noir-ish and I thought matched the lyric well. But it had to be finessed, so a chord that could sound dissonant would blossom into something wonderfully evocative.

Rob, fabulous guy that he is, can sometimes be a tad impatient. And when he heard the first read-down from the orchestra, he exclaimed, "What is *that*?" I explained I just needed a few minutes to find the right balance with the strings, but Rob kept pacing and rubbing his head, exclaiming, "What is *that*?"

I didn't want to give up on my fancy chords, and things were getting rather awkward. Eventually, Eric came out from the booth, strolled over to me at the conductor's stand, and said, "You know, Marc, I think those chords at bar fifty-three are just a bit too... attractive."

What an elegant way to say, "Stop showing off, simplify it, and move on!"

A few years later, it was my good fortune to once again write music to accompany Jack Nicholson (and Morgan Freeman) in a Rob Reiner movie. This one was *The Bucket List*, a phrase coined by screenwriter Justin Zackham which became part of the lexicon. And I say good fortune because my agent, Richard Kraft, negotiated for me to take a small upfront fee and then get bonuses based on the box office results—not the studio accountant's version of grosses, but what is reported in the trades each Monday morning. Although the movie was clobbered by critics, audiences loved it, and it turned into my biggest payday. Hooray Richard!

But the Rob Reiner film I hold closest to my heart is 1995's *The American President*, a perfect romantic comedy. Its main title sequence is a montage of American presidents for which I tried to summon music that would evoke appropriate respect. I was honored the Academy deemed the result worthy of an Oscar nomination, in a year that had me sharing the category with, among others, that giant of film music, John Williams.

Usually when you go up against John Williams, you're pretty sure you're going to lose to John Williams. But not this time! This time, I lost *with* John Williams (to *Pocahontas*). So, see? John Williams and me? We're equal!

In 2020, when Rob and I were both honored at the Sedona Film Festival, they showed a pristine print of the movie. It is among the few of my scores I don't beat myself up over, and I'll watch if I come across it on television. But it had been over twenty years since I had seen and heard it on the big screen. Since I had already gotten my honor the night before, it was my job after the movie finished to introduce Rob. I had planned to crack a few jokes, but the movie overwhelmed me. As I tried to express my gratitude for the opportunity to score such a stunning film, I lost it (yes, I am a crier) and barely uttered a word between the gasps and foot stomping that are all I can manage when emotion gets the better of me. No matter, the tears spoke volumes; I was happy to let Rob, and the audience, know how much he meant to me.

I would add that if I'm ever asked to score a movie about the American president who won non-consecutive terms and isn't named Grover Cleveland, I'll simply write some circus music and leave it at that.

16

WHAT COMES FIRST?

The first question songwriters are always asked is: "What comes first, the music or the lyrics?"

Legendary lyricist Sammy Cahn used to answer: "First comes the phone call."

The next question is always: "How long does it take to write a song?"

To that, my first soulmate and cherished co-lyricist Scott Wittman always answers: "A lifetime and three days."

So true.

For the last forty years, almost every song I've written has been with Scott. But there are a few songs (and many scores) I have written on my own, and here are a few examples.

Back in '88, my sister Joyce was marrying a doctor, so you can imagine the joy that sparked within our Jewish household. I was inspired to create a song to sing at the reception, written from my mother's point of view:

"A DOCTOR, A DOCTOR"

A DOCTOR, A DOCTOR
MY DAUGHTER JOYCE IS MARRYING
A DOCTOR, A DOCTOR
SO IF YOUR KIDS NEED SHOTS,
JUST CALL UP MY DAUGHTER
AND ASK FOR HER HUSBAND THE DOCTOR!
GEVALT, I MAY PLOTZ!

ACTUALLY RIGHT NOW, HE'S AN INTERN
BUT SOON, HE'LL BE A UROLOGIST
SO YOU SHOULD ALL MAKE APPOINTMENTS
IF IT BURNS WHEN YOU *"PISH"*
EVERY CHECK-UP BUYS A SET-UP
AND A SERVING DISH!

A DOCTOR, A DOCTOR,
OH WILLY, I'M KVELLING
IT'S A JEWISH MOTHER'S DAY
BECAUSE NOW I CAN COMPLAIN
ABOUT EVERY ACHE AND PAIN
AND NEVER HAVE TO PAY!

(OY VEY!)

When I got back to LA, I sang "A Doctor, A Doctor" for Bette, who got such a kick out of it that she put it at the end of a scene in *Beaches* where, as fate would have it, her character C.C. gets engaged to a doctor. So, ya never know when a ditty you write for your sister's wedding is gonna end up being a royalty check for decades to come!

♫

Another song I wrote on my own took a more meandering path. I first conceived its music in the '80s, when I had a melody and some chords in my head that I used to play over and over. But as it wasn't attached to a story Scott and I were musicalizing, I could never figure out what the lyric should be. Also it was a waltz, meaning it was in three-four time, making it more of a Rodgers and Hammerstein number than anything that was destined to become a pop song.

Sometime after composing this melody, I went to LA to work with Bette at her house for a week, to run through songbooks and gather material for her next album. At one point, Bette went upstairs to take a phone call in her kitchen, and I used the opportunity to check in with Scott back in New York. This is when we were romantic as well as writing partners. Scott was in a blue mood, and when I told him Bette had asked me to stay for a few extra days, he got kind of upset, asking, "Why aren't you here, home, with me?" I assured him I was only staying in LA to work with Bette a few more days and there was no other subtext to being away.

After I hung up from this melancholy conversation, I found myself doodling my wordless melody as I tried to understand how Scott was feeling. Bette came down from the kitchen as I was playing, still lost in thought. She said, "Okay, back to work. Marc? Marc, you're drifting!"

"Drifting"—eureka! That word fit the melody, the song, and Scott's mood perfectly. And as soon as Bette and I finished work that day, I wrote the lyric, trying to place myself into Scott's emotion. The lovely thing about writing songs is that it allows you—forces you, really—to either be very open about your emotions or, if you are writing for a character, to empathetically place yourself into the heart and mind of someone else.

Either way, you strive to find the right words to convey a specific feeling, while staying conscious of how those words "sit" on the melody. Or, if you are working the other way around, how a melody can "lift" the lyric. In a song, you can repeat a phrase as you never would in an actual conversation, but layered with just the right music, it can seem perfectly natural. Just think of the chorus of The Beatles' timeless "Let It Be."

A few years after that day with Bette, Harry Connick Jr. and I were at the piano gathering material for his 1990 album *We Are in Love,* which we co-produced as our follow-up to the *When Harry Met Sally* soundtrack. After we sang through "Moon River"—and you can only imagine how gorgeously he sang it—Harry said, "No one writes songs in three-four time anymore."

"I wrote one once," I said, "but I've never played it for anybody."

"Let me hear it," said Harry, and I proceeded to sing my secret song, now called "Drifting."

"I am singing that on this album!" he proclaimed, and I sure am grateful he did.

And oh, I wasn't drifting. Scott and I remained a couple for another fifteen years. But here's what I imagined he was thinking that day:

"DRIFTING"

I SEE YOUR EYES
DRIFTING, DRIFTING
I'M REALLY NOT THAT NAÏVE
YOU WEAR A SMILE,
BUT IT'S DRIFTING, DRIFTING
WHILE I WEAR MY HEART ON MY SLEEVE

I FEEL YOUR COLDNESS AGAINST MY SKIN
I KNOW WHAT FOLLOWS THE AUTUMN WIND

AND THOUGH YOU SAY YOUR HEART ISN'T
DRIFTING, DRIFTING
THE WORDS SIMPLY DON'T RING TRUE
YOU'RE DRIFTING AND I'M LOSING YOU

♫

You never know where, how, or in whom the muse will present itself. In the case of a score cue from *City Slickers*, it manifested in the play button on a VCR and Aretha Franklin.

That particular morning, I sat down to compose music for the huge cattle stampede scene in *City Slickers*. They had temp-scored it with music by Elmer Bernstein, the great film composer who defined the sound of the cinematic western with his classic score for *The Magnificent Seven.* I had already written a lot of music for *City Slickers* in the classic Western style but found the stampede intimidating. It called for a lot of music without any pesky dialogue, which is usually a composer's dream, but between its length and the Bernstein temp music, I was daunted and paralyzed. It happens from time to time to most creative people and can quickly spiral into full-blown imposter syndrome.

After sitting awhile in abject terror that I had reached the limit of my film-scoring abilities, I decided to clear my head by putting on some music that was completely unrelated. At the time, I was listening to Aretha Franklin's *Amazing Grace* album a lot, a live recording of the church music she was raised on. It's an extraordinary album that I devoured, and I would always have a certain climactic moment cued up for plane take-offs. I figured if I was listening to it when we crashed, I'd be one step closer to salvation than everybody else.

Back in the early '90s, I would get the film work on VHS tapes. I paused the film at the beginning of the stampede to put on Aretha and get lost in the bliss of that amazing record. But it turned out my VHS machine would only "pause" for five minutes. So, as Aretha, the band, and the choir were ripping through their exhilarating rendition of the gospel classic "Old Landmark," the tape machine went back into "play" and the cattle stampede was suddenly showing onscreen. With Billy and his castmates running about, arms in the air, I was immediately struck by how their body language and the gospel music seemed perfectly matched.

"Hallelujah!" I shouted.

And that is why you hear the possibly incongruous but ultimately joyous choice to score the *City Slickers* stampede like some bizarre mid-cattle-drive revival meeting. Thank you, Aretha!

♬

Aretha's music also played a role in creating a bond with my friend Jenifer Lewis.

We met while filming the song "Otto Titsling" for *Beaches*. Bette, Jerry Blatt, Charlene Seeger, and I had written it years earlier for Bette's comedy record *Mud* Will *Be Flung Tonight*! For the movie version, we needed a buxom lass to play Brunhilda, a character whose oversized bust inspires the invention of the world's first "over-the-shoulder boulder holder."

Bette said, "I know just the gal!" And Jenifer, who had been on the road with Bette as a Harlette, was cast, and, with Jenifer outfitted with breasts even larger than her own, we all had a great time in between takes.

We were filming at the Wilshire Ebell Theatre and during a break for lighting, we spied a piano in the pit and Jenifer and I proceeded

to perform a fifteen-minute version of Aretha Franklin's "Think." But the moment Jenifer and I became inseparable was when Jenifer and I discovered a shared love of a "deep cut" from Aretha's brilliant *Young, Gifted and Black* album, a song called "First Snow in Kokomo." Neither of us had ever met anyone who could also sing the lyrics to this obscure song, and that thoroughly cemented our friendship.

From that point on, Jenifer and I would write songs to score our lives. After hearing her say "Black don't crack" a million times (referring to how many Black women don't get wrinkles as they age), I wrote her this song (which we update from time to time).

"BLACK DON'T CRACK"

NOW THERE'S MISS DIAHANN CARROLL
LENA HORNE AND EARTHA KITT
THEY STAYED ON TOP FOR AGES
BUT THEIR LOOKS JUST NEVER QUIT

NOW WHEN WHITE WOMEN GET OLDER
THEIR SKIN GETS CREASED AND LINED
BUT BECAUSE OF MY RACE, JUST LOOK AT MY FACE
IT'S AS SOFT AS A BABY'S BEHIND

BECAUSE BLACK DON'T CRACK
I TELL YA BLACK DON'T CRACK

NOW BEYONCÉ AND SERENA
CERTAINLY KNOW HOW TO MAKE A BUCK
BUT HITTIN' TENNIS HEIGHTS
OR ON GRAMMY NIGHTS
THEY DON'T NEED NO NIP AND TUCK!

NOW HARRIET HAD HER RAILROAD
SOJOURNER HAD HER TRUTH
SO SHIRLEY CHISOLM AND KAMALA
COULD BE A CHOICE IN THE VOTING BOOTH

OPRAH WINFREY'S GOT HER BILLIONS
AND MICHELLE HAS GOT OBAMA
AND I STILL LOOK GOOD OUT IN HOLLYWOOD
PLAYING EVERYBODY'S MAMA

AND THAT'S CAUSE BLACK DON'T CRACK
I'M SAYING BLACK DON'T CRACK

NOW JUST LOOK AT TINA TURNER
SHE STAYED AS AGELESS AS CAN BE
WHEN SHE DANCED IT WAS HARD TO BELIEVE
SHE WAS TWO HUNDRED AND SIXTY-THREE

SO WHITE GIRLS GET YOUR FACELIFTS
TILL YOUR FOREHEAD'S ON YOUR BACK
BUT I'LL BE HAVING FUN OUT IN THE SUN
CAUSE BABY…BLACK DON'T CRACK!

After an Aretha Franklin concert at the Greek Theatre, Jenifer and I crashed Aretha's after-party and performed "Black Don't Crack." When we finished, Aretha said, "Jenifer, I didn't know you had *chops* like that!"

I have written many songs with or for Jenifer: some for her cult film *Jackie's Back,* others about our obsession with Scrabble, her endless trips to her therapist, and our most infamous ditty, written while riding across a stretch of the Gobi Desert, "My Pussybone Broke (On the Back of a Two-Hump Camel)." I'll leave those lyrics to your imagination (psst, you can Google it!), but it proves you can write a song about just about anything.

♬

In November 2008, although my friends and I were celebrating the election of Barack Obama, we were also in a state of shock that Proposition 8 was voted into law in California. Prop 8 made it legal to prohibit same-sex marriage, and few imagined that such a bill could pass—particularly those of us living in the bubble of the entertainment community.

I then learned, because donation records are public, that a gentleman who worked at a regional theater in Sacramento which had recently put on *Hairspray,* had donated $1,000 to support Prop 8. I was nauseated that a man who works in musical theater, and had lined his pockets from their production of *Hairspray,* would have turned his back on so many friends and collaborators. I started emailing everyone I knew, going on and on about how upset I was.

I probably went a little overboard with the emails. Which is why writer/director Adam McKay, who created the website Funny or Die (and with whom Judd Apatow and I had co-written a song for Will Ferrell and Jack Black at the Oscars), wrote me and said, "Why don't you stop with all the fucking emails and do what you actually do—write a song about it!"

Gee, why didn't I think of that? I thought.

I decided to write the kind of original musical that would be put on by a community theater—located in Sacramento, for obvious reasons. So, this purposefully corny seven-minute musical poured out of me in pretty much the same amount of time it takes to perform it. The only thing I changed from my first day of writing was that I originally had Liza Minnelli (who I had the great pleasure of playing piano for a few years earlier at a GLAAD benefit and for whom Scott and I would write a song, years later, on the television show *SMASH*) appearing to teach the crowd wrong from right. But when we learned that Liza was unavailable on such short notice, I switched Liza to Jesus. Why not? Both lived through some tough times and were known for their spectacular comebacks.

With the help of Adam and Mike Farah of Funny or Die and my friend, director/choreographer Adam Shankman, we put out a lot of "asks" all over town and were delighted to receive a lot of yeses. On a Saturday morning, we all congregated at a small theater in Santa Monica; Adam staged the number and we started filming *Prop 8: The Musical*.

Everyone worked pro bono: hair, make-up, wardrobe, you name it. And the cast list was incredible: John C. Reilly, Allison Janney, Neil Patrick Harris, Jenifer Lewis, Maya Rudolph, Margaret Cho, Kathy Najimy, and Jack Black as Jesus. It was one of the most uplifting experiences I've had, and because everyone was doing it for the purest of reasons, there were no egos involved (except, of course, mine).

So, the inspiration for a song can come from anywhere: your sister's wedding, your boyfriend's fear of rejection, social justice, or even just riding a camel with your best friend in the Gobi Desert.

17

MY SCOTT RUDIN ERA

The Addams Family, Sister Act, The First Wives Club, and More

’88–

Thank the Lord that when Scott Rudin offered film composer Danny Elfman the gig of scoring *The Addams Family*, Danny turned it down.

At the same time, Scott read the *New York Times* article on me that said, “Broadway’s loss is Hollywood’s gain.” So, he called me out of the blue and set up a meeting. Before you could snap your fingers twice, he had hired me to score *The Addams Family*—all without hearing a single note I had ever written.

Not only did he hand me that plum assignment, but there was also a spot in the movie for a musical number featuring Raúl Juliá, who played family patriarch, Gomez Addams. Scott hired the legendary team of Betty Comden and Adolph Green to write the lyrics. While I was in Manhattan appearing on Broadway with Harry Connick Jr., I would go up to Betty Comden's apartment to write the song that would be christened "The Mamushka" after a made-up Cossack dance.

What a mind-blowing thrill it was to sit with two gods of MGM and Broadway musicals, playing a piano that their composing partners—giants like Jule Styne and Leonard Bernstein—had also played. At the same time, I was also writing themes for the party scene in which "The Mamushka" would be performed.

After playing Betty and Adolph what I thought would be "Morticia's Theme," the three of us wrote some lyrics:

> LOOKING LIKE SOMETHING THAT ROSE FROM THE GRAVE
> HOW CAN I HELP BUT TO KISH' YA?
> MORTICIA
>
> EVEN THE SUN CAN'T SPOIL OUR FUN
> WE'LL KISS IN THE COBWEBS TILL DAYLIGHT IS DONE
>
> THEN AS THE NIGHT CHOKES THE LIFE FROM THE DAY
> YOU'LL LEAD THE VAMPIRE'S MILITIA
> MORTICA, LEAD THE WAY!

Scott Rudin was making a lot of my dreams come true: I was writing with Comden and Green and would soon be scoring a film based on characters straight out of my childhood. And I love arranging existing music as much as writing it, so figuring out fun ways to make use of Vic Mizzy's classic theme song from the *Addams Family*

TV show was a total pleasure. And let's face it, if not for the TV theme that became such a large part of pop culture, no one would be making a major motion picture.

I even appeared in the movie, playing the conductor of the band at the party, which required getting into an insane wig and beard every morning for ten days. That cured me of ever wanting to be in the movies I scored.

I got to write gothic, romantic music for the film, which luckily was a huge hit. But it was devastating when, after only one preview of the movie, the studio decided—for pacing purposes—to cut the main body of "The Mamushka" out of the film. Bummer. Only three decades later would they restore it for the 4K release.

Even before I finished *The Addams Family*, however, Scott put me to work on the film *Sister Act*. Paul Rudnick had written the script for Bette Midler, who turned it down, famously remarking, "My fans don't want to see me in a wimple."

Luckily, Whoopi Goldberg—whom I had met while working on the first *Comic Relief* HBO telethon—said, "Bring on the wimple, bitches!"

We got along great, but she admitted to me right away that she was nervous about singing. So, I called my friends Charlotte Crossley and Jenifer Lewis (both former Harlettes) to play her back-up singers. I knew Charlo and Jenifer were just the right people to make Whoopi comfortable with our shared sense of humor, and we all laughed so much that Whoopi forgot she was afraid of singing.

Around the time of *Sister Act*, my friends and I used to play a game called "Co-Star," where one person would say the name of a movie actor, and the players had to name a chain of co-stars until somebody got stumped. One person might start with Barbra Streisand, for example, and the next person might say Robert Redford, and the next person could say Jane Fonda, and so on. It was always great if John Travolta came up, because then you could say his co-star from *Saturday Night Fever*, Karen Lynn Gorney, and you'd win because she was never heard from again.

I will never forget a car ride Scott Rudin, Scott Wittman, and I took where the two Scotts played the Broadway musical version of that game, amazing me with their encyclopedic knowledge. Later, Scott R. had our friend, the casting director David Rubin, round up all the great character actresses from the Golden Age of Broadway who were then living in California—like Susan Johnson of *The Most Happy Fella* and Ruth Kobart of *How to Succeed in Business*—to play the nuns. Rehearsing with those ladies was a theater queen's fantasy, and we hardly got anything done due to constantly asking them about the classic shows on their résumés.

Paul Rudnick's script originally used classic '60s songs like "Chapel of Love" and "Your Love Keeps Lifting Me Higher and Higher." But the Disney Music Department told me that, due to a contractual dispute, I couldn't use any song written after 1962. That eliminated the material Paul had hoped for, and really cut down my choices since the movie was supposed to be scored with "girl group" songs, and they didn't really start until 1963.

But as I combed through the pre-1962 Billboard charts, although they weren't recorded by "girl groups", I was relieved to find "I Will Follow Him" which nuns could easily sing about the Lord. Then I saw "My Guy" and wondered, *Dare we switch it to "My God"*? Which I did, to great success. I devoured hymnals and was delighted to come across "Hail Holy Queen," with its refrain of "Oh Maria!" That sounded to me like something that could have been sung by a girl group on a stoop in the Bronx, so I put a '60s groove to it and off we went.

When filming was complete, Scott Rudin and I went to a screening room to see the "rough assemblage" (which is when you watch all the scenes shot for the movie, before editing), wondering if it worked. Even then, *Sister Act* jumped off the screen, and it became a big ol' hit. Every day after the film opened, I would look out my window to see if Disney had sent me a new car with a big red ribbon around it. Thirty years later, I'm still waiting.

Scott Rudin and I seemed to be a match made in heaven. Right away, sequels were planned for both *The Addams Family* and *Sister Act*, and I signed on to do them both.

At the same time, Rob Reiner, my other match made in heaven, for whom I had just scored the monster hit *A Few Good Men*, told me about *his* next project. *North* sounded like a spectacular film to score, so my agent floated the idea to Scott that I oversee someone else to score the *Addams* sequel, making use of my themes from the first film.

In response, Scott Rudin exploded.

Although his temper was often uncalled for, he had a right to be angry then; after all, I *had* committed to *Addams Family Values*. Things got very ugly, very quickly. He refused to help figure out a way for me to continue both partnerships, and I felt that after his initial and understandable outrage, he could have dealt with the situation more calmly.

At the time, I was working in Toronto on another Scott Rudin/Disney film called *Life with Mikey*, starring Michael J. Fox. Scott and I had such a horrible fight on the phone as he was heading to the airport from New York that I went and stayed in the room of the movie's choreographer, Diane Martel, for fear of what would happen if he came a-bangin' on my door. Not just what he would do to *me*, but what I would do to *him*!

Thankfully, after a few days of ignoring each other, things calmed down and we worked out a schedule that would allow me to do both *Addams Family Values* and *North*. But then *Sister Act* opened and was such a hit that, ironically, Scott took me off *Life with Mikey* to have me start work on *Sister Act 2*.

On that film, Disney music exec Matt Walker told me the plot would revolve around a student gospel choir, and they wanted to bring in a real gospel arranger to work with me. "I love gospel music and can do it myself," I cried.

But then Matt said, "We wanna reach out to Mervyn Warren."

I stopped dead in my tracks. "The brilliant arranger of Take 6, the incredible a cappella jazz/gospel singing group whose CD I have listened to, dare I say, *religiously*, since it came out? *That* Mervyn Warren? Bring him on!" Merv and I bonded immediately and laughed ourselves sick every moment we were together.

When it came time to cast the young lead, they sent two contenders up to my studio for Merv and I to evaluate. One was Tanya Blount, who sang like Whitney Houston had entered her body.

The other candidate, from my home state of New Jersey, was none other than Lauryn Hill. Up at my studio, I asked what "older" songs she knew (that I might also know) and she said "Bridge Over Troubled Water." When she began to sing, every hair on my body stood up. She didn't have Tanya's unending top range, but there was something mystical about her voice; a unique tone and the emotion of an old soul came through with every note. It was clear to us that

Lauryn *had* to play the part. Tanya also appeared in the film, and they duetted gorgeously on "His Eye Is on the Sparrow."

Sadly, the director of *Sister Act*, Emile Ardolino, a sweetheart of a man, had passed away from AIDS. So, a director named Bill Duke was brought in to helm the sequel.

Then came *Addams Family Values*, which to me is the better of the two films. Among its great set pieces, the Thanksgiving play staged at Wednesday Addams' summer camp is a highlight, featuring a song Paul Rudnick and I co-wrote lyrics for called "Eat Me." There was also a wild tango number for Gomez and Morticia that I scored using both my "Morticia's Theme" and Vic Mizzy's TV theme, joined together in an orgasmic mash-up.

I had played Scott and director Barry Sonnenfeld a demo of the tango at my home studio, orchestrated with all the new digital orchestral sounds that were then coming into use. It was big and bombastic, wildly romantic, and extremely theatrical. They loved it and left very happy.

Some weeks later, I recorded the tango with the actual orchestra. Barry was so satisfied that it sounded great, he was cracking jokes and barely even listening to the recording.

But when Scott came in, I immediately sensed he was *in a mood*. You could practically see storm clouds circling his head. He listened as the orchestra finished and said, "What's this?"

I turned to him quizzically and said, "What do you mean? It's the tango."

"This is *not* what you played us!"

"Um, Scott, this is *exactly* what I played you, note for note."

"Well, it must be orchestrated very differently from what you played me."

"No, actually, this is exactly what my home demo implied it would be. You're just hearing it now with an actual orchestra. My orchestrator Jeff Atmajian beautifully recreated what I had mocked up at home."

To avoid a scene, we went back to his office and he said, "Well, the orchestration is all wrong. I want it redone by someone else." Seeing that there was no way around Scott's obstinance, I suggested Michael Starobin, an orchestrator who had just made a big splash with Sondheim's latest triumph, *Sunday in the Park with George*.

"That's a great idea," said Scott. "I'm going to New York tomorrow. I will meet with Michael and tell him what it should be like myself."

"Okay," I said, "I'll send Michael the music, a tape of my demo as well as what we just recorded, and I'd be more than happy for you to explain what you didn't like about today's version." And that was that.

A few days later, Michael Starobin called me and said, "I have no idea what to do differently. Jeff's version is superb and is a perfect realization of your demo."

I said, "Well, Michael, do whatever you can that will please Scott."

Two weeks later, a session was booked to re-record the tango. I was on the podium with my conductor, Artie Kane, when we began playing down Michael's new orchestration and…it sounded virtually identical to Jeff's. Yes, maybe an oboe played in a spot instead of a clarinet, maybe a French horn now played what had been a trombone, but to almost anyone's ears, it was identical.

Oh my God, I thought. *Scott Rudin is going to think I'm in cahoots with Michael and trying to pull a fast one on him. He's going to kill me*!

I looked behind me and, sure enough, here comes Scott from out of the control booth. I truly thought the orchestra was about to witness a murder. I tensed up, preparing for the worst, but Scott just looked up at me and said, "Sounds great, doesn't it?"

I just smiled and said, "Yes. It does."

Next, Scott hired me for *The First Wives Club*, starring Diane Keaton, Bette Midler, and Goldie Hawn.

In the film, their characters were once in a college singing group together. So, besides scoring the movie, it was my job to collaborate with these three fabulous (and not unopinionated) co-stars to choose a song they would sing. We settled on Lesley Gore's early feminist hit, "You Don't Own Me." We mapped it out, including who might sing which lines, and I wrote the arrangement we ended up recording.

It started simply, but morphed into the magical style of a musical, where the principals were suddenly singing to a swelling accompaniment, with other voices joining in.

After filming was complete, in a total reverse of the day Scott and I watched the assemblage of *Sister Act*, when we met to watch the rough assemblage of *The First Wives Club*, we left the Paramount screening room in mourning. The movie seemed like a disaster. I think I might have actually said out loud, "Can you just release it quickly and put it out of its misery?"

But then I learned a lesson about how editing can save a movie. Scott had long banished the film's director from the lot, but he and editor John Bloom went to work and cut every ounce of fat. There was a subplot in which Goldie's character has a sweet affair with a photographer (played by a very young Jon Stewart) that they completely excised. And when you can remove an entire subplot that doesn't affect any other scenes, you know it was meant to go. They (pardon the technical term) frame-fucked the movie into the classic it now is, and I was awed by what they achieved.

Even though that ingenious editor John Bloom seemed to actively despise my score during the dub, I got an Oscar nomination. Cheers!

Next on my Rudin journey was Albert Brooks' *Mother*, starring Debbie Reynolds in a performance that really should have gotten an Oscar nomination. Once during the orchestral recording sessions, I remember Albert was flummoxed that the orchestra had to take a union-mandated break every hour.

"Ten minutes every hour, that's the union rule," I told him.

He responded, "Well, I'm glad airline pilots don't have the same union!"

Right after that, Scott hired me for another film that featured Ms. Reynolds, the wonderful Paul Rudnick romp *In & Out*. It was directed by Frank Oz, starring Kevin Kline and the brilliant Joan Cusack, who was deservedly Oscar-nominated.

I also worked on the Rudin films *South Park: Bigger, Longer & Uncut* and its creators' follow-up, *Team America: World Police*—but stay tuned, they get their own chapter.

Although I never saw or heard of any physical altercations, I did observe Scott's infamously explosive temper with his assistants. More than once I said, "Did you ever stop to think they would make fewer mistakes if they weren't so scared?"

He was notorious for crossing names off his "call list" by having assistants call long before most humans are awake, so that the ball would be in that person's court. But one night, I was still up at dawn, composing. And when I actually answered the phone, the poor underling was so flustered not to get an answering machine that he hung up on me. I called Scott's New York office back, asked to be put on speakerphone, and said to his army of minions, "Guys, no matter what your orders are, don't ever hang up on me again!"

Scott also went on to conquer Broadway before his "cancellation." Complicated as he is, one cannot deny that he is a genius producer with taste, smarts, and a phenomenal track record and I for one am glad to hear he has worked on himself and is coming back where he belongs.

18

"ONE FOR MY BABY"

My View of Johnny Carson's Final Night

'92

When a talk show host sees me in the wings, I must appear to them like the Specter of Death, because I have the odd distinction of having played off all the greats.

I helped Nathan Lane serenade both Conan O'Brien and David Letterman in their final weeks, and with Billy Crystal, I helped bid *adieu* to not just David Letterman, but to Jay Leno on *both* of his final *Tonight Shows* (the second Leno farewell allowing me to write, rehearse and perform with a wildly disparate cast of characters, including Sheryl Crow, Jack Black, Kim Kardashian, Jim Parsons, Carol Burnett and Oprah Winfrey!)

But the most precious farewell occurred the night of May 21, 1992, when I collaborated with Bette for her performance as Johnny Carson's last guest on *The Tonight Show*.

Years later, on the day Johnny died, as news coverage repeated the clip of Bette singing to him over and over again, I was overwhelmed with the memories of that great night and the days that led up to it...

When Bette asked me to help put together her performance as Johnny's last guest, I was overjoyed. The whole country was watching every night, as star after star made one last appearance to thank him. It was a great honor to be part of his final evening with guests; the very last episode was simply him talking to the audience.

Bette and I got together with our friend and frequent collaborator Bruce Vilanch, and we immediately thought of writing new lyrics to the Judy Garland version of "You Made Me Love You." A very young Judy had sung it in worshipful tribute to Clark Gable, and the song seemed perfect. We wrote:

YOU MADE ME WATCH YOU
I DIDN'T WANNA DO IT
JACK PARR HAD PUT ME THROUGH IT

YOU MADE ME WATCH YOU
I LOVE THE JOKES YOU'RE FLOGGIN'
WHEN YOU ARE MONOLOGUE-IN'

I WATCHED YOUR HAIR TURN SLOWLY
FROM DARK TO WHITE
AND WHEN I CAN'T SLEEP
I COUNT YOUR WIVES AT NIGHT

(That line got a huge reaction, especially from Johnny. It is uniquely satisfying to write something like that, knowing it is going to be sung to the actual person, and then watch him crack up.)

I'D DROP MY DRAWERS FOR
THE KIND OF BUCKS YOU'RE MAKING
FOR SIMPLE DOUBLE-TAKING

BEFORE YOU BID ADIEU
DON'T BE CHEAP
PUT DE CORDOVA[10] TO SLEEP

JUST THE THOUGHT YOU'RE LEAVING SURE GIVES ME THE SHIVERS
ARSENIO IS AT THE GATE AND SO'S JOAN RIVERS!
YOU KNOW THEY MAKE ME WATCH YOU!

HOW I'LL MISS THE SOCIAL INTERCOURSE SO VARIED
NOW I'LL HAVE TO HAVE IT WITH THE GUY I MARRIED
YOU KNOW I'D RATHER WATCH YOU!!

Well, the number played fantastically. I was playing it over with the band, beaming with pride. Playing for Bette any time is beyond thrilling, but co-writing lyrics and watching her bat them out of the park is positively orgasmic.

After that I went backstage to the on-set piano, where she would, after talking, come to sing...*the ballad*.

When she first called, I tried to come up with the ultimate "I've talked to you for years and now you want to go home and I just want to thank you" song. "One for My Baby" popped into my head while I was in the shower, and I almost had a stroke, I was so excited. I called Bette dripping wet: "I've got it, the most perfect song!"

10 Johnny's longtime producer

Her reaction, as usual, was, "What else ya got?"

But I could hear it in my head, and despite her fear that she'd be too nervous in the moment to hit those notes, she came over and we rehearsed it. We even started to toy *ever* so slightly with the lyrics to the final verse, making it more specific to Johnny, but she was still apprehensive about tackling a song that both Fred Astaire and Frank Sinatra had made iconic performances of.

Cut to: Sound check, the afternoon of the show. Bette asks the guys in the band what Carson's favorite song was. In unison, they all say, "Here's That Rainy Day."

Oh no, what's she planning? I thought. *Is "One for My Baby" doomed*?

Well, after "You Made Me Love You," I'm seated at a different piano, behind the curtain. I'm ready to play "One for My Baby" in the next segment but on the monitor I see and hear Bette ask Johnny to name his favorite song. After he responds, she starts singing "Here's That Rainy Day" a cappella.

It's my worst fear come true. *No*! *They're gonna run out of time for our masterpiece*, I think. *AAIIIEEE*!

Meanwhile, Carson has started singing along, completely sincere and totally in tune. I wait to see if the band's piano player joins in, since it is now clear they are gonna sing the whole song. When he doesn't, I jump in, hoping I am mic'd, but who even cares? I am an accompanist, it's a reflex—I hear people singing and I have to play for them!

I am also having a schizophrenic discussion in my head. *This is so exciting*! *You're playing for Johnny Carson*! versus *Stop playing*! *This moment is gonna spoil the incredible one we planned*!

Well, they finish, we go to commercial, and I am sure they are about to tell me the final song is cut for time.

God smiles! It isn't!

Bette takes her place on a stool in front of me. The entire staff of the show is huddled in the wings, watching her live and on the monitors. They are *very* emotional; this is *their* final night of the regular show as well.

We come back from commercial, Johnny intros Bette, and we start.

IT'S QUARTER TO THREE
THERE'S NO ONE IN THE PLACE EXCEPT YOU AND ME...

I am playing the song in the style of Bette's first two albums, in which her musical director, Barry Manilow, created beautiful arrangements of standards using the kind of moody, dreamlike chords associated with 1970s songwriter, Laura Nyro. To say you could hear a pin drop would be an understatement. Whenever I rewatch this moment, I am reminded there were little "licks" I meant to play between lyrics—but it was so tender and I was on such pins and needles, my fingers didn't attempt anything but the simplest accompaniment.

Then, right before the final verse, they cut to a new angle—one never before used on the show. Over Bette's shoulder, we could see Johnny mesmerized, as everyone was, by her performance. His eyes lock with hers as she sings our adapted lyrics:

FOR ALL OF THE YEARS
FOR THE LAUGHS, FOR THE TEARS
FOR THE CLASS THAT YOU SHOWED
MAKE IT ONE FOR MY BABY
AND ONE MORE FOR THE ROAD...
THE LONG...LONG...ROAD

I swear, I felt like I was floating on a cloud. There is no other way to describe it.

On the final measures, I did what any other gay musical director would have done and incorporated "The *Tonight Show* Theme," which brought forth a knowing smile from the host.

We finished, and the place went insane. Bette was so overcome that, after placing the customary Hawaiian lei around Johnny's neck, she ran backstage.

I myself was in a daze as I walked past the show's staff, all sobbing.

And as we all celebrated backstage, Johnny disappeared into the night.

Bette won an Emmy award for her performance, and it remains a rare thing for me, something I can watch or listen to and feel that it is...perfect. That collaboration between Bette and I is something I will cherish until the day that I myself set down that long... long...road.

19

SLEEPLESS WITH NORA

'93

In 1992, I was on a work visit to New York and had time one afternoon to catch a movie. It was Nora Ephron's directing debut, *This Is My Life*, and I was so charmed by the film that I called Rob Reiner's office to get Nora's home number.

We had never met in person, but I figured it was okay to call since we had recently enjoyed a great success together, *When Harry Met Sally*, which she wrote. Doing something I should do more often—and others should do more often to me!—I called her out of the blue to say how much I enjoyed the movie, and its original songs written by her friend, Carly Simon. (As this story unfolds, it's important to remember that I love Carly Simon!)

It was a totally pure phone call—I had no ulterior motive, I just knew the movie was not setting any box office records and that the person who made it would probably love to hear directly from a fellow film compatriot.

Who knows if what came next was due to that call or, hopefully, just the good work I had been doing. But the following year, my agent called to say Nora wanted me to work on a film called *Sleepless in Seattle*. I would both compose an original score and serve as music supervisor, meaning I'd help her choose the songs and records that would work in tandem with my score for the soundtrack. My kind of gig! I love arranging music as much as composing it, and love choosing just the right song as much as writing just the right song.

For example, I chose the Hank Williams song "Back in the Saddle" to play as Tom Hanks realizes it's time to jump back into the dating pool. The audience's uproarious reaction to that at the first preview of the movie was one of the great thrills I've had in a movie theater (my assignation during *Funny Lady* notwithstanding).

When the time came for me to start work, they sent me a rough cut of that charming and romantic movie, and I started work. Nora came over to my studio in Los Angeles and seemed remarkably happy with what I was writing. Corny as it sounds, I can still remember her actually dancing around the room as I played my ideas for themes for the movie. My piano, via MIDI, would also have a lovely string sound playing the same notes I was playing on the piano, and she loved how the strings just seeped out of the piano like magic.

Since *An Affair to Remember* featured in our film, the theme from that movie, "Our Love Affair," would become part of the fabric of the soundtrack. So I devised a theme for Meg Ryan's character (which we first hear when she calls Rosie O'Donnell's character from Seattle) that, when Meg later runs to the Empire State Building, would fit right on top of "An Affair to Remember," a musical trick that Irving Berlin perfected. (Think of Ethel Merman singing "You're Just in Love" from *Call Me Madam.*)

The next time I saw Nora was probably when things started getting a little lopsided. I visited her apartment in New York, and in the kitchen was a framed black-and-white photo of a couple that looked like they were dressed up at a Bar Mitzvah or wedding in the early '60s. Knowing Nora had very sophisticated parents who were screenwriters themselves, I innocently asked, "Oh, are those your parents?"

"No," she replied acidly. "*That. Is. A. Diane. Arbus. Photo.*"

I died a little death, since I knew Arbus was famous for photographing human oddities. Oh boy.

Back in LA, Nora continued to come over to my home studio and still seemed to really like what I was writing for the film. There were two spots I thought called for music: as Meg Ryan listens to Tom Hanks talk about his ex-wife on a call-in radio show, and the scene where he consoles his young son after a nightmare. Nora wasn't sold on the idea of music in those spots, but said I should go ahead and follow my instincts. Great!

We also talked about the original song she had left a spot in the movie for: the dialogue-less section when Meg gets to Seattle and trails Tom. I suggested New Orleans lyricist Ramsey McLean because I had enjoyed working with him on the songs Harry Connick Jr. co-wrote for the album *We Are in Love*. (At that point, I didn't jump at being a lyricist as much as I would later in my life.) I played her Harry's songs with Ramsey's lyrics; Nora was impressed and said to proceed.

Then, on yet another trip to New York, Ramsey and I met in my room at the Carlyle hotel, and we whipped up the song "A Wink and a Smile." When I got back to LA, I played it for Nora, and she was ecstatic. *Really* ecstatic. We sent Harry Connick Jr. the song and, much to our delight, he agreed to record it. We were all very happy.

I thought.

But two weeks later, I was working on a Sunday morning (showbiz knows no weekends or vacations) and heard my fax machine go off. Spilling out was what appeared to be a handwritten poem, decorated with hearts and flowers in the margins. At the bottom it said, "love, Carly."

Although excited to receive any kind of message from Carly Simon (whose *No Secrets* album was on constant rotation on my record player when I was twelve years old, and is one I still love to listen to from beginning to end), I had to wonder—what is this?

I called my co-music supervisor, Nick Meyers, a skilled music editor who worked on all of Nora's films (and sadly passed away, far too young, of cancer). Nick said Nora had decided she would like Carly to write a new lyric to my melody.

"She seemed so happy with Ramsey's lyrics. This is so sudden," I said. "Why didn't she tell me herself instead of me just receiving this fax from Carly?"

I had to give Ramsey a heads-up that there was strangeness happening. Being the sweetest man on Earth, he took it in stride. But as the session with Harry drew close, things were getting awkward.

The movie's producer, Gary Foster, told me Nora agreed to have both lyrics with us at the session; we would try each one and make a decision. Unfortunately, it appeared that he told Nora something completely different, telling everyone what they wanted to hear just to get us all in the same room.

That kind of thing can sometimes work. It didn't this time.

On the Saturday when Harry was booked to record the song with his band, Ramsey and I were the first to arrive at Capitol Studios on Vine Street, in the historic Studio A where Frank Sinatra recorded all of his classic 1950s records. Nora walked in, and, with it being the first time we were seeing each other since the dark turn, things were kind of icy. But not as icy as it got when she looked directly at Ramsey and said out loud, right in front of him, "What is *he* doing here?"

I felt the blood leaving my body.

"I really don't know what you mean, Nora," I said. "Gary said we were gonna sing both sets of lyrics to make a decision based on how they sounded coming out of Harry Connick Jr.'s mouth."

"That was not what I was told," she replied, and stepped away into the engineers' booth.

Ramsey and I were standing there in absolute shock when Harry came in with his band. I told Harry what was happening, and like a knight in shining armor, he said, "I agreed to sing the song with Ramsey's lyric, and that is all that I am singing today."

You don't say no to a director, and there is no director on Earth who likes to hear that word. But Harry put his foot down, and we proceeded with him singing Ramsey's lyric. We asked Nora if there were certain words or phrases that she would like something different on, but she only asked for the word "Cadillac" to be changed. Ramsey quickly suggested "Pontiac," and that is as you hear it in the movie.

We recorded with a small band, a rhythm section, and a few horns. We used a "head chart," meaning the band all gets the same music with basic chords and melody but works out amongst themselves who's going to play what. Harry's band was used to this kind of thing, and it came together really well. I can't even remember if Nora stuck around for the remainder of the session.

I went home with the track and Harry's vocal and wrote a string arrangement to work on top of it, because we had left holes for where strings would go.

With these unsettled feelings, we began the week of big orchestral sessions to record the score for the film. Most of the sessions went well, but Nora was famous for her dry delivery—she could knock you out with laser focus. After the orchestra rehearsed and played the cue I had pitched for that "nightmare" spot in the film to flow into "Bye Bye Blackbird," she said loudly and condescendingly, "It's very pretty music, Marc, I just wish I had someplace in the movie to use it."

At another point she asked, "What is that instrument playing?"

"That's an oboe," I replied.

"Well," she witheringly said, "I just found out I don't like oboes."

And so, an awful lot of rewriting had to happen on the spot. That's normal for a movie. What's *not* normal is to have such a strange feeling in the air. If you could bottle the feeling, you'd never open the bottle.

Midway through the week of scoring, Nora and I were summoned to meet with Sony Pictures music executives who wanted to include a whole bunch of contemporary songs in the movie. Walking over to the music bungalow, Nora whispered, "Help me."

So, at the meeting, as they played one contemporary song after another that had absolutely nothing to do with the music Nora wanted in the film, I fell on my sword and was the one to keep saying, "Next. Next!"

I even interrupted around the fifth song to say, "Do we have to finish listening to this? With all due respect, you guys know this is not what Nora wants the music in the movie to be." Now I not only had Nora playing the ice queen, but also had just alienated the entire music team at Sony Pictures.

Wonderful!

Still, there *was* one amazing moment that week. We had transcribed the gorgeous cue from *An Affair to Remember* (composed by the fabulously named Hugo Friedhofer) for the scene on top of the Empire State Building when Tom and Meg meet and fall in love at first sight. But even though we had the exact notes as the original recording and the best orchestra you could want, we just could not capture the lush sound and style of 1950s recordings. Playing with that throbbing emotional intensity was winnowed out of orchestras in the following decades, so we decided to find and use the original recording.

At that point, recordings for film were still made on what's called mag, a very large reel-to-reel magnetic tape. The mag with the original recording was found in the vaults; we literally baked it to eliminate the condensation that had built up over the years, and then gingerly transferred it onto our tape machines. Then, in a way you wouldn't believe it if you saw it in a movie, the *second* the last note was played, the mag tape disintegrated in front of our eyes. But that recording is what you hear in the movie, right up until they touch hands; afterward, our new recording is used to match the remainder of the scene.

Nora headed back to New York to start the dub, which is when all the elements of the movie are mixed together. And it was time for me to have a three-hour session with a smaller string section to put down their part for "A Wink and a Smile." But suddenly I was told there was no money left in the budget to record the string part. Geez, what did I ever do to piss off the Sony Pictures music department? Oh, right.

That's what you get for falling on your sword at a meeting with the music department.

I told them, "Fine, I'll pay for it myself!" Which resulted in the most glorious three-hour session I'd had up to that point, as I was able to take time to finesse all the parts with no one breathing down my neck.

I got it all recorded and sent the tracks to New York. I have to admit, I wondered if Nora would not use them out of spite. But she obviously recognized those strings were a missing component and used them to complete the arrangement for the film.

I wish I could say the drama ended there.

But then I got a call from Nick Meyers, saying Nora wanted me to redo some cues of my original music. Under the opening scene of Tom Hanks at his wife's funeral, I was now to write an adaption of the intro to the Nat "King" Cole recording of "Stardust" that featured later in the movie. This would replace the cue I had written for that spot, which established Tom's love theme for his late wife. Not establishing that theme as the foundation meant Nora would excise the two other cues which used it—the same theme I'd played on my "magic" piano while she had blissfully danced around my studio.

Side note: My agent, Richard Kraft, has told me that when he speaks to film-score students, he tells them to find a scene in a famous movie with no music under it, so they can compose something of their own to show prospective employers. And that one of my excised theme spots—the scene of Meg listening to Tom talk about his late wife on the radio—serves that purpose incredibly well. I'm just so happy those students have that wonderful scene my music was stripped out of!

Nora went back to New York to complete the dub—but wait, there's more!

Now comes another call from Nick saying Nora wants me to add strings to the glorious Gordon Jenkins arrangement under Jimmy Durante's version of "Make Someone Happy" that closes the film. (Incidentally, that was an album Scott Wittman discovered while I was working on the film, which Nora fell in love with and, if she had her druthers, would probably have scored the entire film with.)

Gordon Jenkins was a master of orchestrations, a god to me, so at that point, amidst the smoldering ashes of my relationship with Nora, I felt no hesitation in saying, "No. I will not bastardize Gordon Jenkins. His arrangement is perfect and works perfectly for the film."

Luckily, they didn't get anyone else to do it, and if you watch the film now, you will hear his arrangement unadorned, doing everything that's needed.

Well, the movie comes out and...is a monster hit. And the soundtrack is a monster hit. Wheee!

But there is absolutely no communication between Nora and me. Later, the film received two Oscar nominations: one for Nora (with David S. Ward and Jeff Arch) for the screenplay, the other for Ramsey and me for our song "A Wink and a Smile." I went very old school and sent Nora a telegram saying, "Well, whaddya know. See you at the Oscars!"

No reply.

She sat right behind us at the Oscars, but we exchanged not a word. (Although, since Ramsey brought Raquel Welch as his date, who even cared? What a thrill!) And if you're going to lose an Oscar (and, to date, the rule is that I am), that was a really good year to do so, because our song was up against Bruce Springsteen and Neil Young for their songs for *Philadelphia,* a Janet Jackson song, and a song that had Dolly Parton singing the lead. Knowing there was no way to beat Springsteen singing a song about the heartbreak of AIDS took the pressure off, and I joined the audience in the standing ovation when his name was called as the winner. Nora also went home empty-handed.

I saw Nora at a few events after that. And at Marty Short's Christmas party, she actually got up to sing and asked me if I knew the obscure (to most) introduction to "White Christmas." Since it's on Barbra Streisand's Christmas album, of *course* I knew it! And the fact I played it in a terrible key for Nora to sing in was truly an honest mistake, I swear, I would never do that to anybody—no, really. How childish it would have been to do that on purpose.

I saw her again at Rob Reiner's fiftieth birthday party and, sick of it all, went up to her and said, "Hey, Nora, I hate having to avoid you and stay on the other side of the room. Can we just call a truce?"

She said, "I don't know what you're talking about."

And from then on, whenever I saw her (such as when my friend Jack O'Brien directed her Broadway play *Imaginary Friends,*) she was completely charming once again. I can say with all sincerity that my heart broke when she died too young.

I'm certain she is in heaven, telling all the angels she doesn't like harps.

20

I'M THE SCHMUCK

'94

There is one *Sleepless in Seattle* experience that brought such *tsuris,* however, it deserves a chapter all its own.

When "A Wink and a Smile," the song Ramsey McLean and I wrote for the movie, was nominated for an Oscar in 1994—my first nomination!—it should have been a time of celebration. But of course, I found a way to spoil it.

Harry Connick Jr. had performed the song on the soundtrack and was asked to do the same for the Academy Awards. But a few years earlier, he had sung a somewhat turgid song from *The Godfather Part III* at the Oscars and wasn't keen on returning. *And* he was recording an album in New Orleans. *And* he was getting married. So, he turned us down.

Was I disappointed? Yes. Was I pissed and hurt? Yes. But also, there was some history between us that might have left me extra sensitive.

At the prestigious Royal Albert Hall in London, during the sound check for the last concert I conducted for Harry during our tour for *We Are in Love,* I complimented him on his remarkable improvisational skills. I also confessed that I'm incapable of improvising a jazz solo; it's a specific talent I simply don't have. I need to sit at home and work stuff out; I don't have fast enough brain cells or the digital dexterity to "blow" (as they call it) a solo. Not to mention it seems so naked an exercise, like exposing yourself in front of an audience. I told him the idea of it absolutely terrifies me.

That night at the concert, as I sat down at the piano to play one of my arrangements, Harry called out an impromptu tune, "Where or When", turned around and said, "Come on, Marc, let's hear it! Take a solo!"

I was mortified. I simply banged out the melody of the song in one-finger style—like when a frustrated Schroeder plays a simplified version of "Jingle Bells" for Lucy to comprehend. I fled the Royal Albert Hall the moment the concert was over, too angry even for tears.

Maybe Harry thought I was fishing and that, if invited, I would play a great solo. Did he want to humiliate me? I don't know. But he did.

Flash forward to the Academy Awards when I discussed with Gil Cates, its elegant producer, who else could sing "A Wink and a Smile."

David Bowie (DAVID BOWIE!) had recently called me out of the blue—he'd heard my work with Harry and asked if I would be interested in collaborating if he ever made a record in that style. (He never did make such a record.) So, we put out an ask to Bowie, who politely declined, saying he was recording in Switzerland. Then Gil thought, since the song was a throwback to Tin Pan Alley, perhaps George Burns could do it. But George Burns was busy approaching death, so he was a no go. Then Gil thought of Tony Bennett.

Tony Bennett! Brilliant! Amazingly, Gil booked him. We rejoiced and for a few weeks, everything was hunky-dory (no Bowie pun intended).

Then, a few days before the Oscar luncheon, where all the nominees gather and take a class picture, we got word that Bennett's people had screwed up his dates. On Oscar night, he would, in fact, be singing for some *important* people in New Jersey it would be unwise—and possibly dangerous—to cancel on.

Joy turned to despondency. Getting nominated for an Oscar should be an ego boost, but now I felt like we had written a turd that no one wanted to sing.

Luckily, Gil pulled a rabbit out of his hat and booked Keith Carradine, who was just coming off the Broadway hit *The Will Rogers Follies*. Not to mention he was a Best Song Oscar-winner himself for "I'm Easy" from Robert Altman's *Nashville,* and his smooth style perfectly matched our song. Whew!

So, off I went to the Oscar Nominee luncheon with Jenifer Lewis as my date. On the ride over to the Hilton, I told her the story. And Jenifer yelling, "It shoulda been *me*! Fuck 'em all!" was still ringing in my ears as I got out of the car and was ushered into the press room, where nominees take questions from reporters.

Who the hell cares about me? I thought, and I swear what happened next was not because of my often-inflated ego.

Quite the opposite, it was because I was certain no showbiz journalist had any interest in me in the year of *Schindler's List* and *Philadelphia,* when Steven Spielberg and Tom Hanks were also in the press room. I just wanted to get out of there quickly—ideally with a laugh. So, when a reporter yelled out (with quite an edge to his voice, I might add), "Why isn't Harry Connick Jr. singing your song?" I replied,

"Well...cause he's a schmuck?!"

That remark got a nice big laugh, just as I hoped. But then, like an idiot who never knows when to shut up, I added, "And you can quote me!"

After the lovely luncheon, I went home and didn't think again about my moment in the press room.

Cut to: The next afternoon, I am in my home studio working with an orchestrator when the phone starts ringing, one call after another. I finally can't ignore the incessant calls and go to the answering machine to discover the messages are all from friends in New York.

"Ha ha, leave it to you, Shaiman!"

Huh?

I listen to the next voicemail. "Never thought I'd hear the word *schmuck* on *Entertainment Tonight*!"

What!?

Yep, even with all the stars at the nominee luncheon, the lead "exposé" that night on *Entertainment Tonight* (which aired three hours earlier on the east coast than in LA) was: "Composer Gets Into a Bit of Yiddish Name-Calling with Singing Star."

I was devastated. When the show aired in LA, I watched through my fingers. I don't *think* there was video of me saying it, thank God. But I so blacked out from embarrassment, who knows? Maybe there was. All I know is that part of me died in that instant.

Then they read a gorgeous response from Harry, something like, "The Oscars are an elegant event and will certainly go on beautifully without me."

For days, I wished the earth could've swallowed me. My apology letter to Harry got no response. And at rehearsal, even Keith Carradine rightly told me I had publicly made him feel like sloppy seconds. How humiliating that I made this lovely man feel that way.

It was a few years before I ran into Harry again, and he was gracious enough to act like it never happened. I am happy to add I recorded something new with him just recently—and no, he didn't ask me to play a solo.

We came up together and will always have that bond. Harry Connick Jr. is a class act. *I'm* the schmuck.

21

SOUTH PARK: BIGGER, LONGER, & UNCUT

And *Team America*: Completely Cut

'99–'04

Scott Rudin caught on to *South Park* very early and smartly secured the movie rights for himself and Paramount Pictures even before the show hit the air. I was lucky enough to see the initial makeshift "South Park" video that was going around like herpes, became obsessed, and—like everyone else—loved the subsequent TV show.

So, imagine my thrill when Scott called in 1999 to say he was producing a *South Park* movie and that it was a musical. He thought I'd be a great partner to work with Matt Stone and Trey Parker, as the older hand (and I was only thirty-nine) helping these young whippersnappers create the musical they imagined in their heads.

How ironic that only ten years earlier, I had been hired for *Big Business* as the young whippersnapper, with Ralph Burns being the old hand. I couldn't care less about having aged into old-hand-hood; I was ecstatic at the idea of getting to work with Matt and Trey. But they had to be convinced that I was on their wavelength, so Scott sent me to meet them.

The morning of our meeting, I was home scoring the movie *Patch Adams*. When I sat down in their office that afternoon, the first thing out of my mouth was, "You guys are going to *so* hate the movie I'm scoring right now. Two hours ago, I was writing music under a scene where Robin Williams uses an enema bulb for a clown nose, bedpans for clown feet, and dances about in a children's cancer ward. I'm doing my job and writing music the scene calls for, but good God, you're gonna hate it!"

It was a great ice breaker, and I think they knew from that moment that my sense of humor matched theirs.

The decade I spent scoring movies in the '90s took me away from my Broadway dreams. A few of them allowed me to dust off my theatrical side, like *Sister Act* and *Beaches,* and even the musical finale of *The First Wives Club*. And of course, those Oscar medleys with Billy Crystal called for old school showbiz flair. But nothing suited me to a tee like *South Park*: *Bigger, Longer & Uncut*. I got to co-write music and lyrics, arrange and orchestrate, and even voice one of the boys in the song "What Would Brian Boitano Do?"

And oh, how could I forget: I make a cameo as myself, playing for Big Gay Al. (It was an honor just to be animated.)

The word gets thrown around a lot, but Trey Parker truly is a genius. He can write music, lyrics, and scenes, perform them as a million different characters, direct, and do it all with a great sense of joy. And while it would be easy to imagine someone like that being unreceptive to other folks piping in, Trey is incredibly collaborative. The script had a couple of ideas about what the opening musical number could be, but he was open to me using them as a point of departure and creating it with him. There are some songs in the movie that are all Trey, and some that have a little bit of my additional music or lyrics. He would send me a tape of a song and say, "Here, I'm pretty much done, but feel free to play around with this."

Trey had enough confidence in me that he never came to a single day of the orchestral recording sessions. That was the best week ever; being with an orchestra without any producer or director, I could just have a great time and get the job done.

On a movie score recording session, when it's time to listen back to a take, usually only a few of the "first chair" players come in to make sure everything sounds right. But on *South Park,* the mixing booth looked like a subway train at rush hour. When the musicians were playing, they could only hear themselves and the click track, because they were concentrating on their own parts. So, when they came in for the playback of "Uncle Fucka" and heard Trey's lyrics for the first time, it was quite a moment. I'll never forget violist Pam Goldsmith walking out, shaking her head, and saying, "All those years in the Conservatory..."

I also had to notify our vocal contractor that the choir would have to sing every dirty word ever invented, and singers shouldn't accept the gig if that was a problem. Many in the Hollywood vocal community are quite religious, and I expected my warning to scare off a lot of the regulars. But on the day of the vocal session, they were all there!

Trey didn't always love my input on the lyrics. I remember rewriting some of "Uncle Fucka" to create perfect rhymes, and he said, "Nope, I like it just the way I wrote it." But another idea I had for the song was to create a tap-dance break for the two fart-obsessed characters, Terrance and Phillip. Instead of tapping, however, they would do it all with farting. Fortunately, Trey loved that one.

By the time I was working on the *South Park* movie, *Patch Adams* had come out and, lo and behold, earned me an Oscar nomination for my score. Sitting across the table from me at the nominee luncheon was a very elegant lady in pearls who asked, "So, Mr. Shaiman, what are you working on right now?"

I simply didn't have the heart to reply, "Well, just yesterday I asked *South Park* to send me every fart sound effect they had in their library, and all this morning, I was editing them into a tap-dance extravaganza!" (In retrospect, I suppose I could've said, "I'm composing for wind instruments," and left it at that.)

I was also at the following year's Academy Awards nominee luncheon, this time for *South Park*. The song Trey and I submitted was "Blame Canada"—not just because it was the only one from the movie clean enough to be performed on the broadcast, but also because it was the song we most co-wrote as equal partners. Trey had written two different songs for this spot, in which Kyle's mother became an "enlarged, red-faced monster on a lightning-struck mountaintop" kind of Disney villain. But when the Columbine tragedy happened, the idea of making parents supervillains for wanting to protect their children suddenly became an issue. One day when Trey was over at my studio, I went to the piano and started playing a march tempo and suggested the idea of the parents placing blame elsewhere. I wrote the first few lines, Trey came and joined me at the piano, and the two of us wrote "Blame Canada" right there, side by side, on the spot.

When it came time to choose a performer for the song at the Oscars, the producers suggested Robin Williams. (Ironic, since my *Patch Adams* story was what got me the *South Park* gig.) Rehearsal was so much fun, and I even got to fly our New York friends Billy Gallo and Tracy Berg out to LA to also be in the number, which culminated spectacularly with two dozen Rockette-style Mounties spanning the stage. (This, my friends, is when you know you're in show business!)

The thing most people remember from that night is Matt and Trey arriving dressed as Gwyneth Paltrow and Jennifer Lopez. They only told me that plan the day before the ceremony, and I didn't want to be the humorless jerk standing between them in a tuxedo. Luckily for me, the Oscars that year hired a woman named L'Wren Scott to be the fashion guru for the telecast, and she quickly helped me figure out an outfit. (L'Wren would later become a respected designer and Mick Jagger's long-term partner.) The blue mink fur and pimp-ish hat I wore came from her closet, and we scrounged around the basement of the Shrine Auditorium, where the Oscars were held, for whatever else we could find to complete the look.

The afternoon of the awards, when the dress rehearsal was finished, I met up with Matt and Trey's limo. My significant other, Scott Wittman, had already joined them, and Trey brought a stripper he met in Vegas a few nights earlier as his date.

Oh, and Matt and Trey were on acid.

I was not brave enough to join them in that. But walking down that red carpet, with them saying nothing but, "What a magical night," and, "Oh look, there's television's Charlton Heston," was something I shall never forget. The fun was only spoiled when Cher came out to announce the winner for Best Song and called out Phil Collins' name for "You'll Be in My Heart" from *Tarzan*.

Now, by this point I was an old hand at losing at the Oscars and, of course, always stayed in my seat with the "it's an honor to be nominated, it's really a celebration for all of us" mentality. But God bless him, Trey said, "Let's get out of here," and on the next commercial break, our group walked up the aisle. I can't speak for Matt and Trey, but only in that moment, I did feel like the guy at a party with the lampshade on his head, but overall it was certainly the most fun I ever had at the Academy Awards. It was also, up until that point, the best movie experience I could have dreamed of.

I could end the story on that happy note, but because it's show business and it's me, there's a darker chapter. Actually, two.

Most horrific is that Mary Kay Bergman, who sang "Blame Canada" in the movie; Robin Williams, who sang it at the Oscars; and L'Wren Scott, who dressed me for it, each ended up committing suicide. So if I ever ask you to be involved with a performance of "Blame Canada"...think twice.

Less ghastly but still soul-shattering was that sometime after the wild ride and Broadway super-success of *Hairspray*, Matt and Trey and Scott Rudin invited me to join them once again on their next film, *Team America: World Police*.

Oh my God, what a funny movie. Every day working on it, my home studio team, Nick Vidar, Dave De Palo, Richard Read, and I were convulsed with laughter. We would watch the scenes over and over again, in fits of hysterics. As he had been on the *South Park* movie, Trey was incredibly trusting and never came over to hear what I was writing; nor did he attend the orchestra recordings.

But on the third day of recording, I got a message to call Trey. It turns out the music editor had shown them scenes with what I had recorded up to that point, and Trey just didn't like it.

I drove down to their office and had the saddest, most awkward meeting I've ever had in my life (and at this point, you know that is saying something). Trey said he wanted the score to be like wallpaper, written like it was from a music factory by someone who had not even seen the movie, which is how he felt about the music from *Top Gun* and other films of that ilk. Matt and Trey asked if I could start from scratch and supply a whole new score with that concept and deliver it within a week to ten days.

I had to be honest and say I didn't think I could pull off that magic trick creatively, physically, or emotionally. I was just too devastated and thought it would be best for them to hire someone else to come in fresh. They understood.

Scott Rudin was a little less understanding—with good reason—since he would now have to pay a new composer. So, he put me under house arrest, and told my agent I was not to leave LA until all the new music had been recorded, mixed, and dubbed into the movie, just in case I might be called back into action. So for almost a month, I sat in my house feeling *very* sorry for myself until I got the call that I was free to go and flew back to New York.

I often wonder, if not for this sad turn of events with Matt and Trey, would it have been me instead of the brilliant Bobby Lopez who would collaborate with them on the mega stage hit *The Book of Mormon*? If it had been, I'd be writing this chapter from a palace somewhere in Bali.

Because of all this, I never saw the finished version of *Team America*. In fact, after the premiere of the *South Park* movie, it also took me two decades to watch *that* film again. Because its reception at the premiere, held at the iconic Grauman's Chinese Theatre, was *so* tumultuous—with laughter and stomping like I have never heard at a movie—I decided to never watch it again, preferring to preserve that memory. Even if it happened to come up while I was channel-hopping, I would just keep going.

It wasn't until the twentieth anniversary of *South Park: Bigger, Longer & Uncut* in 2019 that I agreed to watch it with an audience for only the second time, at a film festival in Brooklyn where I had been asked to participate in a Q&A. And Lord Jesus, what a great movie it is. It will always be one of my most cherished experiences in Hollywood and I will always revere Matt and Trey for the geniuses they are.

22

THE VIEW FROM THE NOSEBLEEDS

'91–'01

In my '90s film-scoring heyday, I was asked to perform at a charity event entitled "Dinner with my Agent." At the time, I was riding a wave of success, scoring one blockbuster after another, and had the idea to write new lyrics to the classic David Rose composition "Holiday for Strings." I felt its hyper, unrelenting tempo and melody were analogous to how my agent, Richard Kraft, prodded me to take every job.

The lyrics I wrote were a big hit at the dinner:

"YES!"

WHEN A CONFLICT COMES MY WAY
I TELL MY AGENT WHAT TO SAY
"MY SCHEDULE WON'T PERMIT"
BUT STILL, IF IT SOUNDS LIKE A HIT
HE LAUGHS AT MY DURESS
THEN TURNS AROUND AND ALWAYS ANSWERS "YES!"

THOUGH IT'S CLEAR I'M BLANK AND SPENT
HE'S THINKING OF HIS TEN PERCENT
SO THOUGH I'M ON MY KNEES
HE TURNS A DEAF EAR TO MY PLEAS
MY MARRIAGE IS A MESS
BUT STILL MY AGENT ALWAYS ANSWERS "YES"

HE MAKES ME FEEL LIKE A DUNCE
CAUSE I CAN'T WRITE TWO SCORES AT ONCE
AND I WON'T WORK IN GROUPS
LIKE HANZY ZIMMER AND HIS TROOPS
I'M YELLIN' S.O.S.
BUT STILL MY AGENT ALWAYS ANSWERS "YES!"

SO, WHEN HIS BANK BOOK MAKES HIM FROWN
I GET AN ELFMAN HAND-ME-DOWN
I REALLY MUST CONFESS
HE WON'T IMPRESS WITH HIS FINESSE
HE DON'T KNOW MORE IS LESS
HE CAN'T SUPPRESS
THE NEED TO JUST SAY "YES"

AND SO...
AS LONG AS THERE'S A MOVIE SHOW
PRODUCED BY SOME DEFENSELESS SCHMO
I'LL NEVER CONVALESCE
"YES!"

In no way am I pointing a finger at my friend and agent Richard for how I sometimes chose to complete all those film assignments, which was by using cocaine. There are many film composers working at the same breakneck pace who do *not* have to rely on any kind of substance to keep them going. But unfortunately, I had learned at *Saturday Night Live* how cocaine will successfully keep you up through the night when there's a deadline that simply has to be met.

In 1991, I was suddenly scoring one movie after another while also working on a million other things, and it occurred to me to find a cocaine connection in Los Angeles. Which was not hard to do. Scott and I had just moved to a new home in Laurel Canyon where I had a writing studio in a separate house. In lieu of a couch, I had a bed up there and would often sleep in the studio without

Scott being aware of exactly how late I was staying up—or what I was up to.

It happened that I was in the middle of a week of recording with an orchestra for *The Addams Family*, but still needed to write and orchestrate music to be recorded within a few days. So, I was using coke to try and accomplish everything that needed to be done. After binging all night, I finally fell asleep for a few hours. When I woke up, I felt very odd. But I had to keep going, so I took a cold shower in the studio's bathroom, got dressed, and went off to the session. As I sat at the composer's desk in the booth, listening to my orchestrator, Hummie Mann, conducting, my head kept drooping lower and lower. People started asking if I was okay, rubbing my back and getting concerned. At the lunch break, I moved down to the couch and everyone left me alone. But I could barely move a muscle without feeling pain.

I wondered, *Is this the result of overdoing the cocaine?*

By the end of lunch break, it was clear I was very sick. Someone called Scott, who came to the studio, and he and producer Scott Rudin brought me to an emergency room in the Valley. There, they gave me a couple of Tylenol and told me to go home.

But once I got home, it was clear I was getting worse. So, we ended up at another emergency room and I was checked into Century City Hospital. After a bunch of tests, they discovered that I had viral meningitis. That's the "good" meningitis; it's *spinal* meningitis you really have to worry about dropping dead from. But viral meningitis is still not great, and there I was in the hospital.

"Doctor," I confided, "I've been using a lot of cocaine. Is that the reason this happened?"

I really wanted him to answer, "Yes, that is completely why something like this would happen." Because that would have given me a reason to stop what I was doing. But instead, he said, "No, you simply caught a cold in your spine."

"You don't think my cocaine use at least made me so run down that I became more prone to catching this?"

"No."

Even though I had the doctor's assurance the two things were not related, it scared me into throwing away the cocaine (which was still in my backpack) and learning to use copious amounts of Diet Coke to keep me awake during those late nights chasing deadlines instead.

A decade later, in 2001, director Sam Weisman, whom I'd worked with on *George of the Jungle* and the Steve Martin/Goldie Hawn remake of *The Out-of-Towners,* asked me to do his next film, starring Martin Lawrence and Danny DeVito. It was called *What's the Worst That Could Happen*? and never was a title more prophetic.

The temp score was filled with hip-hop tracks. Although I'm smart enough to understand and create my own version of any style of music, I was miscast for this movie, and it was not a happy experience. I kept getting asked to redo cues, over and over again—and did I mention it was a lousy movie they had to keep re-editing? Which meant that with each new edit, I had to rewrite my rewrite. I was also in the middle of getting *Hairspray* on its feet in New York and didn't want to be in California scoring a mediocre movie for which I was not well-suited.

At a mixing session one day, bemoaning my lot in life, I kept noticing the engineer sniffling. And I recognized that sniffle. Finally, I said, "Hey, are you sniffling for the reason I think you're sniffling? And if you are, gimme some to help me get through this terrible gig." And thus began "Cocaine: The Sequel." Once again, whenever it was time to chase a deadline, whether in Los Angeles or New York, I would make a call to "the guy." In LA, "the guy" would leave it in my mailbox; in New York, "the guy" would bicycle to my studio and open his briefcase of goodies.

Although cocaine is known as a party drug, I only used it completely in private. And if anyone realized what I was doing, they did not let on.

One moment that embarrasses me deeply occurred after the great lyricist Adolph Green passed away. Because I had co-written "The Mamushka" with him and his partner, Betty Comden, I was asked to perform at his memorial at the Shubert Theatre.

Everybody who took the stage that day was a luminary, including Hal Prince, Cy Coleman, and Arthur Laurents, and I could not believe I was also in the lineup. Perhaps I was deemed worthy because of the then-very-recent success of *Hairspray*, which was truly an honor. So, I'm ashamed to say that standing amongst all those greats waiting in the wings to go on, I found a corner to take a toot or two before hitting the stage. And although my performance of "The Mamushka" was well received, I am still intensely embarrassed that cocaine taints my memory of an event I was so privileged to have participated in.

Back working in LA, with Scott happily living in New York, my addiction had really taken over. Almost every night, I would snort and snort and when I finally knew I had to try and sleep in order to survive the next day, I would smoke a joint. Yes, I had started smoking pot again just so that I could fall asleep from the cocaine. But from smoking the joint, I would get hungry at three in the morning and eat a bagel with cream cheese and/or a bag of Chips Ahoy. I should go into the Guinness Book of World Records for being the only person who put on weight while being a cocaine addict.

When I finally headed upstairs to sleep, I would have to keep a roll of toilet paper next to the bed and continually shove little wads of it up my nose, because my nostrils were either running or bleeding. I would wake up in the morning to bloodied little pieces of toilet paper surrounding the bed. Or remain awake all night, my heart racing, thinking to myself, *How embarrassing it would be for me to die from a heart attack because of cocaine. I mean, what a pedestrian way to go.*

And so, I am ashamed to say that yes, it was vanity that led me to get myself the fuck together.

I also regret the way I acted during this time. I was certainly on edge and not getting enough sleep, so when situations arose that called for a calm reaction, I was more prone to be belligerent. And yes, I'm sure there are a few people reading that sentence thinking, "That sounds like you every day." Well, the hell with you! And to those with whom I need to make amends (like anyone who worked on the movie *Down with Love*) I am literally about to call you. So, pick up.

While it was my vanity that led me *toward* giving up cocaine, the real moment I quit was the day my housekeeper sat me down. Ana Barrientos, who had really become part of the family, said through tears, "You know I clean up the studio. I can see what's going on and I'm afraid for you. I want you to stop."

Cocaine is a real devil, and I had spent enough time in Hell. Ana was the angel that got me to quit. Thank you, Ana. You saved my life.

23

I KILLED STEPHEN SONDHEIM

'99

After living exclusively in Los Angeles for a decade, and with *Hairspray* rehearsals about to start, it was time for Scott Wittman and me to find a place back in New York. In 1999, we found a fabulous apartment in Chelsea with a soundproof studio in the back, and once again had a home in Manhattan.

On November 19 that year, Patti LuPone made her solo debut at Carnegie Hall. Scott directed the act, and I was lucky enough to be called in to do some of the arranging and piano playing. And let me tell you, until you've played "My Way" for Patti LuPone at Carnegie Hall, you haven't lived.

After the concert, Scott and I hosted a party at our apartment. When we got out of the cab, who should be wandering around outside our building but Stephen Sondheim. He had been at the concert and been given our address but didn't take down the apartment number. So, we ushered him through the front door and accompanied him upstairs.

As a teenager, I would take the bus into Manhattan to visit the historic Colony Music store and buy the piano/vocal scores for *Company*, *Follies*, and *A Little Night Music*. I would play along to the cast albums (when I wasn't playing along to the *Mary Poppins* soundtrack or Bette Midler records) and marvel at the depth and passion of Sondheim's music and lyrics. I'm also a huge fan of the shows he wrote later, but because those three were part of that very formative time in my life, they are still my favorites.

Was I in a state of shock that Stephen Sondheim was in our home? Yes, I was.

The apartment was full of people celebrating, everyone in a great mood. Patti said, "Ya know, Marc, a great ice breaker with Steve is to ask him if he wants to smoke a joint. He loves pot."

Now, I had only recently started smoking pot again, trying to learn how to relax after a decade of high-pressure film scoring. So, I went over and said, "Hey, Steve, Patti mentioned you might like to smoke a joint?"

He quickly took me up on the invitation, so I grabbed two of the other guys who had worked on Patti's concert, conductor Rob Fisher and orchestrator Bruce Coughlin, and off we went to the soundproof studio in the back.

The four of us started smoking, making conversation about music and showbiz, but because he is Stephen Sondheim, we each keep deferentially passing the joint back to him instead of around in a circle. So he is easily taking in four times as much as the rest of us. Not to mention, this is when that new, stronger pot was becoming the norm, so this joint packed a punch.

I started feeling comfortable in front of Stephen fucking Sondheim and began telling him about working on the *South Park* movie (which he adored) as well as sharing other stories and dirty jokes—and actually making him laugh!

Suddenly, he got up and walked across the studio, and leaned against crates the caterers had used to bring in silverware. Seeing him walking away, I asked, "Uh oh, was my last story a little too much?"

But before he could answer…BOOM! Sondheim fell to the floor.

Because the party was loud and the studio was soundproof, no one in the front of the apartment could hear the sound of three jaws dropping as Rob, Bruce, and I freaked the fuck out.

I raced over to him. He sat up groggily and said, "Boy, that pot is really strong."

"Yes it is," I said. "I think we have had enough!"

Sondheim stood up, said he was okay, and we started making conversation again when all of a sudden...BOOM! Down he went a second time.

I placed a pillow under his head and, after a few moments, he said, "I think I should just go home now. Help me to a cab."

So now I'm walking with him down the corridor between the studio and the elevator. He seems fine, we're talking, it really seems like the worst is over—but nope.

TIMBER! Down he goes a third time.

I am now standing over him, looking down at Stephen Sondheim, God of The Musical Theater. I can tell that his eyes have rolled to the back of his head, his complexion is ashen, and I think to myself, *Oh my God, I have done what every musical theater writer has ever wanted to do the year before their musical hits Broadway...I've killed Stephen Sondheim*!

Thankfully, that wasn't true. He came to and we put him in a cab back to his townhouse in Turtle Bay.

I got his number from Patti the next morning and called him to make sure he was okay. "Yes, I am, thank you for calling," he said. "Just do me a favor, wait until I'm dead to tell this story."

Well, Mr. Sondheim, I waited. It was hard, but I waited!

When he did pass away in 2021, everyone was writing gorgeous remembrances full of appropriate praise and deification. I went to Times Square that Sunday and joined in the mass choir that had been invited to sing "Sunday," a song so perfect that I have never not broken into tears upon hearing it. But as I sang and cried, I also thought of this story I wanted to share. Not just because it was a secret I had managed to keep for two decades, but because it humanized him in a way we weren't hearing at the time.

Leave it to me to have an experience with Stephen Sondheim that was so comically surreal. But I feel lucky to have had any kind of time with him. I stopped smoking pot again after that night, but I think I might go out to the local dispensary right now and spark up a joint in his honor.

24

HAIRSPRAY: GOOD MORNING BALTIMORE

'98–'02

The *South Park* movie was not only a glorious gift on its own, but it also led me to the truly promised land: Broadway.

It happened that a producer named Margo Lion had come down with the flu and holed herself up in her Riverside Drive apartment with a bunch of rented videotapes in search of her next project. A divorced mother whose parents died in a plane crash in Egypt when she was only eighteen, Margo was known as an artists' advocate, which is not always the case among Broadway's financier class. In addition to her apartment, she also owned a valuable sculpture by

Henri Matisse and would often put up both as collateral for her productions. She had invested early in Tony Kushner's mega-hit *Angels in America* and had been involved in some key creative decisions, like hiring its director—but most recently, she was coming off a flop called *Triumph of Love*. Perhaps it had something to do with the fact she was also from Baltimore, but the first video cassette she placed in the VHS machine the day she was lying in bed sick was John Waters' film *Hairspray*.

Now, besides the fact that in junior high I was basically Tracy Turnblad with a penis, banging out songs like The O'Jays "Backstabbers" on the school auditorium piano in hopes of impressing my Black classmates, Scott Wittman and I were huge John Waters fans, and would be first on line whenever one of his films opened. *Pink Flamingos, Female Trouble,* and *Desperate Living* were movies that spoke to us like few others. Like all John Waters disciples, his movies made us feel there was someone else in the world who shared our own sick and twisted sense of humor. So we were there on opening day in 1988 to see *Hairspray*, a movie full of demented Baltimore characters with an unlikely teenage heroine who somehow manages to integrate *The Corny Collins Show*, a racially segregated 1960s pop music TV program. Its inspired cast included a combination of music and comedy icons like Sonny Bono, Deborah Harry, Ruth Brown, and Jerry Stiller. The young protagonist, Tracy Turnblad, was played by household-name-to-be Ricki Lake, who would go on to rule the '90s as a daytime talk show queen. Rounding out the cast were stalwarts of the Waters repertory like Glenn Milstead, who performed in drag as Divine.

Milstead and Waters had been friends on the Baltimore underground arts scene since the '60s; Waters said of creating the Divine character, "He wanted to be Elizabeth Taylor and Godzilla put together." Mission accomplished!

By the late '80s, Divine was wildly popular in the gay world. But if he (Milstead's preferred pronoun) was known at all by the mainstream, it may only have been for the stunt of eating fresh (and real) dog poop in *Pink Flamingos*.

Hairspray, however, was a star-making crossover vehicle for Divine, who stole every scene as Tracy's stay-at-home laundress mother, Edna Turnblad. Suddenly, Milstead's phone started ringing with calls from Hollywood. Which only added to the shock when, three weeks after the film opened, he died of heart failure at the Regency Plaza Hotel on Hollywood Boulevard at the age of just forty-two. Whoopi Goldberg sent a wreath to his funeral with the inscription: "See what happens when you get good reviews?"

Since the Broadway community had gone wild for the *South Park* movie, and the *South Park* sense of humor was a direct descendant of John Waters', whenever Margo Lion would ask someone who she should get to write the score for a *Hairspray* musical adaptation, everyone told her: "Get Marc Shaiman." Ironically, it took being ten years away from New York and a big "who needs Broadway?" film career to finally get my name into the mouths of the New York theater community.

Margo called out of the blue one day in 1998, and for me, the timing could not have been better. Although I had been blessed with a success in Hollywood, the flipside of scoring movies for ten years at an alarming pace is that I was thoroughly burned out. I was also now scoring the same kind of movie over and over again and felt I didn't have much left in my vocabulary to keep working in the genre of light, romantic comedies. Like many other people in the '90s, I had sought relief in prescription antidepressants, because on bad days, I would just sit on one side of my studio, not wanting to go over to the piano.

I was at home in Laurel Canyon the day Margo called—quite possibly sitting in that very seat in my studio, staring at the piano across the room, wondering how I was going to gather enough energy to go over there and work. *South Park* had been an exception to the kind of movie I was mainly scoring at the time, and it turned out to be salvation on all levels. Because when the telephone rang, it was almost literally a call from heaven, offering the solution to my malaise.

Before that day, I had neither met nor even heard of Margo Lion. I remember she was businesslike on the phone and sounded very upper-crust—not at all like the typical John Waters fan. She later admitted she had first seen *Hairspray* years before, but it had not left an impression until that second viewing on her sickbed. *Hairspray*, of course, is John's most mainstream film, and I got the sense she would have been horrified by a lot of his other work. If it had been *Desperate Living* she slotted into the VCR that day, maybe she would have died twenty years earlier than she did, only from shock. Nevertheless, she introduced herself and, after some opening pleasantries, asked if I would be interested in writing the music for a Broadway adaptation.[11]

It didn't take me but half a second to respond: "Yes, I would love to write the music for a musical of *Hairspray*!" Then she asked who I would like to have write the lyrics.

Now, Scott had graciously moved out to California with me as my film career flourished. But in LA, he had been deprived of an artistic community, and our relationship certainly suffered for it. So, I knew this was not only a hopeful moment for my career, but also a great way for Scott and me to once again have a project to work on together, on equal footing. "Well," I told Margo, "I write lyrics with my partner Scott Wittman, and I would only be interested in doing this with the two of us writing the lyrics."

Margo said, "Well, I don't know you as a lyricist…"

---

11 In fact, this was the second time a producer had asked me the same question. Scott Rudin also had the idea of musicalizing *Hairspray* a few years earlier and had taken *Sister Act* screenwriter Paul Rudnick and me to lunch at Joe Allen, the theater-crowd restaurant near Times Square, to see if we would be interested. We certainly were but, for whatever reason—perhaps Scott wasn't then ready to ramp up his Broadway operation as he would a few years later—nothing came of that meeting.

Which was frustrating since the credits for the *South Park* movie stated: "Additional Music and Lyrics by Marc Shaiman." In fact, this is my pet peeve: perhaps it's because all my other film scoring credits are only "Music By," but it just seems impossible for people to comprehend that I am *also* a lyricist. It's the reason I correct journalists and even my own friends and cast members when they introduce us to someone and say, "This is Marc, he writes the music, and this is Scott, he writes the lyrics." This, out of the mouths of people who have, for years, been singing lyrics I co-wrote. It bothers me so much I am considering titling this book *He Also Wrote Lyrics*—or maybe I'll just save it for my tombstone. (So passersby can see it and say, "I didn't know he wrote epitaphs...")

Margo continued: "Since I don't know your work with Scott, would you be agreeable to writing a few songs on spec, so I could hear what you would do?"

"That's fine," I said. It would have been naive not to recognize Margo was nervous about hiring a domestic couple as her songwriting team. She must have thought—what if they have a fight, does all the writing stop? But luckily for *Hairspray* and other projects, no matter what was going on in our relationship, Scott and I have always still been able to sit together and write. It's the thing that brought us together, and it's the thing that keeps us together, and I thank God for that every day.

After putting down the phone with Margo, I ran across the yard from my studio to the house and told Scott this incredible news. We were over the moon.

The next day, Scott came up into the studio and proclaimed, "The show should open like *Oklahoma!*, the way Curly sings of the glory of the open prairie with 'Oh, What A Beautiful Morning.' But in this case, it's Tracy Turnblad who has such a positive attitude that she can open her window, look at all the flashers and rats in the John Waters version of Baltimore, and still sing about it with love and pride."

And off to the piano I went.

This is often how Scott and I work: He is also a director and thinks about a song with a director's perspective. Once he sees it in his head, we search for a title, and 98 percent of the time, that title comes from Scott. So, with Scott's description in mind, I wrote a first draft of "Good Morning Baltimore." What I write first is what songwriters call a "dummy" version—one that may have the right melody and tone and may very well have a lot of usable lyrics but also has a lot of gibberish and non sequiturs in order to create a rhythm. One of the most famous examples of that method is when Paul McCartney woke up with only the melody of "Yesterday" in his head, and to remember it, jotted down "scrambled eggs, oh my baby how I love your legs." Which is not to say I'm the cute one in The Beatles; it's just an example of a dummy lyric.

After I complete the first draft, I write out the words to my dummy version, including every syllable of nonsense, and then Scott and I sit down together and start to carve the lyric. After watching *Hairspray* a few times, two lines especially stuck out. At the end of Edna's fashion makeover scene, Ricki Lake, as the ebullient OG Tracy Turnblad, turns to Divine and says, "Mama, welcome to the '60s!" And earlier in the movie, when Tracy comes home from her first day on *The Corny Collins Show*, she proclaims, "Now all of Baltimore knows I'm big, blonde, and beautiful!" Both of those lines worked fantastically as song titles—although we stole "big, blonde, and beautiful" for the character of Motormouth Maybelle, who was also big, blonde, and beautiful.

As we wrote the score, we were inspired by the glorious pop music of the '60s we grew up with, from Phil Spector to Motown. And the great R&B singer Ruth Brown, who portrayed Motormouth in John's movie, inspired the "dirty blues" style in which we wrote "Big, Blonde and Beautiful."

Also in the film is a scene where the white kids go to a dance on the Black side of town, where a man is heard singing soulfully.

(This being a John Waters movie, however, the song continues to play under a make-out session between the two young couples, culminating with a rat running over Tracy's foot, which she nonchalantly flings away.) Scott and I both thought the show could use a moment with the rich, soulful feeling of that music. Each summer we lived in California, Scott and I rented a house right on the beach in Laguna (the movie business had, after all, been very good to me), and we set up a writing space in its garage. It was very cramped with my piano and computer/synth equipment piled up in a corner next to the homeowner's car, was which was very much like James Bond's Aston Martin. The irony has never been lost on us that two white men living in a house right on the beach, one of them nursing a martini, wrote a song about the struggle of the Civil Rights movement of the 1960s.

I remember I was tinkering alone in the garage when the first lines came to me:

THERE'S A LIGHT IN THE DARKNESS
THOUGH THE NIGHT IS BLACK AS MY SKIN
THERE'S A LIGHT SHINING BRIGHT
SHOWING ME THE WAY
BUT I KNOW WHERE I'VE BEEN

I ran to get Scott, who was cooking dinner. "Come listen to this," I said. He squeezed into the garage, and I sang him the verse and asked, "Are we allowed to write the lyric, 'Though the night is Black as my skin'?"

"Of course we are," said Scott. "We're writing for the character of Motormouth Maybelle, not for the white Jew writing a song next to an Aston Martin!" So we wrote "I Know Where I've Been" right there in that garage.

Now it was time to demo the songs, and to put across "Good Morning Baltimore" we knew there was no one better than my old "Leader of the Pack" pal, Annie Golden, whose style was a perfect match. For "Welcome to the '60s," there was a fantastic singer named Josie Aiello who sang the role of Tracy, and we were lucky enough that our friend Nathan Lane was in LA at the time and could sing the role of Edna. For Motormouth's songs, we turned to the one and only Jenifer Lewis, whom we hoped would play the role on Broadway. She sang the demos of "Big, Blonde and Beautiful" and "I Know Where I've Been."

We sent these four songs off to Margo and awaited a verdict.

Need I mention, we got the gig. And those four not only remained in the show, which is practically unheard of for the very first songs written for a new musical, but they also served as the tentpoles of the score. It was just the beginning of *Hairspray*'s charmed life.

In short order, we wrote more songs, and once again Nathan Lane sang the role of Edna (plus that of her husband, Wilbur) on the demo of "(You're) Timeless to Me." When he came over to our studio sometime later in New York, I sang through the song once as he listened intently. "Okay, pull up a chair and let's really dig in," I said. "I'll bang it out for you measure by measure."

And he said: "No need, just put up the microphone."

I thought he was pulling my leg, but he proceeded to sing the entire song pretty much perfectly in one take. As anyone who's ever worked with Nathan knows, you better be prepared, 'cause he comes in the first day of rehearsal "off book." But I had never experienced, before or since, anything like his ability to master "Timeless" so quickly.

Scott and I now became the engine of the show's momentum and Margo suggested playwright Mark O'Donnell to be the book writer. Mark, rest his soul, presented as a very soft-spoken milquetoast, but actually had a wonderful, biting wit. And although the book of *Hairspray* seems to be word-for-word like the film, there's actually hardly a single line from the movie in the play. Mark nailed it. Even so, about a year into the writing, our producers asked Mark if they could bring in the security blanket of book writer Tom Meehan (who had just had great success co-writing *The Producers* with Mel Brooks), and Mark graciously accepted Tom as a partner.

Margo had us meet with various directors, all of them talented and working on Broadway, but none seemed right. When one of them asked why Edna would be played by a man, we replied: "Because we want to stay in the John Waters universe. And…because it's fun?"

But he just didn't get it. It wasn't until Margo mentioned Rob Marshall that our ears pricked up. Scott and I moved in similar circles as Rob, and he was in demand having worked on lauded shows including a revival of *Cabaret* starring Alan Cumming and our friends John Benjamin Hickey and the late, great Natasha Richardson, so we were pleased to meet with him. When Rob signed on as director/choreographer, he warned us there was an extremely slim chance a movie version of *Chicago* he was developing might be greenlit by Miramax Films, which would complicate his availability to work on *Hairspray*.

But we all thought: *Ha, that ain't ever gonna happen. No one's going to greenlight a movie musical these days.* So, we proceeded without giving it much thought.

Next were auditions to find an Edna for our first reading. Our casting director, Bernie Telsey, and his office were bringing in wonderful actors, but nothing was clicking. One morning, I came in and said, "Scott and I watched the movie again last night, and when Divine says, 'I'm tryin' to iron in here,' I laugh. It's not the funniest line, but the sound of his voice and his delivery makes it funny. Who out there has a distinctive voice that just on its own creates character and comedy?"

The next day, Bernie said, "Harvey Fierstein is coming in to audition." Bravo, Bernie!

Harvey himself was no stranger to a dress. In 1983, he won twin Tony Awards for Best Play and Best Performance by a Leading

Actor in a Play for *Torch Song Trilogy*, which he wrote and starred in, portraying a New York City drag queen. The day of his audition, he came in and sang "Frank Mills" from the musical *Hair*—and apparently someone once told him he could only sing in the lowest register of which a human body is capable. So I kept asking the accompanist to raise the key to get Harvey out of that subterranean cave and at least to a place where the human ear could hear him. It was a no-brainer: Harvey was our Edna, and he would go on to create a legendary performance.

Rob and I were back in California (while Scott was still in New York) when the casting department sent a few girls over to my home studio to audition for the role of Tracy Turnblad. My studio was on the second floor, so the first thing we would see of someone as they came up the stairs was their hair. The first hair we saw that day belonged to Marissa Jaret Winokur, and there was a lot of it—I mean, this girl really had it piled up high. She had caught Rob's eye with her small role in *American Beauty*, and when she auditioned, we both loved her. But we couldn't imagine the very first girl to walk in the room would be the best one to hire, so even after each successful reading with Marissa, we kept auditioning. Eventually, however, it became clear the perfect Tracy was also the first person we saw, and she got the part.[12]

Our first reading was at the New York Theatre Workshop on East 4th Street, right across the street from the trailblazing alternative theater, La MaMa. An important part of the process of putting together a Broadway show, readings are a kind of pre-rehearsal for works in progress: a way for the creative team and producers to evaluate the strengths and shortcomings of the material. Typically,

---

12 Unbeknownst to anyone outside her immediate family at the time, when Marissa first started working with us, she was also battling cervical cancer at the age of just twenty-seven. Her sister made her a padded leotard to wear during *Hairspray* readings, to cover up her weight loss. But with aggressive treatment that included a hysterectomy, she beat the disease. Today she is cancer-free, a bona fide Broadway legend, and has a family of her own.

at this early stage, some actors may have been definitively cast in the roles for which they are reading, while others might be filling in or provisional while casting is ongoing. For *Hairspray*, the actors sat in chairs to read dialogue from music stands in front of them and stood to perform their songs. Interestingly, however, there was no dancing, which the show is so much about. Even though we felt from the beginning we were nailing the material, there was no physical representation of the thing Tracy loves so much.

Hairspray went through four readings, but our very first one in the East Village was just Act One and two songs from Act Two: "(You're) Timeless to Me" and "I Know Where I've Been." That day was important for many reasons, not least because John Waters himself was coming. We wanted and needed his approval—and thank God he loved it! He admitted it was bittersweet since the movie, successful as it had been, was intertwined with the memory of losing his friend. But I think he saw the stage version as a chance to revisit everything that had been positive about the original and ensure the character Divine had created lived on.

At our second reading, Scott had the inspired idea to hire Jackie Hoffman—an actress he had seen in an Amy Sedaris show at La MaMa—to come in and simply read the stage directions. He thought her deadpan delivery would add a John Waters touch, and boy was he right. Jackie immediately became part of the *Hairspray* family and ended up playing the "Female Authority Figures"[13] which we tailored for her.

After each of our four readings, Margo, her co-producers, and the dramaturg, Jack Viertel, would say to us, "Guys, it's great, but do we really need that 'I Know Where I've Been' song? Isn't it a bit

13 They are Prudy Pingleton, the bigoted mother of Tracy's best friend, Penny; a sadistic high school gym teacher; and a women's prison matron. These three distinct characters, collectively known as the "Female Authority Figures," are always played by the same actress.

of a drag for a musical comedy? Won't it stop the show dead in its tracks, and shouldn't Tracy have the eleven o'clock number?"[14]

Scott and I always fought back saying we believed in the song, and that without it, the show would be soulless. And cutting it would diminish the meaning of the final triumph, when the bigots are defeated and *The Corny Collins Show* becomes integrated. Besides, what would be more like Tracy Turnblad than for her to acknowledge the eleven o'clock spot belongs to the Black community she loves? And so, the producers would stop bringing it up… for a while.

Then, sometime after the third reading, we got the call none of us was expecting. It was Rob Marshall saying Miramax had greenlit *Chicago*—he was about to start pre-production and hoped we would wait for him for a year. Having by now worked in Hollywood for over a decade, I knew better, and that, in reality, it would be at least two years before the director/choreographer of a movie musical would be finished.

It was a tough decision, but we all agreed there was too much momentum to let it go. To stop now would be like an obstetrician telling a woman in the delivery room, "Stop pushing! Stop pushing!" *Hairspray* was "crowning." And so, we reluctantly parted company and began the search for a new choreographer and director.

Choreographer Jerry Mitchell had been a friend of ours for years and had even appeared in a few of Scott's late-night extravaganzas in the '80s. He was then having great success working with director Jack O'Brien on the stage musical of *The Full Monty*, so we sent our demos and met with them. Jerry and Jack loved the show

---

14 "The eleven o'clock number" is Broadway slang for a show-stopping song that happens near the end of the musical (but is not the finale) and sums up something fundamental about its theme or a principal character. "Rose's Turn," a barn-burner from *Gypsy* in which Mama Rose confronts the consequences of her ambition, is usually held up as the exemplar of an eleven o'clock. Back when Broadway shows commonly started between 8:30 and 9:00 p.m.—up to two hours later than they do today—this number typically would have been staged, you guessed it, around eleven.

and were bursting with ideas; we all fell in love and they quickly signed on as choreographer and director, respectively.

Our fourth and final reading featured our future Broadway cast, many of who would go on to award-winning careers.[15] Potential investor Harvey Weinstein left without writing a check, saying, "Who wants to see a musical about a little fat girl?" No problem, the entire budget was raised that afternoon.

But then the other Harvey, Fierstein, spoke up and said there were elements of the book he felt could be improved upon. With the blessing of Mark O'Donnell and Tom Meehan, Harvey made a deal with our producers and started contributing scenes and ideas—like giving Edna the dream of becoming a designer, so that when she comes out at the end in her own dress, we feel her triumph. And it was also Harvey who adjusted scenes to make it clear Tracy got on *The Corny Collins Show* by learning a dance from Seaweed J. Stubbs, a young Black character. These were not small things, and they really elevated the show.

When the time came to go into rehearsal for Broadway, it was a joy every day. The mood in the room was ebullient, with everyone feeling we were working on something that just, well, worked! There were a few bumps along the road, but, in *Hairspray* fashion, many of them ended up being blessings in disguise.

For instance, the talented and sexy-as-hell James Carpinello was hired to play teen heartthrob Link Larkin, as he had at all the readings. I remember rehearsing with him at the first reading and he was wearing a white T-shirt that kept creeping up, exposing his toned stomach. As I played for James, I looked over and, unbeknownst to each other, Scott, Harvey, and Mark O'Donnell, sitting in a row, were all staring at his rippling midriff.

Partway through rehearsals, however, James got a movie offer he felt was too big an opportunity to pass up, so he quit the show overnight. Suddenly we were back casting, and Bernie brought in

15 Like Laura Bell Bundy, Kerry Butler, and Shoshana Bean.

a few other people, but we also asked an actor in the ensemble who had been Link's understudy to audition. He got the part, and *Hairspray* became just the first of many successes Matthew Morrison has had in theater and on television, including his signature role as Mr. Schue, the teacher on *Glee*.

But there was still one other stumbling block that just wouldn't go away.

The producers came to Scott and me *again* after the fourth reading and insisted "I Know Where I've Been" was too slow and serious an anthem; that it would stop the show in the wrong way. And after four readings, they finally beat us down enough that Scott and I decided it would be professional to take the note and try to write a new, more energetic song for the spot. So, we wrote "Lift Him Up," in which Motormouth teaches that if you climb the ladder you must turn around and help the person behind you. It was a nice thought, and I set it to a gospel groove with lots of harmony. One day during Broadway rehearsals, I pulled aside Kamilah Martin (now Marshall), who had been in the previous readings and knew "I Know Where I've Been."

"Kamilah," I asked, "pardon me for acting like you represent an entire race of people, but what does the Black cast think of the new song?"

Kamilah said, "Well, it's a great groove and the vocals are fun…" She then took a breath and added, "It *is* a little 'cotton-pickin'…"

Oh my God. My heart hit the floor.

Thank goodness she was so honest. I told Scott what Kamilah had said, and then we called our longtime friend and lawyer, Mark Sendroff, who informed us the Dramatists Guild has a clause saying writers must be allowed to see their work performed before it can be cut. So we told the powers-that-be—who were *not* happy—we were taking a stand and putting "I Know Where I've Been" back into the show.

And then off to our out-of-town tryout in Seattle we went. Our venue was the 5th Avenue Theatre, a gorgeous downtown landmark which opened in 1926. Its interiors were inspired by traditional Chinese wooden temples, although the execution is more fanciful than faithful. It's mainly red, with a bit of green, and a whole lot of gold. No one could miss the chandelier in the auditorium, which is a golden dragon's head embedded in the ceiling, holding in its mouth a red Chinese lantern whose centerpiece is a single, huge, electric-globe "pearl." The place has more gilt than a Jewish family reunion.

Inside this jewel of a theater, the technical rehearsals for our show went well. It was great finally seeing David Rockwell's spectacular set, William Ivey Long's costumes, and Kenneth Posner's lighting, all working seamlessly together. And before I knew it, it was time for our first preview.

Up until this point, I think Scott and I imagined the audience would basically be people just like us, with similar backgrounds, interests, and sensibilities. After all, that's what it was like when we were working with and for our fellow freaks at Club 57. When we write, we write to please ourselves—and hope that anyone who shows up will like it too. So imagine our shock when we peeked from behind the curtain and the entire Seattle first-night audience looked like they had just arrived from a George and Martha Washington look-alike contest. The only thing whiter than that enormous dragon's pearl was the sea of white hair and white faces seated beneath. Oh my Lord, we worried—was the excitement we'd been feeling for all these months about to come crashing down around us?

Thankfully, all the Georges and Marthas loved the show. (We had prejudged them unfairly—had the lessons of *Hairspray* taught us nothing?!) From the second it started, it was clear the tryout was a hit.

But I enjoyed no moment more than when Mary Bond Davis as Motormouth started singing "I Know Where I've Been." I was sitting a few rows behind our producers and could see their shoulders go up as the song began. But when Mary Bond and the cast reached the thrilling last notes, the audience erupted, and I watched the body language of each producer go from resistance to acceptance and finally appreciation. The fact we had to fight for that particular song spoke to the very issues of representation that *Hairspray* is about, and so the victory of having it back in the show was all the sweeter.[16]

As I would learn the hard way on future shows, it was a once-in-a-lifetime moment of being out of town with no stress. We continued to fine-tune the show during Seattle previews, such as adding to the midsection of "Welcome to the '60s." But the one number that continued to confound us was the introductory song for Velma Von Tussle, our principal villainess, who is a bigot, snob, and the segregationist producer of *The Corny Collins Show*.

At our first reading, we had Velma and her daughter, Amber, sing a duet called "The Mother-Daughter Cha-Cha-Cha." That song fell by the wayside because it wasn't needed, but we used its melody to write Velma another one called "No One on My TV Show Is Gonna Look Like That." But it wasn't working. It's challenging to write a musical comedy with a bigoted character, whose song has to both represent the ugly way they think but also be entertaining to an audience. We have to make the character amusing, while being clear their ideas are the absolute opposite—and that's quite a tightrope.

Then we wrote a new lyric to that melody called "The Status Quo." Covering the orchestra pit at the 5th Avenue Theatre was black stage flooring, and the day we put "Status Quo" in the show, Linda Hart, who was playing Velma, chalked the lyrics across it, from the stage-left side all the way to the stage-right side. When she

16 Our mensch of a dramaturg, Jack Viertel, tells this story in his book *The Secret Life of the American Musical*. "I fought like a dog to keep [the song] out of the show," he writes, before admitting, "That the authors actually won was a lucky outcome, and, in hindsight, I was fortunate to be wrong."

sang it that night, that was her choreography: walking from stage left to stage right. Maybe it was because the audience sensed she was reading rather than singing to them, but that song also fell flat.

So, Scott and I went back to our hotel room and came up with "(The Legend Of) Miss Baltimore Crabs." We felt it gave the character a song celebrating herself, with her bigotry obvious enough for a villainess, while still allowing the audience to enjoy her narcissism. It was too late to get into the Seattle tryout, but we rehearsed it when we got back to New York and put it on the cast album which—I guess with an awful lot of self-confidence—we recorded before the show even began performances on Broadway. That way we would have the cast album available for people to buy as soon as the show began previews.

But what some may see as self-confidence, others might call hubris. After all, plenty of shows that were promising in out-of-town tryouts stumbled when transferring to Broadway, the big league of American theater. And there was an awful lot at stake: not just financially for the producers, but also creatively and emotionally for Scott and me. We had poured our lives into this show for four years; if it failed, we would suffer professionally, sure, but it would also break our hearts.

So, with more than ten million dollars of investors' money and our entire reputations on the line, Scott and I held our breaths and waited for opening night on Broadway.

25

HAIRSPRAY: YOU CAN'T STOP THE BEAT

'02-

Hairspray was scheduled to have its Broadway premiere in the summer of 2002 at the Neil Simon Theatre on West 52nd Street. With a red brick, neo-Georgian façade and relatively understated interior, the venue opened as the Alvin Theatre in 1927 before being renamed in 1983 for the playwright, who staged many of his works there. But even if the setting was not as flashy as Seattle's 5th Avenue, its history was a lot to live up to; almost all the greats of American theater have passed through its stage doors, and it is the closest thing on secular Broadway to sacred ground. As the Alvin, it hosted openings for musical hits by giants like George and Ira Gershwin (including not only the night in 1930 when Ethel Merman became a star singing "I Got Rhythm" in *Girl Crazy*, but also the first run of *Porgy and Bess* in 1935), Comden and Green, Cole Porter, and Rodgers and Hart. The composer Richard Rodgers—who, with his later collaborator, Oscar Hammerstein, would create *The Sound of Music* that so captivated me as a child—had keys to a private room upstairs where he would conduct his affairs.[17] Later, it would open shows that are still household names, like the original production of Stephen Sondheim and George Furth's *Company* in 1970 and *Annie* in 1977. So, no pressure.

On July 18, the afternoon of the first preview, we had the invited dress, where members of all the other Broadway shows get

17 According to his daughter, Mary Rodgers, in her anything-but-shy memoir, *Shy*.

to watch the rehearsal. And the invited dress for *Hairspray* was one for the record books. It was there I paid tribute to my musical theater mentor Judy Cole before the show, and she got her ovation. Then the performance began, and the reaction was so explosive, the audience almost ripped the walls off the theater. The same energy continued that night, with our first paying audience. That morning, the box office had been doing $50,000 in daily ticket sales, but by Saturday—well, I'll let the *New York Times* tell it, from their story on the front page of the same Arts Section I used to read in homeroom during high school:

"By Saturday the box office was bringing in $250,000 a day, just from word of mouth. The day the show opened, on Aug. 15, ticket sales reached $2 million."

For Scott and me, opening night was the greatest night of our lives up to that point. In John Waters' film, Edna says to her husband, "Wilbur, it's the times, they're a-changin'." And nothing proved that sentiment more than when John's mother went up to Harvey Fierstein's mother at the opening to say, "Aren't our sons wonderful?"

When the creative team was brought on stage at the curtain call, I was handed a mic. And after thanking everyone, I said, "I wish that balcony went straight up to heaven, so that all the friends we've lost to AIDS could be watching and celebrating with us."

I've never understood when people advise after a negative reaction to work, "Don't take it personally." If I help create something from my heart and soul, of course I am going to take how you perceive it personally. But with *Hairspray,* that's a good thing. Because I feel if you like *Hairspray*, you like me—and luckily, just about everyone likes *Hairspray*. This show is who I am—or at least try to be.

A more social perk was that Scott met someone from Veuve Clicquot, and they said if you can get a bottle on stage in the show, we will supply cases of Champagne for you every weekend. And that is why, when Corny Collins walked across the stage during Tracy's fantasy wedding in "I Can Hear the Bells," he was holding a bottle of Veuve, which Scott planted into actor Clarke Thorell's hand—and voila!—a case of Champagne was delivered to our apartment every week. Celebration was certainly called for, because *Hairspray* was the hit of the season and everyone loves a hit. Scott and I finally got to know what that felt like.

The show took a gamble and opened in August, which at that point was pretty much unheard of because summer is traditionally thought of as a slow season for Broadway. Also, it's a long way from then until the Tony Awards in spring, when the initial excitement around a show may have ebbed. Fortunately when the Tonys did roll around, however, we didn't have to worry. That year, they were held at Radio City Music Hall and hosted by the triple-threat Hugh Jackman, who was just about to open on Broadway in *The Boy from Oz,* a musical about the life of my late friend and collaborator Peter Allen.

Hairspray was nominated for thirteen Tonys and won eight. Jerry Mitchell unfortunately lost Best Choreography to Twyla Tharp—but would go on to win two others in the ensuing years. Two members of our cast were nominated against each other in Best Performance by a Featured Actor in a Musical, and Corey Reynolds (as Seaweed) probably knew in his heart he would lose out to Dick Latessa (as Wilbur), because Dick was so beloved on Broadway that his win was heavily tipped.

It is a great privilege to be able to create something that enables others to be recognized, and for *Hairspray* to get director Jack O'Brien his first Tony—not to mention one each for Harvey Fierstein and Marissa Jaret Winokur in their respective Lead categories—was deeply gratifying. We also won for Best Musical (announced live from Los Angeles by our friend Martin Short, who was starring there with Jason Alexander in *The Producers*), Best Book (Mark O'Donnell and Thomas Meehan), and Best Costume Design

(William Ivey Long), but sadly missed out in the categories of Orchestrations, Scenic Design, and Lighting Design.

Scott and I are great friends with Matthew Broderick[18] and Sarah Jessica Parker, and rather than wait to see if they would be asked to present at the Tonys that year, they went to the producers and said, "We would very much like to announce the Best Original Score award." That could have been a jinx...but thankfully it was not, and Scott and I had the extra thrill of hearing two friends announce our names as the winners. We bounded on stage, and this being only a few months since Adrien Brody had bent back Halle Berry and planted a kiss on her when he won his Oscar, Scott and I did the same to SJP and Matthew.

At the end of our joint speech in front of the TV cameras, I found myself turning to Scott and saying, "I love this man. We're not allowed to get married in this world, but I'd like to declare, in front of all these people that I love you and I'd like to live with you the rest of our lives."

Well, after *that* declaration, Scott and I did what any other couple on national television would do, even if they were just on *Let's Make a Deal* and had won a refrigerator: we kissed. I can still hear that audience erupting all these years later. And in the days that followed, I could sense that moment had meant a lot to people. Our kiss was reported on around the world, and as I walked around our Chelsea neighborhood, I got the most heartwarming smiles and nods of recognition.

---

18 Let's play a quick round of *Hairspray*-Themed Co-Star, like Scott Wittman and I used to do with Scott Rudin, the show's would-be first producer. In the 1980s, Matthew starred in two of Neil Simon's seminal plays at our eponymous theater: *Biloxi Blues* (for which he won a Tony) and *Brighton Beach Memoirs*. Then, our future stage Edna, Harvey Fierstein, cast him as his lover in the 1988 film version of *Torch Song Trilogy*. Later, Matthew would have huge Broadway success opposite our demo-recording Edna, Nathan Lane, in The Producers (from whose LA stage Martin Short announced Hairspray's win for Best Musical). Then, on the television limited series *The People v. O.J. Simpson*, Nathan worked with our movie Edna, John Travolta, who of course is the penultimate winning move in the game, getting you to...Karen Lynn Gorney. Checkmate!

Unfortunately, not everyone was so thrilled. “I thought they made a spectacle of themselves,” said legendary lyricist Fred Ebb to a reporter the following day. “Your bedroom is not the stage. Say ‘Thank you’ to the people who helped you get where you are and sit down. Nobody has any right to intrude his private life on a mass audience,” he grumbled. “Terrence McNally takes those issues and tackles them [in his art] with taste and clarity and forcefulness. He doesn’t get up there and show his ass.”

Oh dear!

The truth? As a tried-and-true narcissist, I didn’t care what he said, I was just thrilled Fred Ebb knew who I was!

Fred would have also hated the Grammy Awards in February. When Scott and I won for the Original Broadway Cast Album, it was all about a laugh—in fact, the loudest laugh I ever got. It was at the non-televised afternoon ceremony at Madison Square Garden, and I thought if I said something memorable, they might use a clip during the primetime broadcast (which they didn't, goddammit). So, when they called out our names, we ran to the stage and as we accepted the award, I said, "For all of you out there who think the theater is full of nothing but gays and Jews, I have only one thing to say...*oy gevalt*, my lover and I just won a Grammy!" Well, the laugh from a packed Madison Square Garden hit me like a tidal wave, and I shall never forget it. The Grammy was nice, but the laugh was spectacular.

The years tumbled forward, continually bringing new joys—cue montage—like opening new *Hairspray* companies and tours, and expanding the family of cast and crew. Any time a "Tracy" left the Broadway company, Scott and I would come on stage during the curtain call carrying enough boxes of donuts for the cast, crew, and even the audience, which the ushers would distribute. That's a lotta Krispy Kremes! (If only Veuve Clicquot made donuts.)

It was tremendously exciting to open seven years later on London's West End and have the same kind of explosive success, as Michael Ball created an Edna all his own. (Not to mention the eleven Olivier Award nominations, including wins for Best New Musical, Best Actor, Best Actress, and Best Performance in a Supporting Role.) And then, the cherry on top of the cherry was the fact Scott and I got to be part of the movie made from our musical, which is often not the case for composer-lyricists.

The huge success of *Hairspray* on Broadway had made New Line Cinema (which also made the original) interested in developing the property as a feature film. Ironically, New Line's other big inspiration was *Chicago,* the spectacularly successful movie musical which had lured away our first director, Rob Marshall. That film won five Oscars, grossed over $300 million worldwide, and became the biggest-ever hit for Miramax Films—whose boss just happened to be Harvey "who-wants-to-see-a-musical-about-a-little-fat-girl" Weinstein.

Producers Craig Zadan and Neil Meron, who had worked on *Chicago,* also came on board for the *Hairspray* film. And we were overjoyed when our friend Adam Shankman, who had already made a name for himself directing hit movies like *The Wedding Planner,* got the job to direct. An all-star cast quickly fell into place, including John Travolta (who had turned down the role of lawyer Billy Flynn in *Chicago*) as Edna; Michelle Pfeiffer as Velma Von Tussle; Queen Latifah as Motormouth, Christopher Walken as Wilbur, and Jerry Stiller, the original film's Wilbur, who returned to play Mr. Pinky. Rounding out the troupe were younger stars like Zac Efron, Brittany Snow, and Amanda Bynes; discoveries like Elijah Kelley as Seaweed; pros like James Marsden and Allison Janney; and our new Tracy, Nikki Blonsky—all of them bursting at the seams with talent.

Rehearsing with such an elite cast was thrilling. But once again, the subject of Velma's song came up. Adam, Craig, and Neil encouraged Scott and I to see if we could create something even better than "Miss Baltimore Crabs."

So we wrote two new songs. The first was called "Save Your Applause to the End," in which we imagined Velma trailing new-star-in-town Tracy Turnblad like Wile E. Coyote following the Road Runner, being taken out by a different comic mishap in each verse. We also wrote "Mrs. Von Tussle Says," a new number for the spot of

"Miss Baltimore Crabs" that would be Velma's attempt to be more rock 'n' roll like the kids on the show. Scott and I are lucky to have talented friends to call upon; Christine Ebersole sang the demo for "Save Your Applause to the End," and the late, great Pattie Darcy performed "Mrs. Von Tussle Says." Either song would have been a great addition, but we were all going in circles about which one was right until Scott said, "Why don't we send them to Michelle Pfeiffer and let her choose, since she's the one who's going to have to perform it?"

Everyone agreed and all the songs were sent off to Michelle, who responded, "Fellas, I signed on to be Miss Baltimore Crabs." And that was that.

The cost savings of shooting in Canada, combined with Baltimore's lack of sound stages large enough to accommodate a major movie musical, meant that principal photography took place in Toronto starting in September 2006. Mr. Pinky's Hefty Hideaway is in civilian life a local Starbucks. And unassuming Dundas Street West filled in for the Maryland avenue where Nikki performs the opening number "Good Morning Baltimore"—complete with a cameo by John Waters himself as the flasher. And when she climbs on top of the green garbage truck that carries her to school, it's an homage to Barbra Streisand in *Funny Girl*, hopping a ride through New York harbor on a green tugboat while she sings "Don't Rain on My Parade."

But as well as the production seemed to be going, Scott and I were still nervous about whether our vision would translate to film. The adaptation required several adjustments, with some plot points added and others abandoned. Three songs from the stage show ("Mama, I'm a Big Girl Now," "The Big Dollhouse," and "Cooties") were cut, while others were added, including a star turn for Zac Efron called "Ladies' Choice" and an ensemble number entitled "The New Girl in Town" which was originally in the show but had been cut in Seattle.

When the time came to see Adam's first cut of the close-to-finished film, Scott and I weren't sure what to expect. Would it be great, or would our friendship end suddenly in a disaster of titanic proportions? But within five minutes, my body and psyche relaxed as we realized Adam had done a remarkable job of putting our baby onscreen. Whew!

That didn't mean my work on the film was complete, however—I still had to compose the underscoring. But when that time came, I had just finished six months on Broadway in *Martin Short: Fame Becomes Me* (as composer, co-lyricist, arranger, on-stage piano player, *and* performer) and really needed a vacation. In lieu of having any free time in which to do that, I decided to be extravagant—and instead of scoring the film at my home studio in Laurel Canyon, I rented an oceanfront home thirty miles away in the Malibu Colony. And not just any home, but a 1968 masterpiece by the architect and former Frank Lloyd Wright apprentice John Lautner, with an indoor swimming pool and retractable glass walls that disappeared until the living room was almost literally on the beach.

My idea was to have a vacation while continuing with the score—and it paid off with one of the most unexpected and magical experiences I've ever had while working. One day I was creating new string lines for Link Larkin's pining song for Tracy, "Without Love," that a Broadway string section couldn't pull off because the orchestra pit in a theater doesn't fit enough musicians. With a full orchestra for the movie, however, I could live out my Motown string fantasies. Filled with happiness as I listened back to these new string lines, I turned around to look at the ocean—just as ten dolphins were jumping out of the waves right in front of my opened wall. The sun caught their silvery, curved backs as they dove in and out of the surf, as if they were the living embodiment of the joy I was feeling creating the music. It was a scene from a Disney fantasy, like Cinderella being attended to by her bluebird helpers, and yet another good omen about the musical's transition from stage to screen.

With the underscore delivered, Scott's and my work on the adaptation was finally done. And to our complete delight, when the film opened to the public on July 20, 2007, audiences and critics agreed it was something special. *Hairspray* did more than $200 million at the box office, and the notices were glowing.

In the following years, we got to travel (on producers' dimes!) and see the stage version performed around the world, first in Helsinki, in a production so fantastic and outrageous that even John Waters might have said, "Wow, that was really odd!" And we got to see it in Johannesburg, where apartheid might officially be a thing of the past, but there is still a lot of healing to be done. And when celebrated South African singer Mara Louw, playing Motormouth, raised her hand in a Black Power fist at the end of "I Know Where I've Been," Scott and I both dissolved into tears.

And although we were living in England while rehearsing for "Mary Poppins Returns", we were able to get a feed and, at 3am London time, watch NBC's "HAIRSPRAY Live!" starring Ariana Grande, Kristin Chenoweth, Jennifer Hudson, Maddie Baillio and which finally gave Harvey Fierstein the opportunity to put his defining portrayal of "Edna Turnblad" on film.

Perhaps most amazingly, I also got to see it in different years as the spring musical at both my old junior high and high school—which is particularly satisfying since, when I went to those schools, there were no musicals put on at all. To see a show I co-wrote performed in the same auditoriums where I dreamed of writing for Broadway—and to hear the score played on the very pianos I used to write my first songs—those nights could not be beat.

Over the years, we have made further adjustments to the show to correct some things that needed to be better. I was always bothered that Seaweed's first lines upon meeting Penny were sexual, and I felt uncomfortable that we were perpetuating the trope of the predatory, oversexed Black male. When I finally spoke up a few years ago, in the absence of original book-writers Mark and Tom, who have sadly both passed on, Harvey supplied a couple of great new lines for those moments. Sometimes we've been asked to tone down the ugly things our villainesses say, and we've adjusted a few lines, but if you are telling a story with bigots in it, they are going to have to say bigoted, ugly things. When the show was revived recently on the West End for a limited run, we made more changes, including having Seaweed's sister, Little Inez, be the one at the record shop to have the idea to picket Mother/Daughter Day so that it's not always Tracy being "the white savior." And another big change was adjusting one of Motormouth's lyrics in "You Can't Stop the Beat." She used to sing:

AND TOMORROW IS A BRAND NEW DAY
AND IT DON'T KNOW WHITE FROM BLACK

Because when we opened the show, the concept of being "colorblind" was in fashion—it was the progressive position that a person could be so fair-minded about race that they don't even "see" another person's color. But the culture has evolved since then, and it was time to give that line a tune-up. I had the band at the Palladium in London do a full stop when the phenomenal Marisha Wallace sang the new line, which was a simple adjustment but a real improvement. The new lyric goes:

AND TOMORROW IS A BRAND NEW DAY
AND IT SEES BOTH WHITE AND BLACK

Hairspray's original New York production closed in 2009 after 31 previews and 2,641 regular performances. But even more importantly, it gives me so much pride that our '00s Broadway musical and film, based on an '80s cult movie that was about the '60s, is still thriving in the '20s, bringing pleasure and meaning to new twenty-first-century audiences. It's understandable the chapters of this book about *Hairspray* would be the lengthiest, but enough already. If you want to know even more, give me a call.

26

FAME DROPPING

I know I have used the words *iconic* and *legendary* a lot in these pages. But that's only because Mary Martin and Carol Channing are not the only "legends!" I have had the privilege of working alongside in my career.

On a tour in 1979, for example, Bette hired Luther Vandross to sing additional backups—from backstage. This was about two years before Luther's star ascended, and at the time, he was "only" a hugely successful backup singer on countless records and commercials. Bette wanted to add his luster to the Harlettes' harmonies, but he wasn't interested in being part of her onstage show. Instead, he was content to sit backstage, sing on only about five songs, and eat the dinner he'd prepared earlier each day.

Luther and I became fast friends as we figured out how to add a fourth note to the Harlettes' three-part harmony. I remember his glee during "Boogie Woogie Bugle Boy" as he jumped from an added second to a sharped eleventh to an unnecessary flatted ninth. We had him jumping all over the harmonic map and were as giddy as two music theory nerds could be. Adding notes to songs with no need for them just gave us ridiculous joy.

Also on that tour, Bette's choreographer, Toni Basil (herself two years away from the stardom her breakthrough hit "Mickey" would bring) added poppin', lockin' street dancer Shabba Doo to Bette's show. This was right before *his* ascension to stardom five years later via the *Breakin'* and *Breakin' 2: Electric Boogaloo* movies.

Shabba Doo, Luther, and I were like the Three Musketeers, acting like children and laughing at everything, especially ourselves. We were each extremely respectful of each other's talent, but were also constantly poking fun, with probably the most juvenile stunt happening in Tempe, Arizona. One morning before Luther awoke, Shabba Doo and I collected every tray that guests had placed outside their rooms during the night and piled them all in front of Luther's door, implying he had ordered room service thirty times. This was long before we all had cameras in our pockets, but I so wish I had a picture of the three of us collapsing in hysterics when Luther stepped out of his room.

When we got back to Manhattan, Luther booked himself into a cabaret on 46th Street called Barbarann and came over to my apartment to have me write out some rudimentary charts. He wanted to do his own version of "A House Is Not a Home." I could be wrong, but I believe I had the honor of being the first one to play that song for him as he created his now iconic version.

I cannot believe both Luther and Shabba Doo are gone now. They had such great talent, and our time together fills me with bittersweet memories.

♬

In 1985, I worked on an Atlantic City nightclub act with the one and only Raquel Welch. Her show was comprised of then-contemporary hits, and I'll never forget the finale when Raquel sang "We Are the World" draped in an expensive Norma Kamali gown and dripping with jewelry. When she got to the lyric, "There are people dying..." and gestured out into "the world," she sang this compassionate lyric with a diamond bracelet shimmering on her wrist.

At one point in the show, a white baby grand and I emerged through the set with her lying across it, my face right up against her lower torso. As a six-year-old, I remember looking from the side at my brother Ronnie's *One Million Years B.C.* poster to try and see what was underneath Raquel's fur bikini. But I had grown up with different tastes, so what a cruel twist of fate that it was me, not my brother, who was now close enough to find out.

I introduced Raquel to Scott, and we all remained friends. When she visited our summer rental in Laguna, she headed straight into the bathroom as "just" Raquel, but emerged a short time later as "La Raquel," impeccably made-up in a knockout swimsuit, wide-brimmed hat, and wrap-around sunglasses—the perfect "incognito movie-star strolling on the beach" look.

Once, when having to cancel a lunch date with Scott, she left him a message which became a mantra for us: "Hello, my love, it's Raquel…as in Welch. Listen, I have to cancel. I'm laid up in 'H-Wood' with my 'chiro.' I got a fax this morning that back-ended my *entire day*!"

She came to the Oscars with us one year, and we attended her last wedding. When she let us in the front door of her home, she ushered us in, saying, "Quick, the paparazzi have telephoto lenses!"

Raquel Welch was perhaps the last great *movie star*, and despite good notices every few projects, was never truly given her due. She was a hell of a lot of fun, and I was very happy to know her.

♬

Then there was the time I was scoring the 2007 *Hairspray* movie in that rented home in Malibu with a writing studio that sat, literally, on the beach. Shirley MacLaine kept strolling by, walking her dog. So, I finally gathered up the courage to say, "Hey, Shirley MacLaine, I scored your last film, *Rumor Has It…*, and am currently writing the score for my movie musical *Hairspray*, and if you want a sneak preview of John Travolta playing, singing, and dancing as a woman, come on in!"

She raced in so quickly it could have been accompanied with that Hanna-Barbera fast-feet sound effect, and three seconds later, was scrounging through my refrigerator and eating all my frozen White Castle hamburgers.

This led to weeks of her being around, giving me endless unsolicited advice; us going to the movies and even watching the series finale of *The Sopranos* together. When I mentioned I would be going back to New York for a few weeks, she said, "Great, they're doing construction right outside my window. I'm gonna stay in your house while you're gone."

"Um, okay!"

So, I can confirm the rumors are true: I shared a bed with Shirley MacLaine.

♫

A different pop icon I was never expecting to meet, however, came into my life in 2010. Producer Randy Jackson, who became famous as one of the original *American Idol* judges, called me to say, "Dawg, I'd love to hook you up with Mariah. She's making a second Christmas album and I'd love to get your classic musical imprint."

There is nobody on planet Earth who needs to hear a last name to know "which" Mariah, and if there were, the phrase "Christmas album" would eliminate any lingering doubt. Mariah Carey's 1994 *Merry Christmas* album went nine times platinum in the US, and its track "All I Want for Christmas Is You" became one of the best-selling singles in history. And since nothing says Christmas like a Jewish songwriter at a piano on a sunny summer day in Los Angeles, I jumped at the chance to work with her on *Merry Christmas II You*.

I was given an address to meet with her at her Los Angeles home, an elegant mansion in the French chateau style, sitting on manicured grounds in the hills of Bel-Air. And that's where I had my first (but certainly not last) experience of waiting for Mariah to arrive—and I mean *really* waiting. Like "bring a meal" waiting.

When she finally entered the room, I realized that, unbeknownst even to the paparazzi, she was pregnant with twins with her then-husband, Nick Cannon. Monroe and Moroccan would be born the following April, but before then—by the first week in November—she had a Christmas album to get out.

When we sat down at the piano, we hit it off right away. She immediately tuned into my sense of humor, and, although we enjoy collaborating musically, it is that shared humor which bonds us. We came up with the beginnings of a couple songs at that first session; I went away and developed them further, and we worked on lyrics together over the phone.

Mariah has a kaleidoscopic mind, capable of expanding in several directions at once, but there *is* a logic to it—and she certainly knows how to write great hooks. I wrote two songs with her for that album and also orchestrated some Christmas classics. We enjoyed working together so much that our next joint project was to write the title song for an animated movie called *The Star*, about the birth of Jesus told from the perspective of the animals in the manger. It earned us a Golden Globe nomination.

Over the years, in her concerts, Mariah has continued to sing the songs we wrote together, always graciously calling me out from the stage by referring to me as "the *legendary* Marc Shaiman." She even joined the producing team of *Some Like It Hot*, and I had the great thrill of bringing her on stage after a curtain call one night, introducing her to the audience and the cast, who went absolutely wild.

She truly is a very funny woman, and one of our shared loves is Woody Allen's *Bullets over Broadway*. She can recite the dialogue verbatim and perfectly summon each character from the movie with her voice and acting ability—another side of her incredible talent that not everyone gets to see.

It's a pleasure to have such a connection with Mariah, especially since we move in such different spheres of showbiz—me in Broadway and film scoring; her in the stratosphere of pop music and hip-hop high society. But whenever I text her, I make her laugh, and when she texts me, she makes me laugh, and I am honored to be a member of that mutual admiration society.

♫

For sheer star power, few nights can compare with the night in 2015 when *Saturday Night Live* staged its *legendary* fortieth anniversary show. Lorne Michaels put me together with Marty Short, Fred Armisen, and Maya Rudolph to create the introduction for the "*SNL* musical characters" segment. To get to play around with those talents was heaven enough—but then came the after-party to end all after-parties.

Literally everyone there was a superstar except my husband Lou and me. You could just walk up to Paul McCartney or Beyoncé or Jay-Z to shake their hands and say, "Thanks." That would have been enough for us to leave the night on a high. But there were instruments up on stage waiting for a jam session, and for some reason, Paul Shaffer wasn't there that night. So, there sat an empty keyboard as Paul McCartney and Taylor Swift got on stage and started tuning up with the band of whatever musicians happened to be there. Lou grabbed my shoulders, pushed me toward the stage, and said, "Get up there!"

Who was I to say no?

I sat at the keyboard and before I knew it was playing "I Saw Her Standing There" and "Shake It Off" with Paul McCartney and Taylor Swift. Gradually, other musical stars came on stage to sing. I did my best to fill in for Paul Shaffer, the king of jam-session hosting, shouting out a singer and a song—and bam!—we were into it. Ariana Grande singing Aretha; Debbie Harry singing "The Tide Is High"; Miley Cyrus singing some insane song about her dead goldfish.

And then Dave Chappelle whispered to Jimmy Fallon, "Prince is here."

Jimmy got on the mic and said, "Prince! Prince! Are you here? Please, Prince, come on up!"

Suddenly, the crowd parted like the Red Sea and from the side doors, Prince floated toward the stage like an apparition. His presence and aura were out of this world. When he got up on stage with his all-girl band (because Prince clearly went nowhere without a band) and strapped on a guitar, I ran back to the keyboard and found myself playing a ten-minute version of "Let's Go Crazy" with...*Prince.*

Lou was in the audience having 70,000 heart attacks—and if all that weren't enough, we met Alex Trebek on our way out of the party. What is "a night we'll never forget"?

♫

In 2024, when Billy Crystal received the Kennedy Center Honor, producers David Jammy and Liz Kelly involved me with his tribute.

Lin-Manuel Miranda had said while growing up he would memorize all the Oscar lyrics I helped write for and with Billy. So I knew co-writing lyrics with him for an Oscar-style medley for him to perform would make both Lin-Manuel and Billy the happiest boys on Earth.

Robert De Niro, also heading down to DC to honor Billy, let it be known that he also wanted to sing. So I wrote him a stanza to lead into the "It Had to Be You" finale. He arrived, and before even the slightest bit of conversation, we ran through it once at the piano on stage. I took a deep breath and said:

"I never thought I'd say these words to Robert De Niro, but... can I give you a line reading?"

"Sure!" he said. Ya see, the greats don't "how *dare* you!" when offered a little guidance from the funny Jew at the piano. We ran through it again, and he nailed it.

Well, he nailed it at dress rehearsal. The night of the show, he couldn't see the teleprompter, went "off book," and barely sang my lyric. But he kept on singing! And they left it in the show just that way.

♬

Later that year, I also had the honor of performing with Nathan Lane and Matthew Broderick as we saluted Mel Brooks at the Academy of Motion Picture Arts and Sciences Governors Awards.[19] At the age of eighty-seven, Mel was getting an honorary Oscar to bookend the one he got in 1967 for the screenplay to *The Producers*. After having been part of the Kennedy Center Honors for Billy Crystal just a few weeks earlier, I was happy, as a proud Jew, to get to pay tribute to another Hebraic hero.

The Governors Awards audience is full of voting members of the Academy, so it is also heavily attended by folks who are hoping to get nominated. The amount of boldface-name schmoozing is off the charts, and everyone is *very* friendly. When we went to this event the year of *Mary Poppins Returns*, Scott Wittman called it "Bobbing for Oscars."

At the cocktail hour I ran into Glenn Close, who I sorta knew from parties some years ago at Bette Midler's. We traded pleasantries, but a few minutes later she rushed back to me. "I am so embarrassed! While we were talking I mistakenly thought you were Alan Menken," she said, meaning the celebrated Disney composer.

"Don't fret it," I replied. "It happens all the time. In fact, I am writing my memoirs and one title I am considering is *The View from Alan Menken's Shadow*."

She laughed and said, "I feel your pain. For me, it's Meryl Streep!"

After an hour of everyone pretending they were best friends with everyone else, it was time for the ceremony to begin. Our number started with special lyrics I wrote to "We Can Do It," from *The Producers*:

---

19 One summer night at the beach, as a group of us sat out back after a BBQ, Nathan and Matthew, who were about to go back into *The Producers* after a few years off, wondered if they remembered any of the lines. They then proceeded to perform, at full throttle, the opening scene. We were screaming with laughter (they still had it!) when suddenly, from a neighbor's bush, we heard "Ssshh!!". Odd. Nathan and Matthew continued until, once again, the bush uttered "SSHHH!!". How ironic that elsewhere, people were scalping tickets for thousands of dollars to witness their return to the show, but our grouchy Cheshire Cat of a neighbor was having none of it!

HE CAN DO IT, HE CAN DO IT
EVERY MINUTE BRINGS A JOKE
YOU CAN'T TOP HIM, YOU CAN'T STOP HIM
HE'S AWAKE, BUT HE AIN'T WOKE!

Seeing Mel laugh at my lyrics was worth the entire schlep out to Los Angeles.

Before the event was over, however, the Shaiman "*plotz*" begets "*zetz*" Vortex struck once more and Lou was racing me to Cedars-Sinai with an attack of kidney stones. The ER was a nightmare, crowded with people needing an intense amount of attention for their inner pain. Come to think of it, it was not unlike the crowd at the Governors Awards.

♬

But perhaps my most unexpected brush with a celebrity was when Katie Couric, for whom I had written a morning full of farewell lyrics for her last day on The Today Show, called and asked if I would write special lyrics for a star-studded colon cancer charity event she was producing on the Queen Mary, which was docked in Manhattan. And those lyrics would be sung by Harry Connick Jr. and...Donald Trump.

This was when he was only Donald "you're fired" Trump. Katie's idea was for Harry to sing "Manhattan" ("We'll Take Manhattan...") and for Trump to enter and sing a new verse, the theme being "I'll Buy Manhattan...".

"Will do!" I said to Katie, and Trump's office called to set up a rehearsal at his apartment. How embarrassed I was the day of the rehearsal when I called his secretary to ask for his address and she barked "TRUMP TOWER!" (with "you idiot!" only being implied by her tone). I guess I only thought of Trump Tower as his office and that perhaps he lived elsewhere. Turns out he was ahead of the curve on the whole "work at home" trend.

When I got to his apartment, my memory tells me that almost everything was gold-plated, including the piano. And then, there he was, not gold-plated but acting as if he were. He sang my lyrics, pretty much in tune, but I found it almost impossible to concentrate on anything but his hair. As much as I could get away with, I stared at this Hairdresser's Origami, this Rubik's Cube of Coiffure, trying to figure out exactly where this Möbius strip of a mop started and where it ended.

The day of rehearsal, he sat next to me and - while still immersed in the study of his hair-don't - I answered his questions regarding who all the luminaries were. The rehearsal with Harry went ok, but at the performance that night, he mixed up the words. I guess this was the birth of the now well-known "Trump word salad."

If only I knew then what I know now, I would have done my best to have talked him into a new career as a nite-club performer instead of the next line of work he pursued. My apologies to one and all!

27

LOOK WHAT HE MADE

William R. Shaiman

1927–2006

I believe I got my sense of humor from my father. Although he wasn't extroverted, he often had a twinkle in his eye, and I hardly ever saw him really mad.

There *was* the day I got suspended from school—for the second time—for cutting gym class and my father had to leave work to come get me. Seething, he drove me straight to a barber and the early '70s mane of hair that I was so proud of was buzzed into oblivion. Not counting fleeting moments when a few unfortunate waiters weren't fast enough with the coffee, that's almost the only time I ever saw him furious.

Except for that night in 2003 at the Tony Awards.

When we won for Best Original Score, Scott and I had to share the short, allotted time for our acceptance speeches. He spoke first, beautifully. But as I started to speak and thank Margo, the orchestra began playing me off—so I panicked and went right to my proposal to Scott (which, by the way, I had *not* pre-planned). So no, I did not thank my parents the night I won a Tony Award.

They had schlepped to, or watched, endless awards shows where I was nominated and lost. But then, when I finally actually won at the Tonys, the orchestra cut me off before I could finish what I wanted to say.

That would've been something like, "We people in showbiz get applauded all the time. But why is there no awards show for people who work their whole lives, and give of themselves, without even a single moment of complaint? Well, when they finally put that show on the air, I can already tell you, the winner is my father, William Shaiman."

Except I didn't get time to say that.

Of course my parents were happy for me and very proud, but when I got back into the audience, my father wasted *no* time letting me feel his anger that he and my mother had gone unrecognized. As anyone who's ever been lucky enough to get an award or even step on any stage knows, you sometimes go into what's called "the white room," where everything you thought of saying goes right out of your head.

The way that affected my father is something I have lived with and will live with for the rest of my life.

But that rare flash of anger was it. I know this world is full of mean, abusive fathers, creating scared children who grow into broken adults. But our father was an uncomplicated man, with neither the time nor inclination to harbor ill will toward anyone. I can honestly say, to paraphrase Will Rogers, no one ever met Bill Shaiman and didn't like him. He was simply irresistible.

My dad developed prostate cancer that spread into his bones. But only once, three days before his death, did he finally answer yes when my mother asked if he was in pain. When my time comes, do not expect that kind of grace from me; I am going to milk it for all it's worth!

When people asked where I got my talent from, I used to shrug. Then, in the last years of my father's life, he started carving charming figures out of wood. At first I (stupidly) thought he had bought some sort of kit that came with a knife and a block of wood with lines on it, like a whittler's version of "Paint by Numbers."

But I soon realized he was taking a block of wood, looking at it, seeing something inside, and then carving away. He just took his knife and wood and freed the character he saw living within.

When I stop to think about the talent he set aside all his life in order to raise and support us, my heart breaks into a billion pieces. He was an artist. But at least now, when people ask me where I got the gift from, I don't have to shrug. I can proudly say, "My father."

When it was time to write a eulogy for his funeral, an idea for a song came into my head. I drove over to my parents' home, sat in his recliner, and looked at the shelf of his carvings. I thought of him creating something that did not, and would not, exist without him, and wrote this song:

"LOOK WHAT HE MADE!"

WHEN MY PARENTS MOVED DOWN FLORIDA WAY
TO EAT DINNER IN THE LIGHT OF DAY
MY FATHER FINALLY HAD TIME ON HIS HANDS

SO, HE TOOK SOME WOOD AND A CARVING KNIFE
AND A NEW CAREER WAS BROUGHT TO LIFE
AND WHAT ONCE JUST SAT UNFORMED NOW PROUDLY STANDS

LOOK WHAT HE MADE!
HIS OWN CREATION
JUST WITH HIS SWEET IMAGINATION
THINK OF THE WAY HIS FINGERS HELD THAT WOOD AND PLAYED

NOBODY KNEW HE COULD ACHIEVE IT
BUT WHEN HE WAS DONE YOU BEST BELIEVE IT
HIS HANDS AND HEART HAD DANCED IN A TABLETOP PARADE
AND LOOK, LOOK WHAT HE MADE!

NOW, AS WE SAT THERE IN HIS FINAL ROOM
I TRIED TO LOOK BEYOND THE GLOOM
AND I TOOK IN ALL THE FACES THAT LAST DAY

THERE WAS HIS ELDEST SURE AND STEADY
THERE WERE HIS GIRLS BOTH ROUGH AND READY
AND THERE WAS HIS ROCK, HIS DARLING CLAIRE,
TO WHOM I SAY

LOOK WHAT HE MADE!
HIS OWN CREATION
WE CAN STAND TALL ON HIS FOUNDATION
HE WOULDN'T WANT TO KNOW THAT WE WERE SO AFRAID

HE MUST HAVE KNOWN WE COULD ACHIEVE IT
AND THOUGH HE'S GONE YOU BEST BELIEVE IT
HIS LIGHT HAS DIMMED, BUT IT WILL NEVER FADE
CAUSE LOOK, LOOK WHAT HE MADE!

WE WERE HIS WOOD, UNFORMED AND SCRAPPY
HE WORKED HIS LIFE TO MAKE US HAPPY
I KNOW IT'S SELFISH HOW WE WISH TO GOD HE'D STAYED
BUT LOOK!
LOOK WHAT HE MADE!

28

MARTIN SHORT: FAME BECOMES HIM

’06–

Of all the gifts God has given me, none is more precious than my friendship with Martin Short.

It’s no secret that Marty is the most beloved guy in show business. He manages to be a complete sweetheart to everyone he encounters yet has a wickedly biting wit and is fiendishly fun to gossip with. Who else could create the interviewer character Jiminy Glick—and have all the top celebrities lining up to be demolished by his brutal honesty? Marty knows just how to walk that tightrope, and is so adored, everyone happily tiptoes out onto the highwire with him.

When I was being called in to help with musical ideas at *Saturday Night Live* in 1984, Marty, Billy Crystal, Christopher Guest, and I would often hang out in the music room. We were supposed to be creating sketches but usually ended up just schmoozing and laughing at everyone and everything on Earth.

After his yearlong stint at *SNL*, Marty wrote the HBO special *I, Martin Short, Goes Hollywood*. It was directed by Eugene Levy, and co-written with Paul Flaherty and Dick Blasucci, and I was pleased as punch to be asked to co-create songs for this absolutely insane show. I also scored the special, using the rudimentary new equipment that was then coming out. But back in the day, synthesizer strings sounded like a skating-rink organ, so you couldn't pay me now to listen to what must be the most tiny, tinny, and tacky-sounding score of my career. But it was great fun, and along with Billy Crystal's two HBO specials of that time (*Don't Get Me Started* and *Midnight Train to Moscow*), *I, Martin Short, Goes Hollywood* allowed me to dip my toe into scoring.

Around that time, Marty and his no-nonsense wife, Nancy, started throwing Christmas parties. They started small but soon grew to become an outrageous who's-who of the movie business. They were like a throwback to stories you hear about old Hollywood parties, with world-famous stars huddled around the piano, performing for each other.

Marty's upright piano normally stayed in his home office. But around nine thirty, when the buffet dinner finished, he would make me push it into the living room, emphasizing to the A-list guests how stage-starved I was. I would overdo the huffing and puffing while Marty carried a lightweight piano stool, just to show he was "pitching in." He would then climb up on the piano, pretending to crush my fingers. Holding a spoon like a mic, he would launch into our regular opening number, featuring special lyrics to "It's the Most Wonderful Time of the Year."

"IT'S THE MOST WONDERFUL TIME OF THE YEAR"

Marty
IT'S THE MOST WONDERFUL TIME OF THE YEAR
NOW THE PARTY'S JUST STARTIN'
CAUSE HERE COMES STEVE MARTIN
HE'LL JUGGLE A BALL!
IT'S THE HAP, HAPPIEST SEASON OF ALL

IT'S THE MOST WONDERFUL SHOW OF THE YEAR

Marc
CELEBRITY BUTT YOU'LL BE KISSING
WHILE HIGH NOTES YOU'RE MISSING

Marty
AND THIS...FROM A QUEER!
IT'S THE MOST WONDERFUL TIME
IT'S THE HAP, HAPPIEST TIME

Marty & Marc
IT'S THE MOST WONDERFUL SHOW OF THE YEAR!

After that, Marty would usually sing "Too Marvelous for Words," and then start asking, nay, *demanding* guests to perform. You wouldn't believe how petrified some of them—otherwise confident, world-famous movie stars—were that Marty might call on them to perform. Scott used to say that when the "entertainment" started, so many people hid in other rooms that it looked like we were putting on a production of *The Diary of Anne Frank*.

Luckily, there were many who were happy to join in. One year, Nathan Lane performed the number that made Danny Kaye famous, a rapid-fire list of Russian composers entitled "Tchaikovsky." Once Nathan got to the end of the song and we ended with a flourish, he fell to the ground in a mock coma. Another person who also fell to the ground at the end of their performance was the late, great Jan Hooks, my Sweeney Sisters compatriot who had just finished her run at *SNL*. When Marty asked Jan what she would like to do, she solemnly announced, "I would like to perform a monologue from *To Kill a Mockingbird*."

"Very good, then," said Marty. And Jan proceeded to do the entire "Mayella Ewell" witness-stand monologue, so perfectly it was as if we were watching the movie. Just imagine Jan, staring at this room of celebrities, bellowing, *"I got something to say! And then I ain't gonna say no more!"* Jan went on to recite the entire monologue, leading to a complete emotional breakdown, at which point, she threw herself to the floor. I've never witnessed anything like it—certainly not at a Christmas party!

Others who would perform were Tom Hanks, Billy Crystal, and Steve Martin, mesmerizing the crowd with his exquisite banjo playing. One year, Steven Spielberg brought his clarinet and I accompanied him and his wife, Kate Capshaw, as they performed "Hanukkah, O Hanukkah." Later on, I cornered him to ask if I could now say that I had worked with him.

What began as a spontaneous production soon gave way to much preplanning and rehearsing. I would receive music from people weeks in advance, and every year would have to get to Marty and Nancy's home earlier and earlier. People like Victor Garber, Andrea Martin, Catherine O'Hara, Phil Hartman, Glenn Frey of The Eagles, and Kenny G worked themselves into a tizzy as we tried to finish rehearsing before the guests arrived.

(When Kenny G performed and momentarily turned his back to the room, exposing his lustrous, auburn curls, Marty quipped, "Oh look, Bernadette Peters is here!")

By the second year, it was time for me to write something for myself, and it became a tradition for me to sing these "special" lyrics every year:

"MARTY THROWS A PARTY JUST TO SING"
(SUNG TO THE TUNE OF "WINTER WONDERLAND")

EVERY YEAR, MID DECEMBER
COMES A NIGHT TO REMEMBER
WITH ME AT HIS SIDE, WE'LL WATCH THE GUESTS HIDE
CAUSE MARTY THROWS A PARTY JUST TO SING

SEE HIS EYES, HOW THEY'RE GLISTENING
HE DON'T CARE IF NO ONE'S LISTENING
YOU THINK THAT WE'RE GUESTS, BUT NOBODY RESTS
CAUSE MARTY THROWS A PARTY JUST TO SING

NOW THE HOUSE IS BRIGHT AND LOOKING FANCY
ALL THE GUESTS ARE HERE AND LOOKING CHIC
BUT THOUGH THE DRESS IS WORN BY HIS WIFE NANCY
HE THINKS HE'S JUDY GARLAND AT HER PEAK!

HOW HE CRAVES OUR ATTENTION
IT DESERVES AN INTERVENTION
BUT LET'S BE SANTA CLAUS
AND GIVE HIM BIG APPLAUSE
CAUSE MARTY THROWS A PARTY JUST TO SING!

Always spread out on the front-row couch was Marty's beloved manager and agent, Bernie Brillstein. He was such a character; he looked like a cross between Moses and Santa Claus, and, although everything about him screamed old-school showbiz, every fresh young comic dreamed of joining his stable. He had such an eye for talent, and was just as funny as any of his clients.

So it pains me to report that Bernie also featured in the only real blip I ever had in my relationship with Marty. They asked me to be the musical director for *The Martin Short Show*, a late-night talker he hosted in 1999. This was at the height of my film-scoring career, when I was doing six or seven movies a year. So my reps worked with Bernie to negotiate a deal that included building a mini replica of my home studio in my dressing room, so I could work right up until showtime. There were also clauses allowing me to be absent whenever I had to attend an orchestral recording for a film. It was a fool's errand to try and figure all this out, but we almost got there, until finally, inevitably, the deal fell apart.

The next day I received a note at my home from Bernie saying, "I thought you were Marty's friend. Some friend." It didn't go on to say, "Go fuck yourself," but that was certainly implied.

Luckily Marty is so gracious, and our bond strong enough, that our relationship survived that unfortunate incident.

At the Christmas parties, Marty finally met my other half, Scott Wittman. They hit it off immediately, recognizing in each other a shared, sweet-but-twisted worldview. A few years later, after the success of *Hairspray*, Marty asked Scott and I to co-write the songs for his upcoming Broadway show, *Martin Short: Fame Becomes Me*, and for Scott to direct it.

At that time, Broadway was packed with one-person shows featuring celebrities baring their souls and revealing their deepest, darkest secrets. So, the premise for *Fame Becomes Me* was that Marty would try to do the same, even though his life was charmed and he had no demons to vanquish. We wrote and workshopped the show and cast it with an outrageously talented troupe of comic actors: Mary Birdsong, Capathia Jenkins, Nicole Parker, and Brooks Ashmanskas. And then we hit the road.

Unfortunately, unlike the preparation and performances at the Christmas party, the road to Broadway for *Fame Becomes Me* was rockier. Satirizing the confessional form of celebrity one-person shows proved a tad too insidery for folks outside New York, so we scrambled to reframe the humor.

Someone once said, "If you wanna give your enemy pure hell, put them on the road with a new musical." Things were tenser than you would want them to be while trying to put on a musical comedy. Scott even came down with a case of shingles while we were in San Francisco. Meanwhile, despite being a huge ham, I discovered I am really no good at learning choreography. Nor the juggling act of rewriting off stage while performing on stage.

Nevertheless, improvements were made. And by the time we hit Broadway, audiences loved the show, which ran for about half a year.

And oh, did I mention that Scott and I were splitting up as a couple at the same time? Maybe that contributed to the rough patches, ya think?

Still, even with all that *tsuris*, we had an *awful* lot of fun putting on the show. Every night, huge celebrities attended and were often brought up on stage to be interviewed by the "Jiminy Glick" character Marty created for his '90s talk show. And when the performance finished, per showbiz tradition, they would come backstage.

One night, I was standing there after the show as the one and only Kirk Douglas came up the small stairway that Jiminy's guests used to mount the stage. This was after he had suffered a stroke, but was still living a full life. And when Kirk Douglas got to the stage, he looked over, saw me near the wings, and a huge smile came over his face. He walked past Marty and the other cast members, right toward me, and I thought, *Oh my God, Kirk Douglas is about to tell me how fabulous I am*!

And when he got to me, he opened his mouth and said, "Hey, kid, where's the bathroom?"

Sometime after *Fame Becomes Me* finished its Broadway run, Scott and I went up to visit Marty and Nancy at their summer home on Lake Muskoka in Ontario, Canada. It's the comfiest, coziest compound imaginable—even though there are three separate houses on the property to accommodate the endless stream of guests arriving for a week at what the Shorts call Snug Harbor.

One afternoon, they called out to us: "Hey, guys, can you join us in the living room? We need to talk to you."

When Marty recounted this moment in his own memoir, he reminded readers that my imploding relationship with Scott caused more than a few headaches on *Fame Becomes Me*. So, when Scott and I nervously entered the living room, I thought we were gonna get a real talking-to.

Instead, they asked us to sit down and said, "We wanted to tell you ourselves that Nancy has cancer."

Trying to break the gloom with inappropriate humor, I replied, "Oh, thank God, I thought you guys were mad at us!"

Luckily, as I imagined and hoped they would, Marty and Nancy dissolved into hysterics. Painting myself as a self-involved showbiz cretin helped break the ice.

Nancy's battle with cancer was a long and heartbreaking struggle, supported all the way by Marty and their three children. But sadly, on August 21, 2010, she passed away.

A few years earlier, our friend Sarah Jessica Parker had asked me to write music and lyrics for a television commercial introducing her perfume, "Lovely." I returned a few thirty-second mini-songs for her to choose from, and James Marsden sang the one she picked, "Ain't it Lovely Just to Be in Love."

But later, when Scott and I were writing songs for *Fame Becomes Me,* I remembered that one of the other songs I had written fit Marty's view of life nicely. So, we fleshed it out with lyrics that reflected the working title of the show at the time: *If I Saved, I Wouldn't Be Here.* Marty sang it at the end of the evening, dedicating it to the audience, his three wonderful children and his wife and soulmate, Nancy.

"GLASS HALF FULL"

SOME FOLKS SAY HALF EMPTY WHEN THE SWEET WINE FLOWS
OTHERS SEE THE GLASS HALF FULL
THROUGH GLASSES COLORED ROSE
BUT WHEN I RAISE A TOAST, NO MATTER HOW SMALL
I'M JUST GRATEFUL FOR THE GLASS AT ALL

SOME FOLKS CRAVE A PENTHOUSE HIGH ATOP A CLOUD
OTHERS NEED A PRIVATE JET TO LOOK DOWN ON THE CROWD
BUT WHEN THEY SEARCH TO FIND THEIR WAY, WAY UP HIGH
I JUST CLOSE MY EYES AND TOUCH THE SKY

THE GRASS IS ALWAYS GREENER IN SOMEBODY ELSE'S YARD
THEY SWEAT ALL DAY TO MAKE SURE THAT IT'S SO
BUT WHEN I HAVE THE TIME AT HOME
DON'T WANT TO WORK THAT HARD
I'D RATHER SIT AND WATCH THAT GREEN GRASS GROW

SO YOU CAN KEEP YOUR PENTHOUSE TOWERING UP ABOVE
JUST GIVE ME A SWEETHEART AND THREE ANGELS I CAN LOVE
AND LET ME RAISE A TOAST TO DEBTS LONG PAST DUE
FOR IF I'D SAVED I WOULD HAVE NOT MET YOU
YES, IF I'D SAVED I WOULD HAVE NOT MET YOU

A year or so after her death, Marty was doing a live interview on *The Today Show*. Host Kathie Lee Gifford, unaware of Nancy's passing, said, "You and your wife have one of the all-time great showbiz marriages. What's your secret?"

For two minutes, Marty continued the conversation, carefully choosing his words without embarrassing Kathie Lee on live television. She was, of course, mortified when told the truth during the commercial break. But Marty wasn't upset. This moment of grace demonstrates the compassionate man he really is—despite what he may say when he gets in the "Jiminy Glick" fat suit.

My husband Lou and I have gone up to Snug Harbor every summer, with our dog Chops, to have the most glorious five days sitting on Marty's dock. We gossip endlessly, then settle on the couch after dinner to do what Marty loves more than anything else: watch terrible movies like *Boom*! with Elizabeth Taylor and Richard Burton.

In 2023, Scott and I co-wrote a song with Benj Pasek & Justin Paul for Marty and Steve Martin's fabulous television show, *Only Murders in the Building*. We had a blast visiting the set when they filmed our number—and found ourselves nominated for an Emmy for it. At the ceremony, so used to hearing someone else's name read, I turned to Scott and said, "I don't care if we win…I just don't wanna lose!" And lo and behold, we didn't! My second Emmy win, only thirteen nominations and thirty-four years apart!

It gives me great joy to see Marty, after six million years in show business, now even more successful than ever. No one deserves it more, and I love him from the bottom of my heart.

29

THE SECOND TIME AROUND

'06–Till Death Do Us Part!

Around 2005, as Scott and I were co-writing *Martin Short: Fame Becomes Me,* our marriage-in-all-but-name came to an end. After some twenty-five years, our relationship had evolved past being significant others, but we still remained the very best of friends, writing partners, and soulmates. I won't pretend our breakup wasn't painful, but as hard as it sometimes was, we had to—or chose to—continue to work together. At that moment, it meant working on Marty's show, as well as the score for our musical version of *Catch Me If You Can*.

After we went out on the road with *Fame Becomes Me* to Toronto, San Francisco, and Chicago, we hit Broadway at the Bernard B. Jacobs Theatre on West 45th Street on August 18, 2006. But newly single and without an apartment of my own, I took up residence at the Roger Smith Hotel not far from Grand Central Terminal in east midtown, a lonely bachelor for the first time in my life.

One night while performing in the show, as Brooks Ashmanskas and I were waiting in the wings to make an entrance (dressed as angels with huge wings), a drop-dead gorgeous guy walked through the stage door. When he left a moment later, Brooks and I asked our stage manager, Bess Glorioso, "Who was that handsome man with the military haircut?" She said it was a volunteer from BC/EFA named Lou, who was helping our show by holding a red bucket at the door. During the darkest days of the 1980s, two of the largest New York theater-community organizations founded to combat the AIDS crisis were Broadway Cares and Equity Fights AIDS. They later merged, and BC/EFA still raises money from Broadway audiences and across America every year in the spring and fall. Normally a member of the cast makes a speech about the importance of the cause at the curtain call, as many of the other actors wait by the exits to collect donations in red buckets as the audience files out. But since our show had so few people in it, the organization had to send volunteers to help with the collection.

At the curtain calls for *Fame Becomes Me*, Marty had, every few nights, "auctioned" me off to the highest-paying audience member who would like a song written about themselves. The winners would come backstage, share some information with me about their life, and I committed to writing them a short song which I would later email to them—and this helped raise a lot of money. Most of the folks just gave me some basic information about themselves, but one woman named Kate told me the most beautiful story. It turned out that *Fame Becomes Me* was the first time she and her father had taken in a Broadway show since her mother died. Kate told me she was raised in a one-stoplight town in Pennsylvania, and every year her mom would scrimp to save enough money to take Kate to a Broadway musical. It was a beautiful and bittersweet concept for a song. And the fact that my father had died at the beginning of that same year made me even more empathetic to Kate, for whom I wrote what I believe is a lovely song.

Each night after the show, I would return alone to the Roger Smith Hotel. Scrolling through my laptop, clinging to hope that I might still have a future love life, I found myself flirting (via MySpace, which lets you know exactly when this was) with Ryan, a cute guy in the chorus—pardon me, the *ensemble* (as it is now called)—of the non-Equity tour of *Hairspray*, which was then traveling across America. When the tour hit Hartford, Connecticut, I decided to go and see it, not just to finally check out the state of this new tour, but to maybe consummate the flirtation with this adorable guy in the chor…I mean, the ensemble.

I traveled to Hartford on Sunday after the matinee of *Fame Becomes Me* and saw *Hairspray* that night. Luckily, the show was in great shape—but as far as hooking up, I was less lucky. In my room, I made a pass at Ryan, which he gently rebuffed. I don't think I was really his type, and he sensibly said it wouldn't be cool to sleep with a person who was, in a way, his employer. Just then, months and months of loneliness hit, and poor Ryan unfortunately witnessed me, embarrassed and rejected, breaking into tears. I apologized, explained where I was in my life, and we said goodnight.

The morning following that embarrassing encounter, December 4, I was scheduled to perform Kate's song at Gypsy of the Year—the annual BC/EFA fundraising show of music and skits, which since

2018 has been called Red Bucket Follies. But the only way I could get back from Hartford in time was, very extravagantly, to charter a helicopter. As I flew back, the skies over Manhattan were leaden and overcast, which perfectly matched my mood. If this were a movie, the camera would start with a very tight close-up of my face pressed against the helicopter's window as I took in the grey skyline, and as it pulled back to show this small speck in the sky, the voice-over would be just what I was thinking: *Okay, God, I get it. I won't make a fool of myself again like that. I understand that I had twenty-five years of a fantastic relationship. I shouldn't be greedy and expect more; it's time to put my heart and my libido out to pasture.*

God must have thought, *I'll show you.*

Because when I got to the Neil Simon Theatre, where the event was to take place, a man greeted me and said it was his responsibility to take me to the lower lobby where I would sign posters. Which I did, still in a very gloomy daze. I was in such a funk, I didn't recognize this was the same man with the navy haircut who had come backstage to retrieve his red bucket.

When it was time to perform the song I had written for Kate, I became very emotional. It was a combination of her affecting story, which I related to my own father's death; the events of the previous night in Hartford; and the fact that it was an AIDS benefit at the very theater where I had wished on the opening night of *Hairspray* that all our lost friends could once again be part of our lives. So I broke down a bit as I introed the song.

After the performance, stage manager Bess said that there was someone who wanted to meet me. "Okay, sure, whatever." She brought me to a corner of the wings where Louis Mirabal, the gorgeous navy man, handed me a coin. Lou had been moved by my performance and explained that in the navy, when someone does something for you, a custom is to present them with this special coin that represents appreciation.

He also mentioned that many times in the navy, his assignment had been in a submarine. Now, I have met a lot of interesting people, but never someone who has lived in a submarine. I was definitely fascinated and also couldn't help but notice how utterly gorgeous Lou was. I told him I'd love to hear more about his life, and we traded contact information. And started emailing each other that very night. And then had a few very long phone calls. I would soon learn that Lou loves to talk, never leaving out a single piece of information—"blah blah" we call it.[20] I couldn't get a bead on if we were flirting with each other or if he was even gay, so I asked why he had chosen to volunteer for BC/EFA.

Now, Lou is not a man of the theater—in fact, I often say that if he likes a show, he gives it "two eyelids up." But apparently a cousin had dragged him to a show earlier that year and as BC/EFA collected at the curtain call, it occurred to him that volunteering could be both an act of community service and also help expand his activities outside the regimented confines of navy life. Although he was living in Rhode Island while stationed in Groton, on the easternmost coast of Connecticut, he would drive hours every time he was needed in Manhattan to hold the red bucket.

I asked Lou to come meet me after the matinee on Saturday. We walked back to my hotel on my dinner break, and after talking for a while in my hotel room, once again, for the second time that week, I spontaneously leaned forward to kiss a man. But this time, after initially pulling back in surprise, he leaned forward and kissed me back! I would come to learn that this was the first time Lou had been kissed by a man and that, in fact, Lou had lived quite a solitary existence. It made me sad to think such a loving and lovely man had been living so long as a loner.

---

20 I learned in those calls that he was a Marvel comic book nerd, so imagine his (and my) thrill years later when I got the assignment to write a production number for the Marvel TV series *Hawkeye*.

I shan't share any more details of our afternoon, but will tell you that after dropping me at the theater, when Lou got to Port Authority that night to take the bus to his mother's house in New Jersey, he was in such a pleasant haze that he got on the wrong one—which is why we celebrate "Wrong Bus Day" every year on December 9.

Lou started driving in each weekend, and we would spend every waking hour entangled in each other's arms in that room at the Roger Smith Hotel, falling more deeply for each other with every heavenly moment. By the time the show closed on January 7, 2007, and it was time for me to head back to LA to start scoring the *Hairspray* movie, Lou and I were hopelessly in love.

And after many years of a torturous long-distance romance—at various times Lou was stationed everywhere from Hawaii to Virginia to Afghanistan—when same-sex marriage became the law of the land in summer 2015, I proposed. Shortly afterward, when he retired from the navy as Lieutenant Commander Mirabal, we decided to piggyback on that ceremony—March 26, 2016—as the time and place to also get married. Wanting to keep the focus on his twenty years of serving his country, however, we did not tell his family about our marriage plans, so they wouldn't overlook this accomplishment amid the excitement of a wedding. But I certainly told all *my* friends, 'cause I knew, much as they liked Lou, none of them were going to schlep to a VFW Hall in Bogota, New Jersey, for his retirement ceremony. But for a wedding? Yes, it turns out, they would schlep for that.

That afternoon, one side of the room was Lou's friends and family, ready to applaud his service, while the other side was a celebrity-filled group, all trying hard not to let on what they knew. I don't think the denizens of this VFW hall ever expected to see Bette Midler, Whoopi Goldberg, Jenifer Lewis, Darlene Love, Nathan Lane, and Patti LuPone among the spectators of a retirement ceremony. They must've thought a USO tour showed up at the wrong address.

Esteemed playwright Terrence McNally attended with his husband, the producer Tom Kirdahy, who had gotten ordained over the internet. And as Lou's glorious and moving retirement ceremony came to a close, Tom stood up to say there was still one last thing to do. I will never forget the mixture of surprise and elation on the faces of Lou's friends and family as they realized what was happening. As he concluded the wedding ceremony, Tom gleefully added: "Ladies and gentlemen, I give you an officer and a gentleman."

I will never know what I did in some former life to deserve the love of not one, but two great men. And the fact that I can work with Scott all day and then go home to my husband Lou is, even for an Eeyore like me, a reason to rejoice.

30

CATCH ME IF YOU CAN

'03–

After *Hairspray,* we got a lot of offers, and one of them was to write a musical of the old chestnut *Stage Door,* a play and classic film from the '30s starring Katharine Hepburn ("The calla lilies are in bloom...").

When Scott and I went to the Drama Book Shop in the Theater District to buy the play, we noticed a new coffee-table book about the making of Steven Spielberg's movie, *Catch Me If You Can.* Scott picked it up and said, "I'd rather write a musical of this." And that was that; we never bought the script for *Stage Door.*

Instead we went home, watched *Catch Me* on DVD, and immediately saw a chance to tell a great father-and-son story with the Rat-Pack-era sounds we both adored—a side of the '60s barely represented in *Hairspray.*

The first song we wrote was called "Fifty Checks," inspired by the wonderful scene in the movie where Christopher Walken (as Frank Sr.) gives Leo DiCaprio (as Frank Jr.) his first checkbook. Our song sounded straight out of the Sinatra repertoire. The next songs included a Judy Garland/Édith Piaf solo for Frank Jr.'s mother, along with his opening number, which could have been performed on the TV Show *Hullabaloo.* A concept was starting to form naturally, from the songwriting, to present the show in the style of a classic television special of the early- to mid-'60s. As Frank told his story, the songs became presentational performance pieces; a way of conning the audience into seeing these events *his way.*

To get the rights, I bypassed agents and lawyers and contacted Spielberg directly. (After all, ever since Marty's Christmas party, I'd considered him a "colleague.") I sent him the demos we had recorded, he responded enthusiastically, and we were off and running.

Scott and I asked our *Hairspray* cohorts, Jack O'Brien and Jerry Mitchell, to join us, and they suggested esteemed playwright Terrence McNally to write the book. I booked a recording studio for a reading, which went encouragingly. *Hairspray* producer Margo Lion came. She didn't respond over-enthusiastically to the material but wanted to continue her relationship with the *Hairspray* gang. In the same way, Hal Luftig, who had produced Jerry's directorial debut, *Legally Blonde*, wanted to continue that relationship and partnered with Margo. The big lesson here was that getting into bed with folks who love working together—but only *like* the material—can lead to heartbreak down the road.

At our out-of-town tryout in Seattle, the song "Fifty Checks," which until that point had been our calling card for the show, was not getting across the footlights. It came early and stopped the show—not in a good way—by being "presentational" rather than story-based.[21]

It became clear we had to get Frank Jr. to Manhattan as soon as possible, and that Frank Sr.'s song had to have more story-engine to it. Losing "Fifty Checks" was a sign that our original concept just wasn't coming across.

But these show-business travails seemed trivial when an unimaginable tragedy befell our co-lead Norbert Leo Butz, who was playing the Tom Hanks role of Detective Carl Hanratty.

---

21 At intermission of the very first performance in Seattle, I saw Tom Wopat walk out the stage door and approach that lobby entryway. "Um, Tom, where ya going?" I asked. "I'm gonna go sell my CDs at the merchandise table," he replied. "Tom, it's intermission, this audience has to only see you as your character, you can't go in there now and hawk CDs!" Tom stared at me with such focused rage that I braced myself for a jaw-breaking punch to the mouth. Thankfully, he turned around and retreated back to backstage. Whew. I don't think I would have survived a punch from Tom Wopat.

One day after rehearsals, a bunch of us had a wonderful sunset dinner with his sister Teresa, who lived in Seattle with her fiancée, Jennifer. Just two days later, we learned that Teresa and Jennifer had been brutally attacked by a mentally ill intruder who had climbed in through their window. He raped and stabbed them both, resulting in Teresa's death.

We were stunned. How could this be? How could Norbert survive this? That night on the news, there was dear Norbert standing in front of the police tape. He brought his sister back to their hometown of St. Louis, and asked us to wait for him, so previews were postponed. After ten days, he returned and stoically and beautifully asked only that we, in honor of Teresa, not hate Seattle. Somehow, he was able to jump back into the show and we finished our out-of-town tryout.

The show got promising reviews there, but our producers felt someone else needed to come in to make the book work. Terrence McNally being replaced was traumatic and we ended up with a very unfocused creative team. But by opening night on Broadway, it seemed like we had figured it out, and during the creative team curtain call, I said, "We dedicate tonight to all of our fathers—and to one of our sisters."

Then off to the party we went, where Scott and I learned about the mixed reviews when an investor came up to us and said, "We don't care *what* the *New York Times* says, we love the show!"

(By the way, if you're ever about to give feedback to a Broadway composer/lyricist that starts with the phrase, "We don't care what the *New York Times* says," consider leaving that part out.)

The show still scored four Tony nominations, including Best Musical. Larry Blank and I were nominated for Best Orchestrations, and, although humiliated and depressed that our score had not made the cut, I went to the Tony nomination press event. But the second I walked in without Scott at my side, I burst into tears. A publicist quickly pulled me behind a door, patting my back as I tried to get the sobs out. After ten minutes, I put on a brave face and walked back into the event—at which point the tears returned, so I ran out the door and straight home.

Writing about seating for the Tony Awards at the smaller-than-usual Beacon Theatre, Michael Riedel, then the Broadway columnist for the *New York Post*, said, "the Catch Me team might as well get seats across the street." I will never forget how hurtful that was. The show *did* win one Tony, thankfully, for Norbert Leo Butz, in no small part due to his spectacular performance of "Don't Break the Rules," the lyrics for which speak very much to America today.

"DON'T BREAK THE RULES"

IT STARTS VERY EARLY ONCE THE BABY TOYS ARE GONE
A KID ON THE PLAYGROUND
HAS TO CHOOSE WHAT SIDE HE'S ON
IT'S THE BULLIES OR THE GOOD GUYS
BOY, THERE AIN'T NO MIDDLE GROUND
THOUGH HOODLUMS TRY TO BLUR THE LINE
AND TWIST THE TRUTH AROUND
THEN THEY CALL THEMSELVES A WINNER,
BUT THEY'RE SELF DECEIVING FOOLS
CAUSE THE GAME AIN'T WORTH WINNING
IF YOU'RE BREAKING ALL THE RULES

THE LAW IS LAID UPON US WHEN AS KIDS WE FIRST ASK WHY
OUR PARENTS SET THE RULES
WHEN "CAUSE I SAID SO" THEY REPLY
AND THOUGH I THOUGHT I HATED THEM
AND SCREAMED WITH ALL MY MIGHT
THE NEXT TIME THAT I HAD A CHOICE
GEE WHIZ, I DID WHAT'S RIGHT
NO, I NEVER SNUCK A DRINK, I NEVER STOLE A PACK OF KOOLS

CAUSE THE GAME AIN'T WORTH WINNING
IF YOU'RE BREAKING ALL THE RULES

DON'T BREAK THE RULES – OR ELSE WE'RE LIVIN' IN THE WILD, WILD WEST
DON'T BREAK THE RULES – GOD'S KEEPING SCORE AND YOU DON'T WANT TO FAIL THAT TEST
DON'T BREAK THE RULES – YOU THUMB YOUR NOSE RIGHT AT THE LIFE FOR WHICH I STRIVE
BUT THOSE RULES, THOSE LAWS KEEP US ALIVE

IT STARTED BACK WITH MOSES WHEN HE LED AROUND THE JEWS
AND CLIMBED WAY UP THAT MOUNTAIN
TO PICK UP GOD'S DAILY NEWS
HE SCHLEPPED UP OL' MT. SINAI
CRIED AND BEGGED ON THEIR BEHALF
THEN ALMOST DROPPED THOSE TABLETS
WHEN HE SAW THAT GOLDEN CALF
NOW WE TEACH THE TEN COMMANDMENTS
EVERY SUNDAY IN OUR SCHOOLS
CAUSE THE GAME AIN'T WORTH WINNING
IF YOU'RE BREAKING ALL THE RULES

SO GO SNEAK INTO A MOVIE, RUN A RED LIGHT, SELL SOME POT
IT'S ALL THE SAME TO ME
YOU'RE EITHER GUILTY OR YOU'RE NOT
IF WE ALL DID WHAT WE WANTED EVERY TIME WE FELT THE URGE
THE WORLD WOULD BE TOTAL CHAOS, IT'S ALREADY ON THE VERGE
YES IT'S LAWS THAT KEEP US HUMAN
CAUSE WITHOUT THEM WE'RE JUST MULES
AND THE GAME AIN'T WORTH WINNING
IF WE'RE BREAKING ALL THE RULES

DON'T BREAK THE RULES – OR ELSE WE'RE LIVIN' IN THE WILD, WILD WEST
DON'T BREAK THE RULES – GOD'S KEEPING SCORE AND YOU DON'T WANT TO FAIL THAT TEST
DON'T BREAK THE RULES – YOU THUMB YOUR NOSE RIGHT AT THE LIFE FOR WHICH I STRIVE
BUT THOSE RULES, THOSE LAWS KEEP US ALIVE

Despite Norbert's Tony win, we closed a few weeks later after only half a year.

Now any time Scott and I see a production of the show, it's like being in the locker room as a coach plays film of and critiques the game. Still, the show gets produced all over the world and people have a great time putting it on. But for us, it is a bittersweet memory, with Norbert's perseverance and fortitude being the only thing I can marvel at. I don't know how he did it. God bless you Norbert, Teresa, and your entire family.

31

CHARLIE AND THE CHOCOLATE FACTORY

'09-

In February 2009, Scott and I were asked to meet with representatives from the Roald Dahl estate, Warner Bros., and Sam Mendes' producing partner, Caro Newling. They wanted to see if we would be interested in writing a brand-new musical adaptation of Dahl's book, *Charlie and the Chocolate Factory*, for London's West End.

They wanted a completely new score, because the author had hated the songs in the 1971 film, *Willy Wonka & the Chocolate Factory*. In December of that year, he fired off a scathing letter to its producer, David Wolper, about "getting some of those ghastly songs cut...particularly the opening number, 'The Candy Man.'"

Tim Burton had just directed a hugely successful remake that did not include the famous songs by Leslie Bricusse and Anthony Newley, so we naively thought audiences would not picket the theater if they didn't hear "The Candy Man," "I've Got a Golden Ticket," and "Pure Imagination." But we were about to learn that nostalgia is a powerful thing and that audiences aren't on the same page with Roald Dahl when it comes to those so-called "ghastly" songs.

Writing songs for the show and collaborating with book writer David Greig and director Sam Mendes was a lot of fun, and we all felt good about the project. Sam was also then directing his first James Bond movie, *Skyfall*, and would often call or email from exotic locales.

Not that it ever showed up in the writing, but I saw the story as positively biblical, with Willy representing the vengeful, Old Testament God, and Charlie as the more loving, New Testament Jesus. Maybe I should have pressed for that to be part of the show—it could have earned us some badly needed divine intervention!

As the show prepped for rehearsals in London, Sam took us on a stroll that Scott refers to as the "Fredo in *The Godfather* walk." He said that Warner Bros. now insisted "Pure Imagination" go in, and it got the "eleven o'clock" spot for the glass elevator ride that finishes the show.

Sadly, the song we wrote for the entry into the Chocolate Room in the West End production, "Simply Second Nature," came where "Pure Imagination" comes in the movie, and when the audience didn't hear what they expected, their disappointment flowed like the chocolate river itself. But the song spoke to the very nature of Willy's (and Scott's and my) need to create.

"SIMPLY SECOND NATURE"

A PAINTER NEEDS NO REASON
TO MAKE A THING OF ART
YES, THERE'S NO SWITCH TO STOP AND START THE FLOW
A GARDENER HAS HIS SEASON,
HIS GREEN THUMB AND HIS HEART
DON'T ASK THE MAN "WHY DOES YOUR GARDEN GROW?"

A POET SITS FOR HOURS
WITH WORDS UPON HIS TONGUE
HE CANNOT HELP BUT RHYME HIS DOOM AND GLOOM
SO IF YOU TASTE MY FLOWERS
YOU'LL SEE THAT I'M AMONG
THAT LUCKY TROUPE, THAT CERTAIN GROUP FOR WHOM...

...IT'S SIMPLY SECOND NATURE TO WISH AWAY THE GRAY
TO TAKE A LICORICE STICK AND MAKE A TREE
YES, THERE'S NO RHYME OR REASON
I WAS SIMPLY MADE THIS WAY
WHAT'S STRANGE TO YOU IS NATURAL TO ME

IT'S SIMPLY SECOND NATURE TO PAINT OUTSIDE THE LINES
IT MERELY IS THE WAY THAT I WAS BORN
YOU SEE I'VE BEEN SELECTED
TO CREATE THE UNEXPECTED
AND MAKE EACH DAY FEEL JUST LIKE CHRISTMAS MORN

PICASSO TOOK A TORSO
AND TURNED IT ON ITS HEAD
IT ISN'T RIGHT OR WRONG, IT'S WHAT HE FELT
AND DALI, EVEN MORE SO
WOULD POSITIVELY DREAD
EXPLAINING WHY HIS HANDS OF TIME SHOULD MELT

AND ME, I TAKE SWEET HONEY
AND MAKE A TASTEFUL ROSE
WHAT CAN I SAY, IT'S SIMPLY WHAT I DO
SOME MEN MAKE POTS OF MONEY,
THEY'RE HAPPY, I SUPPOSE
BUT, BE GRATEFUL THAT FOR JUST A LUCKY FEW...

...IT'S SIMPLY SECOND NATURE TO DREAM
OF SOMETHING NEW
THE MIND IS SUCH A WONDER TO EXPLORE
AND THOUGH SOME NIGHTS I DREAD
ALL THE VOICES IN MY HEAD
I'D RATHER BE THIS WAY THEN BE A BORE!

IT'S SIMPLY SECOND NATURE TO MAKE AN EVENING SING
TO WAKE ON FIRE AND TRY TO SCULPT EACH DAY
IT'S NO BLESSING, IT'S A CURSE

WAIT, NO, STRIKE THAT AND REVERSE
I WOULDN'T HAVE IT ANY OTHER WAY

The sets for the show in London were spectacular, and once the reviews came out, let's just say the audience seemed to leave the theater humming the sets. When it came time for the Olivier Awards (the West End's Tonys) Scott and I were not just overlooked, they actually nominated the pit orchestra for a revival of *Merrily We Roll Along* in what would have been our slot.

When the show came to Broadway in 2013, Sam chose not to direct. More songs from the film were included to make the audience happy. But, after the huge expense of the scenery in London, the misbegotten decision to save money and have the audience simply use their "pure imagination" to see the sets proved disastrous, and we limped along before closing after only nine months.

It seemed to Scott and me that we would be paying for the success of *Hairspray* for a long, long time.

32

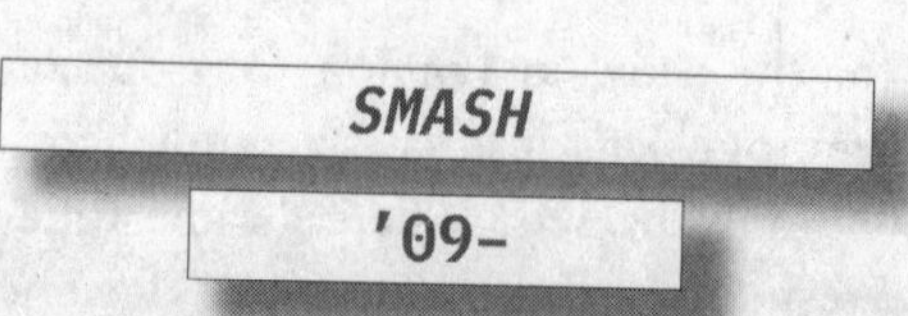

SMASH

'09–

Scott and I were watching TV at our weekend home in the country (good God, that sounds awfully posh) when producers Craig Zadan and Neil Meron called.

I first worked with Craig in 1979, when I was only nineteen. He asked me to be musical director for songwriter/performer Peter Allen, with whom he was creating an autobiographical Broadway concert called *Up in One*. Since then, Craig and his eventual business partner, Neil, have constantly run in and out of our lives. They produced our movie-musical version of *Hairspray*, as well as Rob Reiner's *The Bucket List*, which I scored (and was also my biggest payday, hence the country house).

Now Craig and Neil were on the phone saying, "We're sitting here with Bob Greenblatt and Steven Spielberg and were wondering if you'd be interested in working on a television show about people writing a Broadway musical? We'd like you guys to write the musical that the characters on the TV show are writing, and we hope that every year, a new musical is written and then actually put on Broadway. Are you interested?"

Were we interested? "Are you insane? Of course we are!"

And thus began the saga of *Smash*, a TV show about the trials and tribulations of creating a Broadway musical, with Steven Spielberg co-producing. Finally—a more legit claim to "working with Spielberg" than our piano/clarinet duet on "Hanukkah, O Hanukkah" at Marty Short's Christmas bash.

When that call came in, Bob Greenblatt was head of Showtime. But shortly after we started work, he and the project both moved to NBC. So, our show had to become less adult and, unfortunately, more like a prime-time soap opera.

After playwright Theresa Rebeck signed on, the team congregated at Spielberg's office in Los Angeles. Finally, all in the same room together, we tried to pinpoint what the first year's musical would be. Theresa suggested a "Three Musketeers"-era kind of show, but then Scott said, "How about a musical about Marilyn Monroe? That way, everyone tuning in would be familiar with who the musical is about, which would help. And her life has so many different chapters that relate to everything about showbusiness, being a woman in show business, and just being a woman on Earth. We could write things about Marilyn that would also mirror what's happening with the characters on the show."

Well, for the first *and last* time on *Smash*, everyone quickly agreed it was a great idea. There had already been a failed Marilyn musical on Broadway in the '80s, but we thought that fact could be used as fodder for the characters on the show, letting them know what they were up against. And so off we went.

After carving out the main characters with Theresa, she delivered her script for the pilot. It was very good, but Scott and I were surprised and disappointed that it said "Created by Theresa Rebeck" on the front page. Since we had been so involved with the choices, we felt our input merited us being included on the "Created by" credit. But we were told by everyone—our co-producers, agents, lawyers, and NBC—that there was no fighting City Hall. Theresa wouldn't budge on having *that* title, by herself, and we needed to get over it. Which we did, because we had to continue collaborating with Theresa, and look her in the eye without resentment.

The pilot script called for three original songs, so Scott and I got to work. He was fascinated that Marilyn was so well-read, and a devotee of William Butler Yeats' poetry, so we took his poem "Never Give All the Heart" and turned it into a song.

Here is Yeats' poem:

Never give all the heart, for love
Will hardly seem worth thinking of
To passionate women if it seem
Certain, and they never dream
That it fades out from kiss to kiss;
For everything that's lovely is
But a brief, dreamy, kind delight.
O never give the heart outright,
For they, for all smooth lips can say,
Have given their hearts up to the play.
And who could play it well enough
If deaf and dumb and blind with love?
He that made this knows all the cost,
For he gave all his heart and lost.

And here are our lyrics:

AS A GIRL, I LIVED IN A MILLION HOMES
SO I ALWAYS WOULD KEEP TO MYSELF
AND MY LESSONS WERE LEARNED
FROM THE STORIES AND POEMS
I WOULD STEAL FROM A LIBRARY SHELF

YES, THE BOOKS LIKE THE ROOMS WEREN'T MINE TO KEEP
BUT THE WORDS WEREN'T LEFT BEHIND
AND I THINK OF THEM ALL NOW WHEN I CAN'T SLEEP
AND A POET WHO READ MY MIND...

AS THE WISE MAN ONCE WROTE
"NEVER GIVE ALL THE HEART"
WELL, IT'S EASY TO SEE
HE WAS WRITING FOR ME
I JUST WISH I COULD PLAY THAT PART

YES, HE SCRIBBLED THAT LOVE ISN'T WORTH THINKING OF
THAT IT FADES OUT FROM KISS TO KISS
IF I JUST LEARNED THOSE LINES
WELL, JUST THINK OF THE MISERY I'D MISS

AS THE IRISH MAN SAID
DON'T PUT YOUR HEART UP TO PLAY
WHEN HE WARNED OF THE COST
AND THE HEART THAT HE LOST
MISTER YEATS REALLY PAVED THE WAY

FOR THE MEN THAT I'VE KNOWN
WELL, THEY'VE CLEARLY SHOWN
THEY'VE BEEN READING HIM FROM THE START
'CAUSE WHEN IT COMES TO ME
WELL, THEIR KISSES COME FREE
BUT THEY NEVER GIVE ALL THE HEART

YES, EACH TIME THAT I FALL
THEY NEVER GIVE ALL THE HEART

I think this is a good example of taking a poem from 1904 and turning it into a mid-century torch song that Judy Garland would have broken your heart with.

The next song for the pilot was a production number. Scott and I were salivating to create numbers for *Smash* in the classic style of Marilyn's films, staged by the visionary Jack Cole, who made them the height of sophisticated sex. We decided to musicalize an imagined moment from Marilyn's life, meeting fiancé Joe DiMaggio's New York Yankees teammates, for the song "The National Pastime." The title pertains to both baseball and sex, and the song became a whole ballgame of double entendres, which choreographer Josh Bergasse pushed into extra innings.

Our third song for the Marilyn musical (eventually titled, by Scott, *Bombshell*), like many others we wrote, also spoke to the emotions of the characters on *Smash*. When we delivered "Let Me Be Your Star," Bob Greenblatt said the song was good, but the lyrics were too specific to Marilyn.

He said, "Think of how 'Don't Rain on My Parade' from *Funny Girl* perfectly suits the emotions and intent of that moment in the plot. But other than when Fanny sings, 'Hey Mr. Arnstein, here I am,' there's not a single lyric that is specifically about Fanny or Nick's life, or even the time period it's taking place in."

With that very easy-to-grasp note (and if only *all* notes from executives were as easily understood and gently delivered as Bob Greenblatt's), we sat down to rewrite the lyric. Our new version, with only one fleeting mention of "Norma Jean," was met with bravos from the creative team, and we now had our three songs for the pilot.

It was our great good fortune to have Kat McPhee and Megan Hilty cast as the two ingénues, very different types of character who are both desperately hoping to land the lead role of Marilyn in *Bombshell*. For the next two years, I would email Megan or Kat a demo of me singing their next song; they would have a day to learn it (while filming!), then come downtown and sing it at our home studio in Chelsea.

But for the pilot, things were a tad more relaxed, and on "Let Me Be Your Star," we cut the vocals at the Power Station, a renowned recording studio in Midtown Manhattan. That vocal session was where we felt something special was happening. Both ladies have outrageously huge ranges, not just in octaves but also emotionally.

The moment they sing even one syllable, you zoom right into the emotion behind the word. To have them sing our song as a duet, work out the harmonies of the last verse, and then experience the way they held the last note and perfectly synced their vibratos, was magic.

Pilot director Michael Mayer really outdid himself filming that song. NBC held a premiere at the Museum of Modern Art, and the show played great. When Megan and Kat sang "Let Me Be Your Star" in the last four minutes, you could feel the audience on the edge of their seats. And on the final chord, when the screen cut to black and the word *Smash* appeared, people went wild.

Just a few nights later, watching it in real time on our TV, Scott and I were amazed to think that it was being broadcast to millions of people. The pilot was so well-made, we thought we were in for the ride of our lives.

Which we were—it just wasn't the ride we had hoped for.

Almost right away, as new episodes were written, Scott and I were perplexed that no one wanted any of our input on what happens behind the scenes during the making of a musical. We were quite literally forbidden from entering the writers' room. Scott and I had so much experience that could inform the plot and character arcs, but within a ten-foot radius of the writer's room, we were personae non gratae.

No matter what was going on behind the scenes, however, we had to write at least one song per episode. Fortunately, we learned to write well under that time constraint. Usually it takes us days just to get in the room together, and then there's a day or two of us just staring at each other, chanting "Paralyzed with fear! Paralyzed with fear!" over and over, until one of us says a phrase that might indicate what the song could be about. And then the other says something back, and thus begins a game of phrase association that delivers us from our state of catatonic terror.

Scott's desk is covered by butcher's paper, as if he splits his time writing and wrapping brisket. (He likes the broad space for jotting down thoughts and ideas.) During *Hairspray*, I was the more traditional yellow-legal-pad kind of guy. Eventually I moved on to my laptop, but I wish that I hadn't. We have so much archival material from *Hairspray* because I didn't throw out any legal pads. But on the laptop, I would not always save copies, and many of the first, second, and third drafts of songs were lost forever. It's a shame not to have that trail to look back on—especially when writing a memoir.

During season one of *Smash*, I would supply a track of the accompaniment for the song the performers would sing at the table read. Sometimes the actors did not yet know the songs, so they would just play my demos, with my "not very easy to listen to for any length of time" voice. We started getting notes that the songs were too long and were frustrated over the reaction to how they worked at a table read. It seemed no one could picture how differently they would play when performed by the brilliant cast within the actual scenes and staging.

And have I mentioned how many chefs were in the kitchen cooking *Smash*? There were Scott and me, Theresa, Michael Mayer or the director of that week's episode, plus Craig and Neil, Bob Greenblatt, Steven Spielberg, and Bob and Steven's legion of NBC and DreamWorks executives. These executives all seemed like very nice people and, I'm sure, did a wonderful job on traditional dramas and comedies, but none of them had any history with musicals. So a lot of time was spent trying to explain how a song could work as both inner and outer monologues for the characters. It was like inching through the Everglades every single day.

The powers-that-be were also becoming concerned that our songs were staying too true to the Marilyn era. The original thought was that cover versions of popular songs would balance things out stylistically. But I sensed my musical style was being perceived as part of the reason ratings, which were so phenomenal for the pilot, were dropping off.

My ego prefers to think it was the ridiculous plot lines.

It was a nightmare. The show went from the universal acclaim of the pilot to something that attracted two different factions of viewers: one that was loving it, and another that was "hate watching." In fact, the very term "hate watching" was coined by a *New Yorker* magazine critic in reaction to *Smash*.

Luckily, our songs were never the butt of online jokes the way that Debra Messing's scarves, or her husband's endless making of salads, or the schizophrenic writing for some characters were. That split reaction taught me to stay away from the Internet. (Although one woman, Rachel Shukert, was writing recaps so hysterical that she would have been a wonderful addition to the writing staff.)

Another false note was that no matter what is happening during the creation of a real musical, there is always laughter in the rehearsal room—and none of that was put on screen. I thought calling the show a soap opera would have been a slur but was shocked when it was mentioned in a meeting to describe what we should be creating.

By the time we got to the end of season one, the mood on the show was very much like *Game of Thrones*: dark, bleak, and mired in carnage.

A few months later, Craig and Neil had Scott and me meet with Josh Safran, who was taking over as showrunner. We responded to his upbeat demeanor and liked his idea to create a rival musical, *Hit List*, as competition for *Bombshell*. That could be written by other young Broadway songwriters, which would give the show a contemporary sound that Scott and I couldn't deliver while writing a Marilyn Monroe musical.

Because we adored his work, we suggested Joe Iconis as one of those new writers. His "Broadway, Here I Come," featured on the season two premiere, is one of the most astonishing songs I've ever heard. Also brought on board were those whippersnappers Pasek and Paul, who wrote phenomenal theater songs that also sounded like they could be on the radio. (A decade later, Scott and I would stand next to them on the Emmys stage as the four of us shared an award for a number in *Only Murders in the Building* that would tip them into EGOT status.)

But in a twist we didn't see coming, the writers' room was still off-limits to us. History repeated: the plots for the show were too melodramatic, with the endearing actor Jeremy Jordan forced to hide his charm under a cloak of gloom and doom. Things just did not get better.[22]

When we started season two, Scott and I wondered what else we could possibly write for a Marilyn musical that we hadn't already covered. Yet it turned out we wrote some of our best songs that season, including one that doesn't just portray the feelings of Marilyn and Megan Hilty's character, Ivy Lynn, but also everyone on the show (both on- and off-screen). We took our own frustration, confusion, and anger and turned it into "They Just Keep Moving the Line." Scott and I wrote it over the phone, and I am proud to say it is one of the few songs we have co-written that bears a title I came up with. Who knew a sports analogy would ever come out of *my* brain?

I'm also proud of its internal rhymes. The title of the song at the end of each verse, paired with my music, meant we had to use every possible rhyme for "line." After making a list of those words, we figured out how they could come naturally at the end of phrases that communicated the song's emotion. And then, also due to the structure of the music, the first, third, and fifth lines of the verse had their own rhyme pattern, like a sonnet. These three words

---

22 I did get a wash of happiness when Bob Greenblatt was presented costume sketches for the number "Public Relations." When Bob suggested dressing Kat McPhee in yellow, the designer responded, "Yellow is not a good color for a woman on screen." To which Bob, a gay man who had obviously seen MGM's *The Band Wagon* countless times, replied, "Well, it worked for Cyd Charisse!" (Kat ended up wearing yellow)

would have to rhyme with each other while also flowing into the phrases that rhymed with "line."

Also, by this point in season two, I figured out that if I composed and recorded our songs with a whole bunch of key changes, they would be harder to edit down for broadcast. (Sneaky, you say? Why, thank you.) I'm very happy to say that this entire song remained in the episode, complete from beginning to end, with Megan Hilty, as usual, knocking it out of the park.

"THEY JUST KEEP MOVING THE LINE"

THE FIELD WAS BRIGHT WITH CLOVER, I SAW THE FINISH SIGN
I STARTED AS A ROVER AND THEN VICTORY WAS MINE
I THOUGHT THE RACE WAS OVER
BUT THEY JUST KEEP MOVING THE LINE

THEY CHEERED AT MY PERSISTENCE
BUT PRAYED FOR MY DECLINE
THE PATH OF LEAST RESISTANCE LED TO HOLLYWOOD AND VINE
I TRIED TO GO THE DISTANCE
BUT THEY JUST KEEP MOVING THE LINE

I JUMPED ALL OF THE HURDLES TO BREAK OUT OF THE PACK
I STARTED ON THE OUTSIDE AND THEN HIT THE INSIDE TRACK
I LEFT THE OTHER FILLIES BACK AT THE STARTING GATE
WAS READY, ON MY MARK, I GOT TO SET TO...HURRY UP AND WAIT

SO TALENT AND AMBITION WON ME A CHANCE TO SHINE
I ACED THE BIG AUDITION BUT IT'S RAININ' ON CLOUD NINE

CAN'T BEAT THE COMPETITION
'CAUSE THEY JUST KEEP MOVING THE LINE

I HANDLED EVERY CORNER, EACH BUMP ALONG
THE TRACK
AND WHEN I SAW THE RIBBON,
WELL THERE WAS NO TURNING BACK
I WON THE PHOTO FINISH, I POSED FOR ALL THE MEN
BUT BEFORE I GOT MY TROPHY, WELL, THE RACE BEGAN AGAIN

SO I MADE FRIENDS WITH REJECTION
I'VE STRAIGHTENED UP MY SPINE
I'LL CHANGE EACH IMPERFECTION
TILL IT'S TIME TO DRINK THE WINE
I'D TOAST TO RESURRECTION
BUT THEY JUST KEEP MOVING THE LINE
PLEASE GIVE ME SOME DIRECTION
'CAUSE THEY JUST KEEP MOVING THE LINE!

The show limped along, but there were bright spots, like Scott and me getting to write songs like "I Can't Let Go" for Jennifer Hudson. My advice to any songwriter is, "Have Jennifer Hudson sing everything you write," because she infuses each word with such deep emotion, and has the range and tone to make every note and phrase a miracle.

We even got to write a song for the other musical, *Hit List*. I hope Scott won't mind me saying that he just threw up his hands at this point, and I wrote the song "The Love I Meant to Say" on my own, which Jeremy Jordan sang with such heartbreaking emotion.

We got word while writing the final episodes of season two that *Smash* was ending. At that point, Scott and I were working on the West End production of our new musical version of *Charlie and the Chocolate Factory*. As viewers "hate watched" *Smash*, we wrote the show's final song, "Big Finish," at a rehearsal studio on the outskirts of London, in a tiny room right next to the toilets. What a perfect showbiz ending: writing "Big Finish" with both a figurative and literal stink in the air.

But, ah, the story of *Smash* would not end there. A few years later, as a benefit for the Actors' Fund at the Minskoff Theatre, the cast reassembled for a concert along with an orgasmically large orchestra. And for one night, Scott and I got to feel like Taylor Swift, because every note was met with a roar. It was incredibly exciting and moving, and as I tried to give a curtain speech thanking the music team, expressing how hard they work without bravos, I characteristically broke down and couldn't continue.

Yep, *Smash* brings out all the big emotions. But wait, there's more!

In April 2025, a Broadway version of *Smash*—with a book by Bob Martin and Rick Elice, directed by the multiple Tony-winning Susan Stroman, and starring Brooks Ashmanskas and Broadway's "Ivy" and "Karen," the amazing Robyn Hurder and Caroline Bowman—opened to a rave review in the *New York Times*. If God had my sense of humor, someone would have walked up to Scott and me at the opening night party and said, "We don't care *what* the *New York Times* says, we *hate* the show!"

But if you've read this far, you know for every *plotz* there is a *zetz*. In the grand tradition of *Smash*, there were many who loved the Broadway incarnation, but the hate-watchers only watched from afar and didn't buy tickets.

We had an omen things were not going to go our way when, one afternoon during a rehearsal at the theatre, the lighted letters of the "Bombshell" sign that started the show broke, and as they repaired them, the words "Bomb" and "Hell" took on a life of their own, flickering and taunting us all!

And after running only ten weeks, we closed that June.

Devastating. Heartbreaking. Showbiz.

33

MARY POPPINS RETURNS

'15–'18

In 2015, our representatives Richard Kraft and Joe Machota told Scott and I that Disney had just hired Rob Marshall and his husband/producing-partner John DeLuca to create a sequel to *Mary Poppins*. There had been talk of a sequel over the years, but this was real, a done deal, it was truly happening!

Serendipitously, about a year before this announcement, I had ventured into a vinyl shop that recently opened around the corner from my upstate home. What an absolute joy it was to flip through albums, reminiscent of the days when you could leisurely browse through a record store. I already had a large stack of records in my basket when I stumbled upon a true gem: the *Mary Poppins Original Cast Soundtrack*.

And it wasn't just any version—this was exactly like the original album, direct from my childhood, complete with a "gatefold" cover that opened like a magazine to reveal a cornucopia of fascinating information. As I would later learn, this kind of album cover was also a nifty tool for separating seeds from pot before rolling a joint (back when pot still came with seeds).

That day, I was with my music co-producer, Scott Riesett, and when we got back to my house, I followed the mantra of the current generation: "Pictures or it didn't happen." Scott filmed the moment I placed the needle on the album, and as the glorious opening notes sounded, I looked like a heroin addict who had just shot up. It transported me back to the years of joy I experienced as a child.

About a year later, a meeting was set up between Rob and John and me, while Scott was on vacation in Italy. Never mind the drubbing we had just received for daring to craft new songs for a different beloved character created by an iconic British writer, we were determined to get this gig. I was passionate at our lunch meeting, and upon returning home, remembered the video from the day I found the vinyl. I promptly emailed it to them, writing, "Can you not just see how the music courses through my veins? Please let Scott and me, with you guys, create a new chapter while also writing a love letter to the first film!"

The thought of someone else getting this job haunted me. I imagined moving to a desert island to escape the agony of witnessing ads, posters, and trailers for a *Mary Poppins* sequel that I hadn't gotten to write.

The anticipation during the selection process was almost unbearable. We spent months waiting, and when we learned we were among the finalists, the tension was excruciating—especially for anyone around me. I spent two weeks constantly refreshing my email, like Mark Zuckerberg in *The Social Network*.

Then the practically perfect news arrived—they had chosen us!

Scott and I immediately began collaborating with Rob and John, alongside the talented and warm-hearted screenwriter, David Magee, at an Upper East Side hotel suite booked by Disney. Their concept involved Michael Banks (the younger son in the original film) being a recent widower, struggling along with his children to cope. As we structured the movie, it became clear that although Mary Poppins ostensibly comes back down from the sky to care for Michael's children, it is really Michael himself, along with his sister Jane, whom she is still looking after.

Meticulously we built upon this foundation, crafting the story scene by scene. We determined where our songs would fit with each plot point. But even with my encyclopedic knowledge of *Mary Poppins,* it was Scott who brilliantly suggested that a moment in the original movie, when George Banks slams the tuppence young Michael wanted to use to feed the birds down on the bank table, that it was secretly invested, and should save the day in our sequel. I couldn't have been prouder of him, or more jealous that I hadn't thought of it myself.

(Unfortunately, a few months later, in a shocking repeat of what happened on *Smash,* we were left off the "Story by" credit. But as with *Smash,* there was no time to sulk. Actually, that's not true. I may have kept working but I sulked, I sulked!)

After those wonderful five weeks of hotel-suite story-construction, Scott and I embarked on the daunting task of composing songs for our new *Mary Poppins* movie. We were fully aware that whatever we created would inevitably be unfavorably compared to the timeless classics from the original film. As a card-carrying pessimist,

I accepted this fact, and we just tried to focus on achieving the emotional depth the story called for, rather than worrying if every measure contained an "earworm."

But the subject of earworms did come up with the initial song we wrote for Mary Poppins to sing to the children (which, we were reminded daily, would be "the first time Mary Poppins has sung in a movie since 1963"). We had written a lively late-'20s swing number entitled "Stuff and Nonsense" (demo sung by Megan Hilty), loving the idea that Mary would be up on the popular musical styles of the day.

Although we had a successful reading of the script with this song in it, Rob called us from England one day and said, "You know what, guys, we are filming tests for the underwater sequence the song is in, and whenever we say, 'It's time to film 'Stuff and Nonsense,' we find that we *say* the title but we don't *sing* it. Maybe you should go back to the drawing board with that in mind and come up with something that you can't *help* but sing when you say the title."

And so, back to the drawing board we went. After several attempts, we landed on the title "Can You Imagine That?" The phrase served a dual purpose, as Mary Poppins used it not only to express her trademark condescension but also to encourage the children to expand their imaginations and get back in touch with their lost sense of wonder.

After completing this new song, Scott had a stroke of genius when he said to me, "Before you send them the demo of you singing the song, you should also play it in the style of a film score, so they can hear how it could also become the main theme of the movie." So I figured out how to slow down this snappy tune and find something deeper, with the richer chords you would use in a film score. Happily, Rob and John DeLuca responded enthusiastically, and we had our song.

Two other songs we had to write for the film were both emotional challenges. The first ended up being titled "A Conversation."

Disney was repeatedly asking David Magee to quickly make Michael Banks more empathetic as he struggles to move past the grief of losing his wife. Being an extremely tasteful screenwriter, his scenes tried not to hit audiences over the head too hard, but those weren't satisfying the executives. Finally, Scott and I piped up and said, "Hey, it's a musical—let us write a song for that moment."

Music and songs allow characters to express feelings that might seem too on-the-nose in spoken dialogue. Lyrics can express things you would never say in a scene, because in a song, you don't have to hide the subtext. Quite the opposite, in fact: a song should express the ideas and emotions lying just beneath the surface of everyday human interactions.

When we sat down to write Michael Banks' song, we recalled how our friend Martin Short told us that after losing his wonderful wife, Nancy, to cancer, he found great comfort in continuing to converse with her, discussing everything going on in his life. He also revealed that at times, he would simply look up and say, "Nan…where'd you go?" It was a heart-wrenching story, and now we were tasked with composing a song to express exactly that kind of moment. And since no one understands that "everything's showbiz" more than Marty, we had the *chutzpah* to ask his blessing to draw from his real-life experience.

He responded, "Fellows, of course, I'd be honored. As would Nancy."

Here are our lyrics:

"A CONVERSATION"

WE HAVEN'T SPOKEN IN SO LONG, DEAR
THIS YEAR HAS GONE BY IN A BLUR
TODAY SEEMS EVERYTHING'S GONE WRONG HERE
I'M LOOKING FOR THE WAY THINGS WERE
I KNOW YOU'D LAUGH AND CALL ME TRAGIC
FOR EVERYTHING'S IN DISARRAY
THESE ROOMS WERE ALWAYS FULL OF MAGIC

THAT'S VANISHED...SINCE YOU WENT AWAY

THIS HOUSE IS CROWDED NOW WITH QUESTIONS
YOUR JOHN'S A WALKING QUESTIONNAIRE
AND I COULD SURELY USE A FEW SUGGESTIONS
ON HOW TO BRUSH OUR DAUGHTER'S HAIR
WHEN GEORGIE NEEDED EXPLANATIONS
YOU ALWAYS KNEW JUST WHAT TO SAY
AND I MISS OUR FAMILY CONVERSATIONS
IT'S SILENT, SINCE YOU WENT AWAY

WINTER HAS GONE
BUT NOT FROM THIS ROOM
SNOW'S LEFT THE LANE
BUT THE CHERRY TREES FORGOT TO BLOOM...

I'LL CARRY ON THE WAY YOU TOLD ME
I SAY THAT LIKE I HAVE A CHOICE
AND THOUGH YOU ARE NOT HERE TO HOLD ME
IN THE ECHOES I CAN HEAR YOUR VOICE
BUT STILL ONE QUESTION FILLS MY DAY, DEAR
THE ANSWER I MOST LONG TO KNOW
EACH MOMENT SINCE YOU WENT AWAY, DEAR
MY QUESTION, KATE, IS...WHERE'D YOU GO?

In a later scene, after Michael Banks' three young children have a shared nightmare, the youngest boy finally expresses what has gone unsaid until then: "I miss Mother." At that moment, Mary Poppins realizes she must find a way to sing about loss in a way that a child can understand and take comfort from.

Something I never knew until working on this sequel was that author P.L. Travers wrote eight *Mary Poppins* books. In one of them, she takes the kids to visit her uncle, who happens to be the Man in the Moon. Once they're up there, he gives the kids little knick-knacks they have lost over the years, saying, "Oh, yes, I keep everything people lose over here, on the dark side of the moon." Pamela Travers was talking about the Dark Side of the Moon long before Pink Floyd!

Scott said, "Let's use the essence of that story as a way for Mary to sing about loss in a way that might comfort the children." And that's how "The Place Where Lost Things Go" was born. I croaked it out at our home studio, we sent it in to Rob and Disney, and—no one suggested going back to the drawing board! That was a nice and rare circumstance.

"THE PLACE WHERE LOST THINGS GO"

DO YOU EVER LIE AWAKE AT NIGHT?
JUST BETWEEN THE DARK AND THE MORNING LIGHT
SEARCHING FOR THE THINGS YOU USED TO KNOW
LOOKING FOR THE PLACE WHERE THE LOST THINGS GO

DO YOU EVER DREAM OR REMINISCE?
WONDERING WHERE TO FIND WHAT YOU TRULY MISS
WELL, MAYBE ALL THOSE THINGS THAT YOU LOVE SO
ARE WAITING IN THE PLACE WHERE THE LOST THINGS GO

MEMORIES YOU'VE SHARED, GONE FOR GOOD YOU FEARED
THEY'RE ALL AROUND YOU STILL
THOUGH THEY'VE...DISAPPEARED
NOTHING'S REALLY LEFT OR LOST WITHOUT A TRACE
NOTHING'S GONE FOREVER, ONLY OUT OF PLACE

SO MAYBE NOW THE DISH AND MY BEST SPOON
ARE PLAYING HIDE AND SEEK JUST BEHIND THE MOON
WAITING THERE UNTIL IT'S TIME TO SHOW
SPRING IS LIKE THAT NOW, FAR BENEATH THE SNOW
HIDING IN THE PLACE WHERE THE LOST THINGS GO

TIME TO CLOSE YOUR EYES

SO SLEEP CAN COME AROUND
FOR WHEN YOU DREAM YOU'LL FIND
ALL THAT'S LOST IS FOUND
MAYBE ON THE MOON, OR MAYBE SOMEWHERE NEW
MAYBE ALL YOU'RE MISSING LIVES INSIDE OF YOU

SO WHEN YOU NEED HER TOUCH AND LOVING GAZE
"GONE BUT NOT FORGOTTEN" IS THE PERFECT PHRASE
SMILING FROM A STAR THAT SHE MAKES GLOW
TRUST SHE'S ALWAYS THERE, WATCHING AS YOU GROW
FIND HER IN THE PLACE WHERE THE LOST THINGS GO

And since it was in a similar spot in our movie, for the orchestral tag that finishes the song after the final lyric, I adapted Irwin Kostal's gorgeous chords from the end of "Feed the Birds" in the first film. A tip of the hat to the master.

After the film was released, Scott and I heard from strangers all around the world, telling us how this song helped them deal with losses they were going through. There is no greater gift a songwriter can receive than messages such as those.

The task of creating new songs that would be compared to classics Robert and Richard Sherman penned for the original film was daunting enough. But our anxiety reached new heights when Rob, John, and producer Marc Platt informed us their choice for the male lead was Lin-Manuel Miranda.

Lin-Manuel Miranda, the genius who had just completed his run in his groundbreaking musical *Hamilton* and was crafting songs for Disney's *Moana*. (And, I must add, is one of the kindest and most loyal individuals you'll ever encounter.) With both the Sherman Brothers and Lin-Manuel to measure up to, I was convinced our songs would get picked apart. Each day, I approached the piano with the weight of that trepidation, feeling as though I had to hoist my arms above my head just to reach the keys.

It was wonderful that Lin-Manuel and Emily Blunt were both in New York and could come over to try on new songs. Our very first composition for the movie was for Lin-Manuel's character, Jack—a song called "(Underneath the) Lovely London Sky."

For this song, Scott and I drew inspiration from the delightful tunes of Flanagan and Allen, a British duo from the 1920s and '30s who wrote charming songs celebrating the common man. While everyone seemed to love this song when we handed it in, things took a turn when we arrived in England and set up at the legendary Shepperton Studios to continue working. As Rob and John began staging numbers, they and Marc Platt gently told us that "(Underneath the) Lovely London Sky" might not be "delivering" Lin-Manuel Miranda in the way that audiences would expect.

So, Scott and I wrote new opening songs, one after another. Lin-Manuel frequently dropped in from the rehearsal room to sing new demos in our writing studio just down the hall. Each song had charm, but the refrain from the team was always a variation on Bette Midler's mantra, "What else ya got?"

Our last attempt drew inspiration from the English music hall song "Any Old Iron," made famous by Stanley Holloway, who portrayed Eliza Doolittle's father in *My Fair Lady*. It was an exuberant number meant to be performed as Lin bicycled around London, featuring rapid-fire lyrics in his signature style while staying true to the period.

As we wrapped up the song, Emily Blunt happened to pass our music room and stuck her head in to inquire, "What's that?"

We explained it was our latest option for Lin-Manuel's opening number. She walked in, took a seat, and requested to hear it. I delivered a spirited rendition of our newly crafted song as Emily smiled, giving away nothing. What an actress!

When I finished singing, she said something like, "Well done." And then she returned to the rehearsal hall where she went straight up to Rob and John and said, "The movie I signed up for started with '(Underneath the) Lovely London Sky.' I really must encourage you to put it back."

Thanks to Emily, the decision was made to reinstate our first, preferred song—just like when Michelle Pfeiffer lobbied for "The Legend of Miss Baltimore Crabs."

Another cherished memory is the day Meryl Streep began rehearsing in the room next door with our musical director, Paul Gemignani. We could hear her through the walls practicing "Turning Turtle," the song her character, Topsy Turvy, sings. Being Meryl Streep, she was exceptional from the first rendition but continued to rehearse with Paul, over and over.

Eventually, I couldn't resist any longer. I grabbed Scott, then we knocked on the door and entered the room. I said, "I just wanted to express how incredibly moving it is to hear someone of your caliber working so tirelessly."

And her response epitomizes show business. She said, "Well, guys, fear can be a powerful motivator."

But it also makes you think, *If Meryl Streep is afraid, then I should be terrified*!

The next exhilarating phase involved pre-recording the songs at London's Air Studios, with Paul Gemignani conducting while the stars performed live alongside the orchestra. Typically in film musicals, the actors pre-record their songs due to the endless number of takes that are shot. This requires them to time-travel with their preparation and envision how they'll perform these songs during the actual filming. However, there *are* instances when performers sing live during filming, such as Michael Banks' first song in the movie, "A Conversation."

A curious and unique thing occurred as we prepared for the pre-recording sessions. Rob Marshall asked me to also write score cues for a few spots in the movie.

"Um, Rob," I sheepishly asked, "how can I write score for scenes that haven't been filmed yet? Everything a composer writes is in direct response to what's on screen, whether overtly or subliminally."

But Rob just said, "I like to have it on set for inspiration, and I know you can do it."

I went back to New York for the Christmas vacation absolutely flummoxed. I couldn't believe, after so many years of being chastised for creeping over budget on my orchestral sessions, that a director was now asking me to record many minutes of music that could never actually be used in the movie.

But Rob gets what he wants, and the studio was willing to pay for it, so I sat down at my music station. I spoke the screenplay for three scenes as if it were a radio play, directly into my computer, saying the stage directions as well as the dialogue. I tried to use my own sense of drama and timing to evoke how the scenes *could* go when I had film in front of me in nine months' time.

When I was happy with my "performance," I wrote music for the scene where the kids chase a kite that has come to life. Just as the winds become treacherous, Mary Poppins appears from a cloud and floats down to Earth. When we recorded, the orchestra sounded fantastic, the conductor matched the tempos of my demos as well as he could, and when we finished, I thought, *Well, I cannot believe we just spent all that time and money on music that will never, ever make its way into the movie*!

Cut to: It's all in the movie, every second of it. It only needed a few additions or subtractions here and there, but through Rob's genius, and I suppose my own natural instincts, it all fit. I never would have believed it if you had told me beforehand.

Scott and I were back in the United States when they filmed the movie, so we could only tune in via Skype as Dick Van Dyke and Angela Lansbury recorded their songs. Despite the choppy connection and the fact we were joining in the middle of the night from New York, there they were: Dick Van Dyke and Angela Lansbury, singing our songs. Can you imagine *that*?

Another cue we recorded "just" for Rob's inspiration was the film score version—that Scott encouraged me to create—of "Can

You Imagine That?" Jeff Atmajian orchestrated my piano performance exquisitely, and Rob played that recording on set, I am told, ad nauseum. Post-production was done back in New York, right down the street from my apartment, and one day Rob told me to come over. He and editor Wyatt Smith showed me the first trailer for *Mary Poppins Returns*, which made extensive use of the recording we had made of the main theme.

I was seeing the imagery for the first time and, just as the recording peaks, the trailer cut to the incredible shot of Mary Poppins floating out of a cloud. With my dream coming true in such spectacular fashion right in front of my eyes, I started sobbing so hard that someone in the next room might have thought Rob and Wyatt were sacrificing a cow.

All the screenings of the film for friends and family were very well received. It really seemed like we had accomplished what we set out to do, which was to tell a new story with humor and emotion while also creating an unabashed love letter to the first film and its creators, most especially the Sherman Brothers. I love adapting existing songs in my scores, and to work with Rob to find just the right spots to quote songs from the first film in the underscore was a thrilling, gratifying, and emotional experience.

But.

When Disney announced the film, for some reason beyond me they seemed unwilling to call it a "sequel," as if it were a dirty word. So, the world took that to mean we were filming a remake. A remake of *Mary Poppins*, which would, of course, have been insane. But that impression created a lot of naysayers before a frame of film was shot or a single song was written.

As we started work on the movie, I knew that anyone expecting to hear "A Spoonful of Sugar" would be let down. In that prediction, I was not let down! But the way Scott and I learned some critics were lukewarm to our songs was when, yet again, a friend texted us the morning the movie opened, starting with, you guessed it, "I don't care WHAT the *New York Times* says..."

So yes, on my all-time dream project, I received some critical lashings. But also two Oscar nominations! Some haters said "meh"—a word I despise over any other—but at a dinner the music branch of the Academy held for all the nominees, I got to sing "The Place Where Lost Things Go" and then play "Feed the Birds" as Richard Sherman himself sang it.

Wow.

Being part of *Mary Poppins Returns* brought with it bipolar highs and lows. We got so many beautiful, emotional responses from folks who went in *without* their arms crossed, especially about "The Place Where Lost Things Go." I think the phrase most heard in theaters playing our movie was, "Mommy, why are all the adults crying?"

Mary Poppins Returns was about our collective memories of the past and love for the first film, and it touched a lot of people. It didn't become the billion-dollar phenomenon Disney wanted—although it *was* a multi-million-dollar phenomenon. But when all was said and done, I am sad to admit it has complicated the pure feelings I held for decades about my beloved *Mary Poppins*. Even now, I sometimes change the channel when one of those timeless songs comes on the radio, due to feeling I dropped the ball, *despite* the Oscar nods.

And the Golden Globe nomination!

And the BAFTA nomination!

In fact, I got nominated for every award you could get nominated for. It's so schizophrenic, and I still battle with those conflicting emotions. But, as the title and lyrics for our final song in the film state, "There's Nowhere to Go But Up."

I just wish I could take my own advice.

34

SOME LIKE IT HOT

'16–

Scott and I now knew far too well about the pressure that accompanies musicalizing beloved books and films featuring iconic performances. So, you'd think we would have said "*No way*!" when they came to us to create a new musical of *Some Like It Hot*.

Talk about a landmine. It's a beloved Billy Wilder movie, featuring iconic performances by Tony Curtis, Jack Lemmon, Marilyn Monroe, and Joe E. Brown, who delivers one of the great last lines in movie history: "Well, nobody's perfect."

And if that wasn't enough, it had already been musicalized in the 1970s with *Sugar,* by a creative team of musical theater giants: composer Jule Styne and lyricist Bob Merrill; playwright Michael Stewart, and director Gower Champion, with a Tony-nominated performance by Robert Morse.

Musicalizing *Charlie and the Chocolate Factory, Mary Poppins Returns,* and now *Some Like It Hot*. What do they say about the definition of insanity being doing the same thing over and over, expecting different results?

Nevertheless, producers Craig Zadan and Neil Meron called to say they had secured the rights to musicalize *Some Like It Hot* and wanted us to write the score. Scott and I had just finished working with them on *Smash,* writing songs in the style of Marilyn Monroe films, including "Let's Be Bad," conceived as a number for that very movie.

Still, the answer was no. "Theatrical quicksand," we said.

But then they said, "We were thinking the character 'Sugar' should be Black. That would subvert any expectation that both the actress and the show will just replicate the movie."

We loved the idea of our Sugar being more like Billie Holiday or Ella Fitzgerald, who both traveled with bands just as Sugar does in the story. She could also have a similar trajectory to Lena Horne, who went to Hollywood and helped break the color barrier. And maybe the Jack Lemmon character (Jerry/Daphne) could go a step further than in the movie, exploring more modern ideas about gender identity.

These two concepts really helped Scott and I have a brand-new perspective on, yet again, tackling an iconic project. And so... we said yes!

Very quickly, Casey Nicholaw, the ebullient director/choreographer of one Broadway hit after another, came aboard. In another inspired bit of behind-the-scenes casting, Matthew López was brought on to write the book. He was in the midst of putting up his groundbreaking epic *The Inheritance*, and was the perfect person to make sure anything in the movie that might offend modern sensitivities would be updated.

And when Amber Ruffin joined the production as Matthew's co-writer, the creative team became properly diverse, with Scott and me taking on the "old white guys" positions.

I'm happy that as the "old white guys" we were never told we couldn't write for characters who aren't also old white guys, because we wouldn't have been able to write the two songs I am most proud of in the score.

For "Sugar", we wrote lyrics explaining how a young Black girl from the south held on to the unlikely dream of becoming a movie-star.

"AT THE OLD MAJESTIC NICKEL MATINEE"

IN A SMALL TOWN IN GEORGIA, YOU REALLY HAD
TO SEARCH
FOR SOMETHING ENTERTAINING TO SEE
SO THE BEST SHOW IN TOWN
WAS EVERY SUNDAY DOWN IN CHURCH
SURROUNDED BY GOOD PEOPLE WHO LOOKED LIKE ME

OH BUT THEN ONE DAY, A PICTURE PALACE OPENED
FOR A NICKEL YOU COULD DREAM THERE DAY AND NIGHT
AH, BUT THOSE WHO LOOKED LIKE ME
COULD ONLY USE THE BALCONY
LIKE THE MOVIES
LIFE COULD BE THAT BLACK AND WHITE...

BUT UP THERE ON THE SCREEN THERE WAS ROMANCE
AND THE MAKE BELIEVE WOULD CARRY ME AWAY
BECAUSE NO ONE I'D EVER SEEN
WERE LIKE THE STARS UP ON THE SCREEN
AT THE OLD MAJESTIC NICKEL MATINEE

IN THOSE MOVIES I SAW, THINGS LOOKED DIFFERENT
SOMEONE ELSE'S WORLD WAS UP THERE ON DISPLAY
FOR NOT ONE VAMP OR WALL STREET WIFE
HELD UP A MIRROR TO MY LIFE
AT THE OLD MAJESTIC NICKEL MATINEE

SO I WOULD PRETEND THAT IT WAS ME UP THERE
BUT WITH MARY PICKFORD PLAYING MY MAID
THAT I WAS THE STAR LIVING LIFE WITHOUT A CARE
WHO NEVER WAS ALONE OR FELT AFRAID

WE COULD NEVER SIT WITH THOSE WHO SAT BELOW US
KEPT OUT OF SIGHT, BUT HECK, IT CAUSED ME NO DISMAY
BESIDES, I WASN'T THINKING OF 'EM,

I WOULD RATHER BE ABOVE 'EM
AT THE OLD MAJESTIC NICKEL MATINEE

A HANDFUL OF NICKELS, WAS ALL I EVER HAD
BUT I BELIEVED THAT SOMETHING HAD TO CHANGE

SO, UP THERE ON THE SCREEN, I DECIDED
THAT A YOUNG GIRL JUST LIKE ME WOULD LOOK ONE DAY
AND DRAPED IN DIAMONDS AND FUR,
SHE WOULD SEE SOMEONE JUST LIKE HER
AND HER HOPES AND DREAMS WOULD NEVER HAVE TO STAY
AT THE OLD MAJESTIC NICKEL MATINEE

And for "Jerry", a man of color who begins to realize that disguising himself as "Daphne" was actually opening the door to a huge self-discovery, we wrote this song:

"YOU COULDA KNOCKED ME OVER WITH A FEATHER"

TONIGHT IN MEXICO, JOE, I FELT SOMETHING CLICK
YES, I GOT TURNED AROUND
WHILE ALL THE OTHER GIRLS GOT SICK
I CROSSED THE BORDER, JOE
AND THANK YOU FOR THE SHOVE
BECAUSE TONIGHT I REALIZED DAPHNE
IS MY ONE TRUE LOVE

AND YOU COULDA KNOCKED ME OVER WITH A FEATHER
YOU COULDA KNOCKED THIS TRAIN OFF ITS TRACK
FOR WEEKS I'VE HAD A FUNNY FEELING
THAT SOMETHING WAS REVEALING
NOW THIS GENIE'S OUT THE BOTTLE
AND SHE AIN'T GOIN' BACK!

YES, I HAVE TRIED TO LOVE MANY LADIES
BACK WHEN I SANG IN A MUCH LOWER KEY

NOW YOU COULD KNOCK ME OVER WITH A FEATHER,
CAUSE JOE
THE LADY THAT I'M LOVIN' IS ME

I LOVE TO BE BELLE OF THE BALL
I LOVE THE SHAPE OF THIS LEG!
SO TAILS AND TUXES, FARE THEE WELL
BECAUSE YOU CAN'T UNDO A FALL
YOU CAN'T UNSCRAMBLE AN EGG
AND NOW THAT IT HAS CHIMED
THERE'S NO UN-RINGING THIS BELL!

YOU COULDA KNOCKED ME OVER WITH A FEATHER
YOU COULDA STOLE THE ICE FROM A CUBE
FOR WEEKS I'VE WRESTLED THE SUSPICION
THAT'S COME TO A FRUITION
NOW YOU'LL NEVER GET THE TOOTHPASTE BACK
IN THE TUBE

I HOPE THE GIRLS I KNEW WILL FORGIVE ME
CAUSE TILL I WOKE UP I JUST COULDN'T SEE
BUT NOW YOU COULD KNOCK ME OVER WITH A FEATHER
CAUSE THE LADY THAT I'M LOVIN' IS ME
YES, THE LADY THAT I'M LOVIN' IS...

YOU ALWAYS LOVED THE WAY THAT I SLAPPED THAT BASS
AND NOW A SPOTLIGHT'S SHINING ON ME
BACK HOME IN 'ILLINOIS'
I DANCED LIKE ALL THE BOYS
BUT NOW I'M RIDIN' HIGH
MY VOICE AND HEELS HAVE HIT THE SKY!

JERRY'S ALWAYS WALKED BEHIND, AND ONLY SURVIVED
BUT NOW I'M LEADING THE PARADE CAUSE DAPHNE'S
ARRIVED
THE DIE IS CAST, IT'S A FAIT ACCOMPLI

NO MORE LIVING IN THE PAST
CAUSE DAPHNE IS FREE! DAPHNE IS FREE!

NO, I COULDN'T'VE STAYED IN FLATS IF I TRIED
I KNOW YOU'RE FINDING IT CONFUSING
THIS SONG THAT I AM CHOOSING
BUT JOE, IT'S TIME TO BLOW YOUR HORN
TO "HERE COMES THE BRIDE"

SO PLEASE BELIEVE ME WHEN I SAY WE'RE STILL PARTNERS
BUT NOW INSTEAD OF JUST A DUO...WE'RE THREE
I SEE THAT I COULD KNOCK YOU OVER WITH A FEATHER
BUT I KNOW THAT DAPHNE IS THE BEST PART OF ME
OH, YEAH! DAPHNE IS WHO I LOVE TO BE!

Still, everyone, especially our producers, was aware that every show was now being put under the microscope. Criticism around casting and representation could sink a show before it even got seen. Our producers brought in trans and non-binary folks from GLAAD to look over all the drafts of the book and lyrics to help us walk that tightrope of humor and responsibility. As Scott and I had lived our entire adult lives in and around trans and non-binary people, even before those terms entered the modern lexicon—loving dear friends like Holly Woodlawn, Alexis Del Lago, and Murray Hill, who had all embraced the gender they felt in their souls—we felt secure that we were on firm ground when writing for Jerry/Daphne.

So, it was galling when our words were misconstrued following an article on Playbill.com, and we were attacked by an angry Twitter mob. Scott and I had explained the show was a chance to write a love letter to our trans and non-binary friends, saying something like, "We have all worked hard to make sure what we were writing was respectful of modern culture."

But when that was paraphrased and condensed into the headline "We Did the Work," the angriest corners of social media tried to throw the "some of our best friends" trope in our face. Never mind the truth that we had lived for fifty years loving and supporting the community.

Luckily, once people started actually seeing our show, hearing our words, and taking in the astounding (and eventually Tony award winning) performance of J. Harrison Ghee, the anger seemed to turn to celebration almost overnight. We received thirteen Tony nominations and four wins—including, most gratifyingly, Best Leading Actor for J.. But in 2022, trying to attract a post-Covid audience that had only just started coming back to Broadway, a musical without songs people already knew was a tough sell.

Many who loved the show called it "a good old-fashioned musical, like they used to make." But maybe only the word "old" stuck in prospective ticket buyers' ears. And even though audiences were enthusiastic night after night, it is naive in this divided country not to think a few people may have left the theater complaining the show was too "woke." So, when we didn't win the Best Musical Tony, our fate was sealed, and the show closed after a year's run.

However, just a few months later, nabbing a Grammy Award for Best Musical Cast Album reinforced my strongly held belief that winning is better!

Even better than the Grammy, a woman who saw the show with their trans son sent me this message online:

> *"I want to thank you for the incredible experience we had at your show. When I first bought our tickets I saw jazz music/Tony winning/Valentine's Day and looked no further into it, I was sold. I had no idea I would leave with a bone deep ferocious appreciation for *everyone* involved. More than the usual feeling of wonder—these events are always fun, always have elements that move you—but we left with something more sustaining than even that.*
>
> *Other than bullying in junior high, our son hasn't faced hate language in person, though he has encountered plenty*

online and is now hearing it from his government, but what people are to this young generations face, is dismissive. Dismissive that is more than passive. Driven by discomfort, bias, or confusion, they look through and around them. The message is that these kids themselves are a phase or a fad. "Come back later..."

*That stage was full of characters saying "hear this!" and "see this!" but for us, watching a person's transition from one state of being to a new awareness of another more FULL sense of being, mirrored so much of our experience as parents of a trans child. It's tricky being a parent! My role in his life is different than my role for anyone else, and it felt scary for minute. What that show demonstrated within all of its other splendor, is how it felt to sit back and ALLOW someone to tell you who they are, instead of telling them who you think they are—and how *rewarding* it is to be invited on that mad cap journey and to meet the fullness of someone, be it a lifelong friend, or even your own child.*

I wish everyone could see this. It was extraordinary.

For our parent hearts, it was medicine...and a sword. We will never, ever, ever, stop fighting.

Thank you so much for writing what you did, musically and lyrically, to reveal the beauty that others want concealed. Thank you."

Well, a message like that can even make an Eeyore like me feel good about what we had created. I believe *Some Like It Hot* pulled off the difficult task of finding a way to tell this story, and retain the humor the mistaken identities create, while also fortifying it with ideas and actions that spoke to how we all now feel about the issues raised in the show. And if there's still someone out there who wants to find fault, well...nobody's perfect!

EPILOGUE

On October 22, 2019, my sixtieth birthday, Lou and I threw a big bash. We booked a space at Chelsea Piers in Manhattan, hired a big band, and invited as many people as would fit, trying hard to represent every corner of my life.

Of course, a show was planned, and a lot of my friends spoke or performed. I gave myself the final slot. My birthday occurred a few months after *Mary Poppins Returns*, and I chose to sing our finale from the film, "There's Nowhere to Go But Up."

As I introed the song, I thanked Bette for singing "The Place Where Lost Things Go" at the Oscars. And it was only then, rather than the actual night of the awards, that it truly sunk in: the full-circle moment I experienced a few months earlier, when my friend and all-time favorite performer, Bette Midler, sang a song I co-wrote with my forever-collaborator, Scott Wittman, for my favorite movie character, Mary Poppins, at the Academy Awards.

As that fact hit me I was, of course, overcome. Cue the waterworks.

During rehearsal the day before the Oscars, waiting for the technical side of things to get set, I sat at the piano and took in being, once again, at the Academy Awards. It was an event I had been part of, as either a writer or a nominee (and on some nights, both), some twenty times. In the darkness on stage, I couldn't shake the feeling that this was my last invitation to the party.

It was very obvious Lady Gaga was going to win Best Original Song for "Shallow" from *A Star Is Born*. In fact, on the red carpet I told reporters, "They are gonna shove that Oscar so far up Lady Gaga's ass that when she smiles, it'll look like a filling." I did harbor some hope I might win Best Original Score, not just for *Mary Poppins Returns*, but maybe as my Susan Lucci moment, as an acknowledgment for my entire career.

But as I sat there by myself in the dark, something told me it wasn't gonna happen. This was it. When Bette was brought to the stage, she asked, "You okay?"

I snapped out of the bittersweet moment just enough to say, "Yes!" and proceed with rehearsal.

I certainly can't complain. I do, but I shouldn't. I understand that everything is cyclical, and the fifty years I have been playing this game is so much more than most get.

But I wouldn't be me if I didn't find something to kvetch about. If the fat lady weren't already singing loud enough: Without involving me in the nitty-gritty, Lou has petitioned the Hollywood Chamber of Commerce for the last four years to get me a star on the Hollywood Walk of Fame. But even after collecting testimonial letters from Bette Midler, Billy Crystal, Rob Reiner, Marty Short, Lin-Manuel Miranda, Kevin Feige, and Steven Spielberg himself, I *still* didn't make the cut. Four years running! And this is for a star which (although no one likes to say the dirty little secret out loud) is something that gets bought. But without a movie studio behind me publicizing a new film, my seven Oscar nominations weren't enough to earn the honor of forking over $50,000.

Music changes, humor changes, the culture changes, and sometimes I'm not sure how I fit in anymore. That's why I wanted to write this book: Get it all down before I forget, and then find a comfortable position in which to rest on my big, fat laurels. With all the "boldface names" who have strolled through my life, I knew I could write chapter after chapter of "fame dropping." But it felt time to do a "life review," to try to take pride in what I've accomplished, and not beat myself up too badly for what I did not.

Besides music, lyrics, and humor, plus *chutzpah*, luck, and longevity, I have also been given two other great gifts. What a blessing to have found great love twice in my life. For that, I am profoundly grateful and astonished. And if you saw me naked in a full-length mirror, you would be just as amazed!

I am also profoundly grateful that I always knew exactly what I wanted to do with my life. There was never any doubt. And Lord knows there is nothing else I could do—ask anyone close to me, I am helpless.

Sometimes I fantasize about escaping show business and being a short-order cook in some greasy-spoon roadside diner, just frying up what people want and then going home at the end of the day. But who am I kidding? Even at a greasy spoon, everyone will be a critic: "My eggs are cold," "I wanted this medium rare." Not to mention, I can't cook. Defrosting those frozen White Castle burgers for Shirley MacLaine is as far as I've ever gotten in the culinary arts.

No, show business was what I was made for, and it has been a hell of a ride. Would I be content just sitting on the couch, watching *Jeopardy*! with my husband and not fretting over trying to compose something "more contemporary, something edgier," or worrying if a lyric I am thinking of is going to "trigger" someone?

Yeah... in fact, couch-husband-Ben & Jerry's sounds pretty good.

All I know is that after fifty years, I am thankful. And if you've gotten to these final paragraphs, I thank you for your interest and patience in taking this look back with me.

And now, I really have to stop typing. Lou's in the TV room with two bowls of ice cream and *Jeopardy*! starts in five minutes.

Never mind the happy—I live it every day.

[END]

ACKNOWLEDGMENTS

I would like to acknowledge every person who appears in this book (each who would have enough eye-rolling stories about me and my neuroses to fill twenty of their own books) and also acknowledge the countless friends and collaborators who I managed to *not* mention in this book (but perhaps you are happy about that). I say to both groups: please forgive me!

I would like to acknowledge Ben Widdicombe, the wonderful writer who guided me through this trek, constantly making sure my trek wasn't dreck. Thanks to Adam Gopnik for his encouragement and the same goes for Matt Roberts. And there would be no book at all without my publisher/editor Gretchen Young, Caitlin Burdette, and everyone at Regalo Press. Thank you all for welcoming and shepherding me and thank you to CAA's Cait Hoyt and Julie Flanagan for the hookup.

Much thanks to my project coordinator Mike Taylor, who proved invaluable beyond words and to Janet Billig Rich and Lisa Moberly for their tireless work clearing a century's worth of lyrics. And to the indefatigable Sam Hoad, who left his beloved Britain in 2018 to be my music/tech assistant and quickly became the absolute nucleus of every project I have done since his arrival, while, most happily, becoming a friend for the ages. And thank you to all the others music/techs that preceded him, assisting me through life, particularly the late great Richard Read.

Thank you to my parents, siblings, and extended family, and of course, unending thanks to the two most important men in my life, Scott Wittman and Lou Mirabal. Each have loved me through thick and thin (not to mention fat and thin) and are both deserving of far more presence in this tome, but I simply had to include that Carol Channing and Mary Martin chapter and I hit my word limit!

Well, I could write a(nother) book with all the additional thank yous necessary. Maybe someday I will. Till then, I thank you dear reader, for making it all the ways to the end of this one.

LYRIC PERMISSIONS

"A Conversation" written by Marc Shaiman and Scott Wittman
Published by Walt Disney Music Company, with special thanks to Disney Music

"A Doctor, A Doctor" written by Marc Shaiman
Published by Universal Music Corp. on behalf of itself and Winding Brook Way Music

"At The Old Majestic Nickel Matinee" written by Marc Shaiman and Scott Wittman
Published by Universal Music Corp. on behalf of itself, Winding Brook Way Music, and Walli Woo Ent.

"Black Don't Crack" written by Marc Shaiman and Jenifer Lewis
Published by Universal Music Corp. on behalf of itself and Winding Brook Way Music

"Don't Break The Rules" written by Marc Shaiman and Scott Wittman
Published by Winding Brook Way Music and Walli Woo Entertainment, with special thanks to Warner Chappell

"Drifting" written by Marc Shaiman
Published by Universal Music Corp. on behalf of itself and Winding Brook Way Music

"Fat As I Am" written by Marc Shaiman, Bette Midler, and Jerry Blatt
Published by Divine S Music Ltd and Winding Brook Way Music, with special thanks to Universal Music Publishing

"Glass Half Full" written by Marc Shaiman and Scott Wittman
Published by Universal Music Corp. on behalf of itself, Winding Brook Way Music, and Walli Woo Ent.

"I Could Write A Book" written by Richard Rodgers and Lorenz Hart
Published by Williamson Music Co. and Chappell & Co, with special thanks to Concord and Warner Chappell

"I Know Where I've Been" written by Marc Shaiman and Scott Wittman
Published by Universal Music Corp. on behalf of itself, Winding Brook Way Music, and Walli Woo Ent.

"I Think It's Going To Rain Today" written by Randy Newman
Published by A Little A Music and Warner-Tamerlane Publishing Co, with special thanks to Warner Chappell

"I've Still Got My Health" written by Cole Porter
Published by Chappell & Co, with special thanks to Warner Chappell

"It's A Wonderful Night For Oscar" (Academy Award Cue) written by William Crystal, Marc Shaiman, and Robert Wuhl
Used with Permission by The Academy

"It's The Most Wonderful Time Of The Year" written by Edward Pola and George Wyle
Published by Barnaby Music Corp, with special thanks to Peer Music

"Just Like You" written by Robert I. Rubinsky and Marc Shaiman
Published by Universal Music Corp. on behalf of itself, Winding Brook Way Music, and Robert I. Rubinsky

"Look What He Made!" written by Marc Shaiman
Published by Universal Music Corp. on behalf of itself and Winding Brook Way Music

"Manhattan" written by Richard Rodgers and Lorenz Hart
Published by Williamson Music Co-A Division of Rodgers and Hammerstein and Piedmont Music Co, with special thanks to Concord Music and Round Hill Music

"Morticia's Theme" written by Betty Comden, Adolph Green, and Marc Shaiman
Courtesy of Amanda Green and Mark Merriman

"My Favorite Things" written by Richard Rodgers and Oscar Hammerstein
Published by Williamson Music-A Division of Rodgers and Hammerstein, with special thanks to Concord Music

"Never Give All The Heart" written by Marc Shaiman and Scott Wittman
Published by Universal Music Corp. on behalf of itself, Winding Brook Way Music, and Walli Woo Ent.

"Never Give It All The Heart" written by William Butler Yeats

"One For My Baby" written by Harold Arlen and Johnny Mercer
Published by Harwin Music Co, with special thanks to MPL Communications

"Simply Second Nature" written by Marc Shaiman and Scott Wittman
Published by Universal Music Corp on behalf of itself, Winding Brook Way Music, and Walli Woo Ent.

"Suddenly" written by Marc Shaiman
Published by Universal Music Corp. on behalf of itself and Winding Brook Way Music

"The Place Where Lost Things Go" written by Marc Shaiman and Scott Wittman
Published by Walt Disney Co, with special thanks to Disney Music

"The Wind Beneath My Wings" written by Jeff Silbar and Larry Henley
Published by Warner-Tamerlane Publishing Corp and Kobalt Music, with special thanks to Warner Chappell

"They Just Keep Moving The Line" written by Marc Shaiman and Scott Wittman
Published by Universal Music Corp. on behalf of itself, Winding Brook Way Music, and Walli Woo Ent.

"We Can Do It" written by Mel Brooks
Published by Mel Brooks Music, with special thanks to Warner Chappell

"Winter Wonderland (Marty Throws A Party Just To Sing)" written by Felix Bernard and Richard B. Smith
Published by WC Music Corporation

"You Can't Stop The Beat" written by Marc Shaiman and Scott Wittman
Published by Universal Music Corp. on behalf of itself, Winding Brook Way Music, and Walli Woo Ent.

"You Coulda Knocked Me Over With A Feather" written by Marc Shaiman and Scott Wittman
Published by Universal Music Corp. on behalf of itself, Winding Brook Way Music, and Walli Woo Ent.

Music Clearance: Janet Rich and Lisa Moberly for Loudspeaker Music Group / Music Coordination, Valerie Braaten

PHOTO PERMISSIONS

Photo on page 19 courtesy of Daniel Burstiner.

Art on page 50 by Vicki Schrott.

Photo on page 64 courtesy of Reggie Lewis/NBC/NBCU Photo Bank via Getty Images.

Photo on page 87 ©2005 Todd Kaplan.

Photos on page 91 courtesy of Mark Sendroff.

Photo on page 113 courtesy of Sony Music Archives.

Photo (Right) on page 117 courtesy of Samuel Hoad.

Photo on page 118 courtesy of ASMAC (American Society of Music Arrangers and Composers) (Glen Lipton).

Photo on page 135 © Paramount Pictures Corp. All Rights Reserved.

Photo on page 140 ©2025 American Broadcasting Companies, Inc. All rights reserved. (ABC/Lou Rocco).

Photo on page 144 © Paramount Pictures Corp. All Rights Reserved.

Photo on page 146 Chris Haston / NBC via Getty Images.

Photo on page 151 courtesy of Carson Entertainment Group.

Photo on page 164 courtesy of Mark Sendroff.

Photo on page 169 ASSOCIATED PRESS (AP Photo/Mark Terrill).

Photo on page 182 Bruce Glikas/FilmMagic via Getty Images.

Photo on page 203 © Sara Krulwich/The New York Times/Redux.

Photo on page 204 © 2003 Broadway.com.

Photo on page 210 Closing number at The New York Pops' Birthday Gala honoring Marc Shaiman and Scott Wittman at Carnegie Hall, April 2014. Photo by Richard Termine.

Photo on page 237 courtesy of Amy Neunsinger.

Photo on page 243 courtesy of Orwin Santa Cruz.

All other image courtesy of the author.